Technopolis

Technopolis

High-Technology Industry and
Regional Development in
Southern California

Allen J. Scott

UNIVERSITY OF CALIFORNIA PRESS
Berkeley · *Los Angeles* · *Oxford*

University of California Press
Berkeley and Los Angeles, California

University of California Press
Oxford, England

Copyright © 1993 by
The Regents of the University of California

Library of Congress Cataloging-in-Publication Data

Scott, Allen John.
    Technopolis : high-technology industry and regional development in
southern California / Allen J. Scott.
        p.   cm.
    Includes bibliographical references and index.
    ISBN 0-520-08189-7
    1. High technology industries—California, Southern.   2. Regional
planning—California, Southern.   3. California, Southern—
Industries—Location.   I. Title.
    HC107.C23H537   1993
    338.6′042—dc20   93-3137
                                                                  CIP

Printed in the United States of America

1 2 3 4 5 6 7 8 9

The paper used in this publication meets the minimum requirements of American
National Standard for Information Sciences—Permanence of Paper for Printed Library
Materials, ANSI Z39.48-1984 ∞

For
N. T. N.

Tout cela est mille fois plus
compliqué encore que je ne peux le
dire, et je ne parviens à l'entrevoir
moi-même que par étincelles . . .
Roger Martin du Gard,
Les Thibault

Contents

Preface

Over the past several years I have been engaged in a many-sided effort to think through the problem of regional growth and development. In two earlier books—*Metropolis* and *New Industrial Spaces*—I tried to deal with this problem by looking in the one case at questions of the social division of labor and urban growth, and in the other at the forces underlying the emergence of new regional manufacturing complexes in North America and Western Europe. In the present volume I attempt to extend the argument on two main fronts. First, the discussion ostensibly moves forward on the basis of a series of dense empirical case studies of the geography of high-technology industry in Southern California. Second, however, these case studies are underpinned by a theoretical leitmotif that runs continuously through the book, and which is focused on issues of industrial organization, local labor markets, and the location of manufacturing activity. The case studies are based on much original data, and collectively they tell a remarkable story about the formation and internal dynamics of what is almost certainly today the world's foremost high-technology region. Despite its size and its overall significance within the U.S. economy, the high-technology industrial complex of Southern California is at the present time facing a number of serious threats to its long-term viability. In the last chapter of the book, therefore, I identify these threats, and lay out some guidelines for the formation of policies to deal with the crisis at hand.

At the outset, a word of warning to the reader is in order about the empirical evidence marshalled in this book. Much of this evidence is based on a series of questionnaire surveys of individual firms and workers in Southern California, and the quality of the data elicited is not always entirely satisfactory. Discussions of the different surveys and their likely sources of bias are provided in several of the chapters that follow. In writing the book, I have tried constantly to keep in mind the limitations of the data. My method in general has been to rely on the multiplicity of the forms of corroboration adduced, so that the argument is built up step by step and from a variety of perspectives. It is my hope that in this manner the acknowledged limitations of the data may to some degree be compensated for by many different pieces of imperfect but convergent evidence. Data problems like these are not likely to be transcended in this kind of research until governmental agencies begin to invest vastly more resources than is currently the case in the collection and publication of detailed production statistics.

Much of the material that follows has previously been published in one form or another, though almost all of it has been considerably revised and reworked for presentation here. I am grateful to the editors and publishers of the following journals for their permission to use this material: *Economic Geography, Environment and Planning A, Growth and Change, Regional Studies, Research and Exploration, Research Policy, Review of Regional Studies,* and *Urban Studies.* In addition, many students at UCLA have worked with me on various phases of this research, and have provided a critical sounding board for my work in progress. Several of them have also helped me at various stages to write up the original research results on which this book is based. I am especially grateful to Jan-Maarten de Vet, Mark Drayse, Donald Gauthier, Eric Kwok, and Doreen Mattingly. It should be noted in particular that chapter 11 is based directly on a master's thesis written by Jan-Maarten de Vet; the substance of chapter 11 is presented here with his kind permission, and I wish fully to acknowledge his role as coauthor of the chapter. The research and writing that I have done jointly with Michael Storper since the mid-1980s inevitably colors much of the following discussion, and I express my appreciation here for his unstinting intellectual support and friendship.

Finally, I owe a special debt of gratitude to the National Science Foundation, which, through grant number SES 8812828, underwrote the entire cost of the research presented in this book.

PART I

Setting the Scene

CHAPTER 1

The Southern Californian Technopolis in Context

INTRODUCTION

Southern California is today one of the world's largest and most dynamic manufacturing regions. Over much of this century, and especially since the end of the World War II, the region has grown at an extraordinary pace, and it now comprises an enormous sprawling conurbation in which some 17 million people make their home.

Southern California began to grow in earnest at the beginning of the twentieth century as irrigated agriculture developed and as rich local petroleum resources were brought into production (Starr 1990). The motion picture industry also contributed to early expansion, and it remains today, along with a constellation of television, recording, and video production activities, one of the mainstays of the region's economy. In the interwar years, a small aircraft industry took root in Los Angeles and to a lesser extent in San Diego, and it soon came to be an important focus of employment. After World War II, the aircraft industry blossomed into a great aerospace-electronics manufacturing complex whose growth was fueled by large-scale federal defense spending over the postwar decades. By the early 1960s the complex had become *the* dominant element of the entire local production system. In addition, since the 1970s, the region has emerged as a major center of low-technology labor-intensive forms of manufacturing such as clothing, furniture, jewelry, and printing, just as it has also grown to be one of the major financial and commercial centers of the Pacific Rim.

This saga of regional growth and development poses innumerable puzzles to the theorist and the historian alike. On the one hand, the available conceptual frameworks of urban and regional analysis seem quite inadequate when faced with the sheer breadth, intensity, and durability of Southern California's rise to industrial preeminence. On the other hand, the narrative sorting out of the detailed empirical events that collectively define the region's trajectory over space and time is a task of daunting complexity. In particular, the circumstances surrounding the birth and subsequent expansion of the many individual industries in the region are frequently quite obscure, as are the ways in which different industries evolved in relationship to one another. I cannot hope, in this book, to achieve much more than a preliminary sketch of some approaches to these questions. Moreover, the focus of the book is on just one ensemble of industrial activities, namely, the high-technology manufacturing complex, and most of the other forms of economic production in the region will be considered only in passing. That said, the great advantage of this concentrated focus is that it allows us to pursue one or two major theoretical and substantive themes with some degree of detail.

In the present chapter, I shall briefly sketch out some of the empirical background to these themes. The chapter that follows enlarges on a few general ideas about problems of industrial organization and regional development, and on this basis I hope to be able to pinpoint a number of important aspects of industrial complex formation. These ideas have been more fully adumbrated elsewhere, and I shall therefore not attempt to argue them out at length in this book. They depend in essence on an effort to capture the logic of the production system as a dynamic complex of interconnected producers articulated with a series of local labor-market activities. This logic, I shall argue, leads under specifiable conditions to *geographically agglomerated economic growth* and hence to the formation of densely industrialized and urbanized regions.

In the light of this conceptual apparatus I shall in subsequent chapters lay out an extended series of empirical studies of high-technology industry in Southern California. Special attention will be paid here to the genesis and growth of the region's aerospace-electronics complex, its changing technological foundations, its structure and organization, its labor force, its extraregional connections, and its evolving geographical pattern within the region. These empirical studies are important in their own right as stories about the development of high-

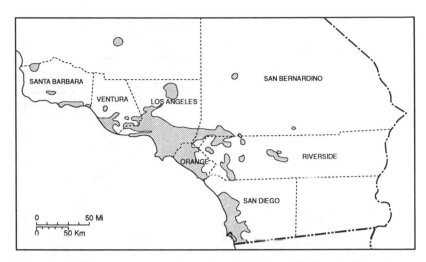

Figure 1.1.   The seven principal counties of Southern California. The primary built-up area is shaded.

technology industry in Southern California. But they are also intended to be read as attempts to operationalize a specific theoretical perspective, and the entire book—despite its profusion of empirical references to Southern California—is meant in the last analysis to stand (or fall) as a series of wider claims about regional development processes in general.

SOUTHERN CALIFORNIA: A BRIEF OVERVIEW OF ITS GEOGRAPHY AND POPULATION

Southern California can be roughly defined as consisting of the seven counties of Los Angeles, Orange, Riverside, San Bernardino, San Diego, Santa Barbara, and Ventura. These seven counties are shown cartographically in figure 1.1. The actual built-up area of the region is also indicated in figure 1.1; it forms a virtually continuous tract of urbanized land sweeping some 230 miles in an irregular band around the Pacific coastline from Santa Barbara in the north, through the central pivot of Los Angeles, to San Diego and the Mexican border in the south.

The whole seven-county area is further subdivided into 188 different independent municipalities so that despite its continuous pattern of land uses it is marked by severe fragmentation of local government and urban-planning activities. These municipalities are connected

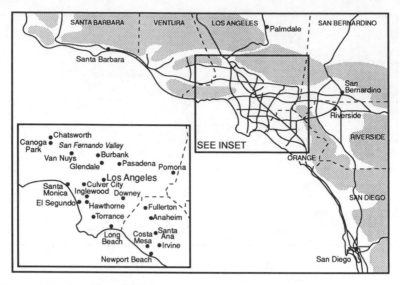

Figure 1.2. Southern California: Freeway system and primary place-names used in the text. Mountainous areas are shaded.

together into a regional system by an extensive network of freeways (fig. 1.2). Over the decades, this network has induced concentrated growth at the core of the region while simultaneously facilitating an enormous shift of both population and industry to peripheral sub-urban areas. Southern California's growth can in significant degree be traced out as a series of ever-widening ripples of lateral urban expansion and outer-city formation.

Population trends in the seven counties are presented in table 1.1, which provides data on each individual county at ten-year intervals since 1970. In terms of total population, Los Angeles County clearly dominates the whole region, with San Diego and Orange counties trailing far behind in second and third places, respectively. The most striking feature of the data presented in table 1.1 is the enormous and steady growth of population in the region in recent decades. The second striking feature is the vigorous population surges of peripheral areas as manifested in the explosion of Riverside and San Bernardino counties in the 1970s and 1980s, and now most recently of all in the incipient expansion of the population of Santa Barbara and Ventura counties. All of this growth has been fueled by the region's extra-ordinary economic vitality, and by its ever-enlarging pool of jobs and economic opportunities.

TABLE 1.1 POPULATION IN THE SEVEN
COUNTIES OF SOUTHERN CALIFORNIA,
1970–1990

County	Population		
	1970	*1980*	*1990*
Los Angeles	7,032,075	7,477,503	8,863,164
Orange	1,420,386	1,932,709	2,410,556
Riverside	459,074	663,166	1,170,413
San Bernardino	684,072	895,016	1,418,380
San Diego	1,357,854	1,861,846	2,498,016
Santa Barbara	263,324	298,694	369,608
Ventura	376,430	529,174	669,016
Total	11,593,215	13,658,108	17,399,153

SOURCE: U.S. Department of Commerce, Bureau of the Census, *Census of Population and Housing.*

The growth in population has been accompanied by a number of important changes in the racial and ethnic complexion of Southern California (see table 1.2). The African-American population of the region currently stands at close to 1.4 million, and it has increased steadily in absolute terms in recent decades. Over the 1980s, however, it actually showed a slight proportional decrease, and it now constitutes 7.7 percent of the total (as opposed to 8.6 percent in 1980). By contrast, the immigrant population has grown enormously since the 1960s, and Southern California has recently become a region of great ethnic and cultural diversity. Two main ethnic groups constitute the major part of this population. First, there is a rapidly growing Asian group consisting variously of Koreans, Vietnamese, Chinese, Japanese, Thais, Filipinos, and Cambodians. Second, there is an exceptionally large Hispanic population originating principally in Central America (Mexico, El Salvador, and Guatemala in particular), with a further admixture of people from South America and the Caribbean. Asians and Pacific Islanders (to use the official census designation) now account for 8.9 percent of the total population, and Hispanics account for 31.0 percent. Los Angeles is today the major port of entry for immigrants into the United States, a position formerly held for most of this century by New York. A large but unspecified proportion of the

TABLE 1.2   RACIAL AND ETHNIC
CHARACTERISTICS OF THE POPULATION OF
THE SEVEN COUNTIES OF SOUTHERN
CALIFORNIA, 1970–1990

	1970	1980	1990
African-American	897,512	1,171,343	1,399,517
Asian & Pacific Islander	n.a.	697,060	1,553,788
Hispanic[a]	1,932,111	3,086,447	5,388,098

SOURCE: U.S. Department of Commerce, Bureau of the Census, *Census of Population and Housing.*
(n.a. = not available)
[a] The specific definition of Hispanic in the 1970 Census was "persons of Spanish language or surname"; the number of Hispanics in 1970 therefore cannot be directly compared with the numbers given for 1980 or 1990.

immigrant population consists of undocumented workers, especially in the case of Hispanics, many of whom enter the country by illegally crossing over the land boundary between Mexico and the United States.

These immigrant populations play a vital part in the economy of Southern California, and they have been absorbed on a massive scale into unskilled low-wage jobs throughout the region. They play an especially important role as a source of cheap and pliable labor in the underbelly of sweatshops that forms an integral part of the region's economy, both in low- and in high-technology manufacturing sectors. African-Americans, by contrast, have not been incorporated to the same extent into either of these sectors (Scott and Paul 1990), and this no doubt helps to account in part for the contrasts in growth between the African-American population and the Asian and Hispanic populations. Several commentators have remarked that with the huge influx of Third World immigrants into the region, social structures and labor markets have tended more and more to become dichotomized between an upper- and a lower-income group. The former group is composed of managers, professionals, scientists, engineers, and other highly qualified workers; the latter is made up to a large degree of unskilled, immigrant workers, a high proportion of whom are women. Between these two strata, there is a middle group comprising the traditional skilled and semiskilled blue-collar working class, but now so small and shrinking with such rapidity that it is commonly referred to as the "disappearing middle" (Ong 1989; Soja 1989).

A SKETCH OF THE REGIONAL ECONOMY OF
SOUTHERN CALIFORNIA

Since the end of the 1960s, economic development in the United States has shifted to a significant extent away from the old Manufacturing Belt in the northeast of the country and toward the Sunbelt, where many new forms of industrialization and urbanization have made their historical appearance. Southern California is in many ways paradigmatic of this change, so the study presented here is not just an isolated investigation of a unique region, but is also in several respects representative of a wider pattern of geographic and economic transformation. Southern California is particularly important as an advanced case of postfordist flexible economic growth.

Over the decade from 1980 to 1990, total nonagricultural employment in Southern California grew by a robust 31.2 percent, as compared to 21.8 percent for the United States as a whole. From the data laid out in table 1.3, it is apparent that most of this growth was concentrated in various service and white-collar sectors. Manufacturing employment in Southern California grew by a modest 3.1 percent during the decade, but this contrasts with a decline of 6.1 percent for the entire country, and several manufacturing sectors in the region grew at a very rapid pace indeed. At the present time, the nearly 1.4 million workers in manufacturing in the region account for 18.2 percent of total nonagricultural employment—a percentage that is just slightly more than the 17.3 percent for the United States as a whole.

The aggregate manufacturing data for Southern California mask a number of important internal differences in this category of employment. We need to note first of all that at the end of the 1960s, once-thriving elements of the region's economy like car assembly, rubber tire manufacture, and steel entered a period of severe crisis. These traditional smokestack and mass-production industries in the region (as in the country as a whole) were subject to an epidemic of plant closures and job losses in the 1970s and 1980s, and they have now virtually disappeared from Southern California. By contrast, two other major industrial ensembles have held their own to a significant degree. These are represented by a group of low-technology labor-intensive craft in-

TABLE 1.3   EMPLOYMENT IN MAJOR
NONAGRICULTURAL SECTORS IN THE SEVEN
COUNTIES OF SOUTHERN CALIFORNIA AND
THE UNITED STATES, 1980 AND 1990

	Southern California			United States		
	1980 ('000)	1990 ('000)	Change (%)	1980 ('000)	1990 ('000)	Change (%)
Mining	23	15	−34.8	1,020	735	−27.9
Construction	245	384	56.7	4,399	5,205	18.3
Manufacturing	1,351	1,393	3.1	20,300	19,064	−6.1
Transportation & public utilities	293	350	19.5	5,143	5,838	13.5
Wholesale & retail trade	1,339	1,790	33.7	20,386	26,151	28.3
Finance, insurance, & real estate	362	517	42.8	5,168	6,833	32.2
Services	1,306	2,127	62.9	17,901	28,209	57.6
Government	903	1,064	17.8	16,249	18,295	12.6
Total	5,822	7,640	31.2	90,566	110,330	21.8

SOURCES: Data for Southern California from Employment Development Department, State of California, *Annual Planning Information* (published for individual counties); data for United States from Department of Labor, Bureau of Labor Statistics, *Employment and Earnings.*

dustries on the one hand, and high-technology industries on the other. Both ensembles of industrial activity employ large numbers of workers, and both have expanded at a fast pace over the postwar decades. Let us look briefly at each.

Employment in low-technology labor-intensive craft industries in Southern California in 1988 is shown in table 1.4. This table is based on data provided by *County Business Patterns*, in contrast to table 1.3, which is based on data in *Annual Planning Information*. The two sets of data are not strictly comparable because of the different ways in which they are collected. In particular, *County Business Patterns* does not ensure a 100 percent enumeration of all business activity. However, *County Business Patterns* gives more complete sectoral breakdowns of employment than does *Annual Planning Information*, and is

TABLE 1.4   EMPLOYMENT AND NUMBER OF
ESTABLISHMENTS IN LOW-TECHNOLOGY
LABOR-INTENSIVE CRAFT-MANUFACTURING
INDUSTRIES IN THE SEVEN COUNTIES OF
SOUTHERN CALIFORNIA, 1988

Standard industrial category	Employment	Establishments
23 Apparel & other textile products	107,765	3,215
25 Furniture & fixtures	54,552	887
27 Printing & publishing	101,112	2,620
31 Leather & leather goods	5,644	108
391 Jewelry, silverware, & plated ware	2,950	207
394 Toys & sporting goods	8,473	148
781 Motion picture production & services	96,367	3,864
Total	376,863	11,049

SOURCE: U.S. Department of Commerce, Bureau of the Census, *County Business Patterns.*

thus used here (as well as in subsequent chapters) as a source of data for detailed intersectoral comparisons. Table 1.4 is based on a mix of two- and three-digit SIC categories defined in terms of the 1987 Standard Industrial Classification. Note that SIC 781 (motion picture production and services) is listed in the Standard Industrial Classification as a service, but given its mode of organization it is probably more appropriately viewed as a low-technology labor-intensive industry (cf. Storper and Christopherson 1987), and hence is included in table 1.4. The major sectors in table 1.4 are apparel, furniture, printing and publishing, and motion pictures, with leather, jewelry, and toys at a much lower level of development (but poised for major expansion). Southern California has now actually edged ahead of New York as the nation's major center of the garment industry. All of these low-technology labor-intensive sectors tend to form specialized industrial districts scattered around the central area of Los Angeles (Scott 1988a). In these districts, they are organized into networks of many interconnected producers and subcontractors, and except for the motion picture industry (much of which is dominated by craft labor unions and subject to closed-shop rules) they also employ large numbers of immigrant workers. The data on number of establishments given in

TABLE 1.5   EMPLOYMENT AND NUMBER OF
ESTABLISHMENTS IN HIGH-TECHNOLOGY
MANUFACTURING INDUSTRIES IN THE SEVEN
COUNTIES OF SOUTHERN CALIFORNIA, 1988

Standard industrial category	Employment	Establishments
357 Computer & office equipment	33,682	340
366 Communications equipment	19,458	172
367 Electronic components & accessories	65,390	959
372 Aircraft & parts	124,938	347
376 Guided missiles, space vehicles, & parts	88,910	47
381 Search & navigation equipment	81,382	147
382 Measuring & controlling devices	27,194	523
384 Medical instruments & supplies	28,943	421
Total	468,897	2,956

SOURCE: U.S. Department of Commerce, Bureau of the Census, *County Business Patterns*.

table 1.4 also indicate that these low-technology labor-intensive sectors are dominated by small production units, averaging 34.1 employees each.

The high-technology manufacturing ensemble in Southern California is made up for the most part of aerospace-electronics industries together with sectors producing various kinds of instruments including medical instruments and supplies (table 1.5). There is also a flourishing biotechnology industry in the region (concentrated in San Diego), but employment data are not readily available for this sector. The high-technology ensemble, defined in table 1.5, accounts for very roughly a third of all manufacturing employment in Southern California. Indeed, Southern California is unquestionably the largest high-technology industrial region in the United States, if not the entire world. The industry is organized in the form of a stratified network of establishments consisting of (a) large systems houses (i.e., small-batch assemblers of extremely complex technology- and design-intensive artifacts such as aircraft or communication satellites), (b) medium-sized producers of components and subassemblers, and (c) many small manufacturers and subcontractors offering specialized services such as

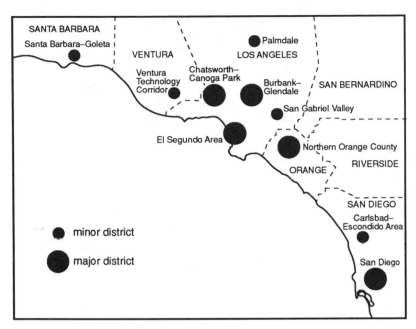

Figure 1.3. The primary high-technology industrial districts of Southern California.

printed-circuit board fabrication, electronics assembly, plastics molding, aluminum foundry work, tool-and-die making, and so on. These establishments, like their low-technology counterparts, also tend to cluster together within specialized industrial districts (see fig. 1.3). The original high-technology industrial districts of the region date from the 1930s and are located in Burbank and the El Segundo area (both of them on the periphery of Los Angeles as it was at that time), and in San Diego. These three districts developed as the region's aircraft industry and associated parts-producing sectors grew. In the postwar decades, new and more diverse high-technology industrial districts have emerged at a series of increasingly peripheralized locations. The collective set of these districts in the region constitutes the Southern Californian technopolis, which is the main object of investigation in this book.

The robust growth of high-technology industry in Southern California since the 1950s has been largely driven forward by the copious spending of the federal Department of Defense over the entire Cold War period. Table 1.6 traces out defense prime contract awards in

TABLE 1.6   DEPARTMENT OF DEFENSE PRIME
CONTRACT AWARDS, U.S. AND CALIFORNIA,
1970–1990

	Total awards				
	Curent dollars (millions)		Constant 1990 dollars (millions)		California as % of U.S.
	United States	California	United States	California	
1970	33,570	5,824	106,747.4	18,519.4	17.3
1971	32,444	5,203	98,015.7	15,718.6	16.0
1972	36,283	6,016	103,902.0	17,227.8	16.6
1973	34,741	6,215	94,774.3	16,954.7	17.9
1974	37,760	6,917	95,485.9	17,491.4	18.3
1975	43,355	7,908	99,418.0	18,134.0	18.2
1976	44,679	8,949	94,928.5	19,013.7	20.0
1977	52,752	10,078	103,804.1	19,831.2	19.1
1978	61,174	10,517	112,504.9	19,341.8	17.2
1979	65,481	11,675	110,872.2	19,768.1	17.8
1980	76,430	13,853	118,965.3	21,562.6	18.1
1981	96,653	16,630	136,772.1	23,532.9	17.2
1982	115,280	22,578	152,054.3	29,780.4	19.6
1983	118,744	26,387	150,267.0	33,392.0	22.2
1984	124,015	28,520	151,193.1	34,770.2	23.0
1985	140,096	29,115	165,683.3	33,432.6	20.8
1986	136,026	27,738	156,683.5	31,950.4	20.4
1987	156,508	24,515	174,899.6	27,395.8	15.7
1988	151,352	23,458	164,145.1	25,440.8	15.5
1989	139,343	23,125	145,016.1	24,066.5	16.6

SOURCE: Department of Defense, Office of the Secretary, *Prime Contract Awards by States.*

both the United States and in California between 1970 and 1990. Un-fortunately, information on prime contract awards for Southern Cali-fornia as such is not readily available over extended time periods, but since Southern California receives from 70 percent to 80 percent of all awards made to the state, the data for California as a whole laid out in table 1.6 can be taken to be reasonably representative of overall trends

TABLE 1.7 HIGH-TECHNOLOGY INDUSTRY
(AEROSPACE-ELECTRONICS) IN SOUTHERN
CALIFORNIA AS DEFINED BY THE
EMPLOYMENT DEVELOPMENT DEPARTMENT
OF THE STATE OF CALIFORNIA: DEFINITIONS
IN TERMS OF 1972 AND 1987 STANDARD
INDUSTRIAL CLASSIFICATIONS

1972		1987	
SIC code	Description	SIC code	Description
357	Office & computing machines	357	Office & computing machines
365	Radio & TV receiving equipment		
366	Communications equipment	366	Communications equipment
367	Electronic components	367	Electronic components
372	Aircraft & parts	372	Aircraft & parts
376	Guided missiles, space vehicles, & parts	376	Guided missiles, space vehicles, & parts
		381	Search & navigation equipment
382	Measuring & controlling devices	382	Measuring & controlling devices

in the region. For both the United States and the state, prime contract awards, in constant dollar terms, grew erratically but continually over most of the period from the 1950s to the 1980s. They reached a peak in 1987, and have declined steadily since then. In view of the prospect of a durable international *détente* throughout the 1990s, this pattern of decline seems likely to persist. Moreover, while Southern California still takes a much greater share than any other state of total money expended on prime contract awards, the share, too, has tended to decline over the late 1980s from a maximum of 23.0 percent in 1984 to 16.6 percent in 1989.

If we look at aggregate annual employment in the core aerospace-electronics complex of the region (i.e., high-technology industry as defined above less medical instruments and supplies), we see that it runs more or less parallel to the course of defense spending. Here, the complex is identified (not entirely satisfactorily) in the terms established by the Employment Development Department of the state of California

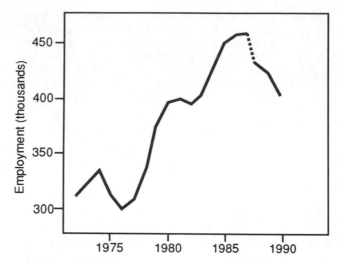

Figure 1.4. Total employment in the aerospace industry of Los Angeles, Orange, and San Diego counties. Note change of definition of industry after 1987. (Data from State of California, Employment Development Department, *Annual Planning Information*.)

(see table 1.7). After 1987, SIC 365 was dropped from this definition, and SIC 381 was added. Fortunately, the discrepancies in the aggregate data series before and after 1987 are probably slight. Figure 1.4 shows absolute levels of employment in the complex from 1972 to 1990 for the three leading counties of Los Angeles, Orange, and San Diego. Over the years of the Reagan presidency, employment in the complex expanded with particular intensity, and this was a boom period for the region as a whole. Since 1987, however, in response to the declines in Department of Defense prime contract awards, significant losses of employment have been experienced. Southern California assuredly remains the world's premier high-technology manufacturing region, though it is now experiencing many difficulties, and serious questions remain as to its future course of development. We shall return to these questions—and the major policy issues that they pose—in the final chapter of this book.

CHAPTER 2

Patterns of Industrialization and Regional Development

BASIC DIMENSIONS OF THE PROBLEM

Industrialization—the transformation of materials and semifinished outputs into marketable commodities—is in both physical and social terms an enormously complex undertaking. In capitalist society it is particularly problematical because in addition to the technical and organizational problems involved, the social relations and accumulation strategies intrinsic to the whole process lead to constant turbulence and crisis, just as they also provoke continual readjustment of the geographical bases of production (Storper and Walker 1989).

As I shall contend later in this chapter, it is useful to think of industrialization processes as embedded within *technological-institutional structures of production* that constitute physical and social settings within which economic activity as a whole is accomplished. These structures are in turn subject to *evolutionary trajectories of development*, meaning that they change over time at varying velocities. Moreover, the dynamic of change can be represented as a branching structure in which the accumulated weight of many small events may lock a particular pathway of development into place over long periods (Arthur 1988; David 1975). In addition, industrialization is, by its very nature, spatially extensive, and therefore it is subject to various *locational logics and leitmotifs*, as expressed in the enormous diversity that we commonly find in patterns of industrial development from place to place. Each of these broad dimensions of the problem is of the

17

first importance in understanding industrial development, and in charting out the rise and fall of regional economic systems. Together, they provide a way of organizing in analytical terms the many detailed inner workings of the production system *qua* sets of technologies, labor processes, input-output relations, locational decisions, managerial viewpoints and ideologies, and so on. In particular, the notion of production as an organized technological and institutional structure differentially unfolding over time and space represents a sort of conceptual road map as we start to examine the complex interrelations between industrialization and regional development.

The investigation now begins with an inquiry into the logic of some of the central building blocks of industrialization processes as they impinge on patterns of regional development (i.e., the division of labor, the organization of production, and the location of industry). This is followed by an account of some of the main temporal and spatial tendencies of production systems in contemporary capitalism, and in which an attempt is made to situate the Southern Californian technopolis both historically and geographically.

FROM THE DIVISION OF LABOR TO SPATIAL AGGLOMERATION

PATTERNS OF INDUSTRIAL ORGANIZATION

In every kind of society there are always productivity gains to be made by specialization and trade. For example, an individual can do all of the work of making a hammer, from cutting down a tree, smelting the necessary iron ore, making a handle and a head, and then assembling the parts into a final product. Obviously, however, in any organized society, it will usually be more economical to carry out this work if there is a division of labor such that individuals concentrate on particular tasks, and exchange what they make against what others make. There are limits to how far such a division of labor can efficiently go, but as it proceeds we say—along with Böhm-Bawerk (1891)—that the "roundaboutness" of the economy is increasing. This is equivalent to the proposition that there is an increasing number of stages or steps between the production of the raw materials on which the economy is based on the one hand, and the production of final outputs on the other. One of the immediate effects of increasing roundaboutness is that it makes possible an evermore finely grained geographical differentiation of economic activity.

Roundaboutness may be expressed in terms of either a *technical division of labor* or a *social division of labor*. The former involves the separation of tasks and the specialization of workers *within* a particular firm. In this case, workers interact with one another via a network of purely intrafirm transactions representing a hierarchy that is coordinated by means of managerial fiat. By contrast, a social division of labor involves the parceling out of different tasks *between* individual production units (firms or establishments as the case may be) in a pattern of vertical disintegration. In this instance, producers specialize in a particular sector or subsector, and they buy and sell among themselves in networks of externalized transactions that are in part governed by market relations and hence subject to price signals (Coase 1937; Williamson 1975). In practice, there is a third organizational modality that is neither purely hierarchical nor purely subject to market forces, but involves various combinations of these two principles, in the form, for example, of joint ventures, strategic alliances, or other kinds of contractual obligation. One of the problems that we face is to determine where these different structural forms begin and end in different sectoral and historical contexts. We may approach this problem by way of a discussion of the relations between technologies, organization, and average costs.

Industrial processes are invariably subject to *internal* and *external* economies. Internal economies, as the name implies, come from cost-reducing relationships that are contained within the individual production unit; external economies come from cost-reducing relationships that lie outside the boundaries of the individual unit. Internal and external economies can be further categorized as being due to the effects of either *scale* or *scope*. Figure 2.1 shows how internal and external economies articulate with scale and scope effects and how each particular articulation is rooted in the broad conditions of production. Figure 2.1 informs us that *economies of scale* are engendered by simple quantitative increases in levels of economic activity (i.e., internally in terms of the amount of product manufactured, especially where large units of machinery and equipment with high fixed costs are present; or externally in terms of the number of individual producers). *Economies of scope* are based on levels of productive variety (e.g., internally in terms of the number of different tasks undertaken such as spinning,

	Internal	External
Scale	size of firm or establishment	aggregate size of economic system
Scope	variety of activities in firm or establishment	variety of activities in economic system

Figure 2.1.   The genesis of internal and external scale and scope effects.

weaving, or dyeing; and externally in terms of the range of different producers in a given industrial complex or economic system). Note that *dis*economies of scale and scope occur when expansion over the same respective dimensions brings about *increasing* average costs.

The empirical circumstances underlying the formation of internal and external economies of scale and scope are many and varied (Gaffard 1990; Tirole 1988; Williamson, 1975), and I shall make no attempt to provide a systematic catalog of them all here. Two major remarks are germane, however. In the first place, where producers face intensified levels of uncertainty (e.g., as a result of increased market contestability, insistent product differentiation, or frequent cyclical ups and downs of the economy) their internal scale and scope economies will be under considerable pressure and will have some tendency to break down. This is a result directly of the circumstance that uncertainty will create inefficiencies in the use of large units of fixed capital, and the problem will be compounded where such units are slaved together in a vertically integrated system so that the inefficiencies will be passed backwards through the vertical structure of the firm (Carlton 1979; Scott 1988a). Conversely, predictability and stability will tend to encourage the quest for scale and scope. In the second place, when vertically related production processes have strong synergetic interactions (as is observable in the case, for example, of manufacturers of military and space hardware, which is commonly subject to rigorous design specifications covering all subcomponents and their interconnections) internal economies of scope are likely to be highly developed. Thus, in this instance, considerable vertical integration is apt to occur and production units may attain great size, even though scale in the strict sense of number of units of output produced per time period may be quite small.

The configuration of any industrial system will be intimately shaped by these different forces. Two extreme cases may be cited to illustrate this point. One is where massive internal economies of scale and scope are present leading to large vertically integrated production units (i.e., hierarchical organization). The other is where internal scale and scope economies dissolve away and where external economies abound. In this second case, we would expect to find the production system fragmented into many small establishments linked together through dense networks of externalized transactions (i.e., vertical and horizontal disintegration). A wide assortment of intermediate cases can be envisaged between these two extremes, as for example, in the Southern Californian technopolis where a number of large, integrated aerospace producers (i.e., systems houses) are caught up in dense networks of small and disintegrated firms.

TRANSACTIONAL NETWORKS

When vertical and horizontal disintegration of the production system takes place, the system typically evolves toward the form of a *transactions-intensive* complex of producers. In brief, more and more of the system is externalized, and interestablishment networks of linkages become ever more profuse and intricate. These linkages or transactions are usually many faceted, and they are often quite problematical in that certain kinds of failures to achieve full transactional efficiency frequently occur.

In the simplest case (which is also probably relatively rare) interindustrial linkages are reducible to spot dealings in which a given quantity of product changes hands at a given price in one finite transaction. In more complex cases, linkages may be based on considerable prior negotiation and discussion, and they may also entail contractual agreements over extended periods of time. Sometimes, the parties involved in any transaction may find it to their advantage actually to form complementary institutional frameworks as a way of ensuring smoother and more reliable flows of information and products. Probably the most advanced case of this latter phenomenon in modern capitalism is to be found in Japanese subcontracting systems where parent firms and dependent subcontractors form durable alliances with one another to guarantee systemwide efficiency and survivability. Joint ventures and strategic alliances represent another means of institutionalizing transactional relations between firms over lengthy periods of time. We may refer to all such phenomena as forms of "quasi-integration" for they represent agreements between otherwise independent firms to renounce a limited portion of their operational autonomy for the sake of superior transactional efficiency. Institutionalist economists of the markets-and-hierarchies school are often accused of evacuating such intermediate forms of organization and transactional interaction from the purview of economic theory (cf. Gordon 1991; Sayer 1990), but as the work of Williamson (1975, 1985) indicates, these forms are actually entirely consistent with the main ideas of this school of thought, and are indeed predictable out of its basic premises about structures of contractual interaction.

One especially important aspect of interindustrial transactions is that *they occur over geographic space*. They thus invariably generate space-dependent costs that increase positively with distance. Often enough, such transactions represent so small a fraction of the total costs of production that they play scarcely any role in the locational decisions of manufacturers. In other cases, they have major impacts on the ways in which productive activity is distributed over geographic space. To sharpen these remarks, we need to distinguish between different kinds of transactions on the basis of their size, formal attributes, and spatiotemporal characteristics.

Thus, transactions that occur in large volumes typically have low costs per unit of quantity and distance because there are almost always significant economies of scale to be obtained in transport processes. Conversely, small transactions tend to incur relatively high costs per unit. Transactions that are in some way difficult to effectuate because of their physical characteristics—in such matters as shape, fragility, packageability, perishability, and so on—also face high unit costs. A special, but enormously important variant on this matter of the formal attributes of transactions is where they necessitate the movement of people who must deal face-to-face with one another for any transaction to be accomplished. This will often be the case where transacting involves the communication of information or advice; or it may occur in relation to a physical flow of materials where a process of mutual education and negotiation is crucial to effective intermediation,—a circumstance that is commonly encountered when work is subcontracted out. The costs of face-to-face contact involve not just ordinary expenditures on transport but also the wages of the person or persons engaged in the contact; and when high-level employees (managers, supervisors, legal counsel, and so on) are engaged, these costs can escalate rapidly. Lastly, the costs of transacting are usually sensitive to the regularity and predictability of transmission and delivery of goods and information. Where transactions are routinized in space and time their costs are likely to fall; and where they are irregular and unpredictable, their costs will rise. The latter state of affairs is reinforced where firms face much randomness in their external transactions (e.g., because of a need for occasional customized components, special kinds of services, machinery repair, and so on) and must, as a consequence, continually find and build new linkage partnerships.

In the light of this discussion we would expect to observe relatively low aggregate transactions costs where groups of producers are linked to one another via large, stable, standardized transactions (especially if these involve little personal contact). But we would also expect to detect much more burdensome transactions costs in disintegrated industrial complexes with many small producers tied together in idiosyncratic and variable linkage networks. If, in the latter case, transactions are problematical so that they must also be executed by means of personal contact (or even, in the extreme, supported by complex institutional infrastructures) then they will be that much more onerous. Indeed, transactions costs may be elevated to the point where they cancel out the advantages that would otherwise accrue from vertical disintegration.

This state of affairs is represented schematically in figure 2.2, which shows two average cost curves for a particular kind of production process—let us say electronics assembly. One of the curves [I(q)] represents average costs of the electronics assembly function under conditions where it is vertically integrated with downstream functions, and where q represents quantity of output; the other curve, [D(q)], represents average costs under conditions where electronics assembly becomes vertically disintegrated from downstream functions. It is assumed that the cost curves in these two contrasting situations have quite different shapes, because the specific conditions of production may vary greatly depending on whether assembly is integrated or disintegrated. Figure 2.2 coincidentally suggests how vertical integration/disintegration may occur in relation to both scale and scope effects. In panel A of the figure there are no distance-dependent transactions costs and vertical disintegration is clearly the optimal solution for this

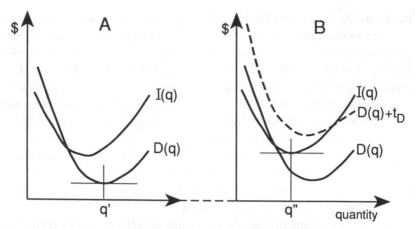

Figure 2.2. Average cost curves I(q) and D(q) as a function of quantity produced (q) under conditions of vertical integration and vertical disintegration, respectively; t_D is the distance-dependent transactions cost involved where vertical disintegration prevails. In panel A (without transactions costs) the optimal solution is production of q' in vertically disintegrated form; in panel B (with transactions costs) the optimal solution is production of q" in vertically integrated form.

particular example. In panel B distance-dependent transactions costs are assumed to be so high that vertical integration becomes the preferred solution, and the greater the distance over which transacting must occur, the greater this tendency will be. Notice that we could add yet another dimension to this discussion by introducing distance-dependent *intrafirm* transactions costs and thus broadening our analytical range to include the possibility of vertical integration *and* spatial separation, i.e., the multiestablishment firm (see Scott 1988a for a more extended exposition of this problem). For the moment, the important point to recognize is that if the distance-dependent costs of external transacting are sharply curtailed by locational convergence of the parties involved, then the advantages of vertical disintegration can often continue to be reaped.

The generalization of the latter remark is immediate. In any transactions-intensive complex of producers there are likely to be benefits for all or for a subset of producers if they locate in close proximity to one another so as to bring transactions costs under control. In brief, depending on the specifics of interindustrial transactions, there will be cases where external economies engendered by fragmentation of the production system can best be secured if they are transformed into agglomeration economies by the locational strategies of producers.

AGGLOMERATION

It is this connection between the social division of labor, external economies, and locational agglomeration that, in part, calls forth the phenomenon of the *Marshallian industrial district*, i.e., a specialized geographical cluster of production activities. The sobriquet "Marshallian" is intended as a reminder of the contribution of Alfred Marshall (1919) who first systematically commented on the disposition of certain kinds of industries to concentrate locationally in specialized areas (see also Becattini 1987). Such districts were extremely common throughout Europe and North America in the nineteenth century, and many of them became celebrated centers of craft industry. Some of these are cataloged by Piore and Sabel (1984, p. 28) in the following terms:

> Silks in Lyon; ribbons, hardware, and specialty steel in neighboring St. Etienne; edge tools, cutlery, and specialty steel in Solingen, Remscheid, and Sheffield; calicoes in Alsace; woolen and cotton goods in Roubaix; cotton goods in Philadelphia and Pawtucket.

Analogous phenomena are still observable today, and as postfordist, flexible production organization has made increasing headway in modern capitalism, many new industrial districts are beginning to materialize. One of the most conspicuous examples of this process is represented by the high-technology industrial districts of the U.S. Sunbelt, and of Southern California in particular.

All such industrial districts are characterized by a proliferation of many different producers, all locked together in mutual interdependence through their transactional relations. Because of the geographical proximity of producers to one another, the velocity of circulating capital through the system is accelerated and this increases the advantages of agglomeration. At the same time, producers have added insurance against rare contingencies that might severely disrupt production. Thus, in the absence of immediate access to suitable suppliers of unpredictable needs (e.g., machine shops or engineering consulting services) production may be severely disrupted over extended periods of time. Industrial districts also represent important centers of employment and local labor market activity. They are invariably surrounded by dense residential districts housing their main work force. Because of the spatial juxtaposition of large numbers of jobs and workers, job-search and job-matching activities are facilitated, and this is often expressed in terms of increased rates of labor turnover in large industrial centers (Jayet 1983). The specialization of workers in local trades and their habituation to place-specific norms of production and work ease the tasks of filling job vacancies and labor-force training. These labor market conditions further underpin the agglomeration economies secured in the first instance by the transactional-cum-locational inter-relations between producers, and they reinforce the competitiveness of the entire complex of industries. Agglomeration economies are yet further amplified where there is active collective provision of infra-structural services and public goods (e.g., roads, utilities, airports, and the like), and where useful immaterial infrastructures emerge such as business associations, information-providing services, educational and research institutions attuned to local production needs, and so on.

Industrial agglomerations thus come to embody significant produc-tivity advantages, and these in turn endow producers with a strong competitive edge. This edge is continually being sharpened by the in-novative activity that seems to occur endemically within industrial agglomerations—both because they are the sites of innumerable win-dows of innovative opportunity, and because they are also places in which the specific individuals best positioned to perceive and take advantage of the same opportunities are located (Russo 1985). These circumstances are manifest in the emergence of *Verdoorn effects* in densely developed regional economies, in that such regions tend to ex-perience rising levels of productivity with rising levels of gross output (Kaldor 1970). The same essential point is to be found in the work of Porter (1990), who has recently argued that one of the major factors behind competitive performance in export markets is the existence of densely developed industrial districts, with their intrinsic productivity and innovation advantages.

Here, an important point of qualification is in order. In modern capitalism, industrial agglomerations are never hermetically sealed off from the outside world. On the contrary, and notwithstanding their strongly centripetal tendencies, they are always connected to a wider economic system through elaborate networks of extraregional transac-tions. Today, these networks are typically global in extent. Indeed, much of the contemporary world economy can be seen as a mosaic of regional agglomerations (marked by localized transactional networks) embedded in far-flung systems of national and international transacting (Scott and Storper 1992). An important corollary of this observation is that the governance of industrial systems involves important tasks of coordination not just at the national level, but evermore insistently at the international and regional levels too. We shall return to this issue.

INDUSTRIAL SYSTEMS AND THE HISTORICAL GEOGRAPHY OF INDUSTRIALIZATION

TYPES OF INDUSTRIAL SYSTEMS

Industrial systems can thus be seen in part as units of production (i.e., constellations of technologies, labor processes, managerial apparatuses, and so on) caught up in transactional networks and local labor markets. A wide variety of geographical outcomes for such systems is possible depending on the specific locational forces at work in any given case. This manner of formulating the problem, however, remains extremely abstract, and we need to inquire into the concrete forms and locational configurations that different types of industrial systems may assume. We must also broach the important issue of the evolutionary dynamics of industrial complexes and agglomerations through time.

We can begin to approach these questions by means of a simple and preliminary classification of industrial systems according to the degree to which they are subject to the sway of internal and external economies (Scott and Storper 1992). In figure 2.3 four major types of system are distinguished. First, a category with low internal and external economies (of both scale and scope) is identified under the designation *the isolated specialized workshop*. Second, a category labelled *process industries* is defined, with low external economies but strong internal economies based on highly capitalized flow-through production technologies, as in food processing or petroleum refining. Third, we can identify *disintegrated transactions-intensive complexes* wherever we find that producers are characterized by low internal economies of scale and scope while simultaneously reaping significant external economies through networks of interfirm transactions. Typical examples of this third category are the craft industries of the Third Italy, or some kinds of high-technology complexes like Silicon Valley. Fourth,

```
                              Internal economies
                          low                    high
                    ┌──────────────────┬──────────────────┐
              low   │ The isolated     │ Process          │
                    │ specialized      │ industries       │
  External          │ workshop         │                  │
  economies         ├──────────────────┼──────────────────┤
                    │ Disintegrated    │ Complexes        │
                    │ transactions-    │ based on         │
              high  │ intensive        │ large-scale      │
                    │ complexes        │ assembly         │
                    │                  │ industries       │
                    └──────────────────┴──────────────────┘
```

Figure 2.3. Types of industrial systems arrayed by internal and external economies. (Based on Scott and Storper 1992.)

complexes based on large-scale assembly industries contain production units that have potent internal *and* external economies of scale and scope. This last category comprises both classical mass-production sectors (like the car industry) and aggregations of systems houses together with their large cohorts of dependent subcontractors. It is the third and fourth types of industrial systems that are of particular interest in this book, because they are the ones that are most closely implicated in the formation of industrial districts.

To be sure, the four main types of industrial systems classified above by no means exhaust the total range of possibilities. Moreover, hybrid forms are conceivable in theory and observable in practice. We can easily imagine, for example, a disintegrated transactions-intensive complex that embodies within itself certain kinds of process industries. The evolutionary transformation of any given complex is also always an open prospect. Allen (1929) shows how the gun industry in Birmingham, England, changed after the 1850s from an intensely fragmented network system to a large mass-production assembly industry based on imported American technology. Over much of the nineteenth century, in both Britain and the United States, the shoe industry was largely organized in disintegrated transactions-intensive complex form, and then with the invention of new shoemaking machinery in the early part of the twentieth century it became something more like a process industry (Hall 1962). The motion-picture industry in Los Angeles, as Storper and Christopherson (1987) have shown, was transformed after the late 1940s from a sector made up of large-scale studios (essentially systems houses) to a network of much smaller disintegrated producers. Changes like these are often, though by no means always, associated with marked locational shifts.

TECHNOLOGICAL-INSTITUTIONAL STRUCTURES OF PRODUCTION AND THE HISTORICAL PERIODIZATION OF CAPITALISM

It is common to find that the sorts of transformations of production systems described above proceed in an extremely wayward fashion. At some times in history one particular sector may be evolving in one direction, while another sector is evolving in an altogether different direction. We might even observe different segments of the same industry changing in diametrically opposed ways, as in the case, for example, of the fragmentation and agglomeration of specialized semiconductor firms in Silicon Valley, in contrast to the emergence of large mass-production semiconductor facilities at dispersed sites across the United States (Saxenian 1990; Scott and Angel 1987). It is therefore a hazardous undertaking to attempt to make any sort of historical generalizations about these processes.

That said, it is sometimes possible to discern certain ordered patterns in the ways in which economic systems are organized at different historical moments. In this regard, it is useful to break any system down into four or five basic tiers of activity, each of which is susceptible to analysis on its own terms, though each of which is also part of an articulated total economic reality. These different tiers involve the following main elements:

(a) an evolving technological system;

(b) a framework of industrial organization;

(c) a regime of labor relations and managerial norms;

(d) forms of competition and market demand; and

(e) institutions of collective economic order and regulation at sectoral, regional, national, and international levels.

We may refer to any composite structure of this nature as a *technological-institutional structure of production*, with any given structure representing a sort of model of political-economic order. The notion has many affinities to regulationist theory as developed by scholars like Aglietta (1979), Boyer (1986), and Lipietz (1986), though at this stage it is my intention to sidestep many of the theoretical issues and debates associated with the regulationist position(s), and simply to concentrate on the descriptive meaning of the notion of a technological-institutional structure and on its use as a heuristic device for periodizing moments of historical geography.

It should be stressed at once that there are probably few, if any, periods in the history of capitalism when anything like a fully coherent, homogeneous, and all-embracing technological-institutional structure of production could be said to be present. However, there are certainly times when we can say that the leading edges of the economy evinced a kind of uniformity and consistency, and when the very success of these leading edges resulted in their identification as models or norms as to how other segments of the economy should and probably would evolve. We can accordingly identify a technological-institutional structure of production as a comparatively stable configuration of economic activities focused above all on the leading edges of the economy as both empirical reality and idealized norm. Different structures may be separated from one another in historical time by abrupt ruptures, or they may fade gradually into one another so that strong continuities are in evidence (Hyman 1991).

Fordist mass production, whose heyday coincided with the period from the 1920s to the 1960s, may be cited as a case of a technological-institutional structure with a strongly identifiable core group of sectors. As the name implies, fordist mass production was focused on large-scale assembly and process industries such as cars, steel, machinery, and domestic appliances. These industries were characterized by highly capitalized lead plants, with large and usually unionized labor forces. Around these lead plants there developed stratified hierarchies of input and service suppliers. The whole system of production and employment gave rise to overgrown industrial cities in the U.S. Manufacturing Belt like Detroit, Pittsburgh, and Chicago. And even though there were many other sectors throughout the period from the 1920s to the 1960s that were organized along completely different lines (cf. Pollert 1991), the fordist mass-production industries functioned as the central motor of the economic system, and as a definite paradigm of technological and managerial order.

During the 1970s, fordist mass production entered a period of crisis and massive restructuring in both North America and Western Europe. As deindustrialization of older fordist centers of production occurred, a number of other industrial sectors—many of which had coexisted with mass production in earlier years—now began to move to center stage. Three major ensembles of industries can be identified as constituting most of this shift. They are (a) various sorts of high-technology industrial sectors, (b) low-technology, labor-intensive industries such as clothing, furniture, jewelry, motion picture and television production, and (c) business and commercial services. These industries are often characterized as being "post-fordist" or "flexible," both of which terms are unsatisfactory in several respects—their very unsatisfactoriness reflecting the circumstance that we still have not achieved a really focused conceptual fix on the technological-institutional structures that sustain them and that have brought them into prominence. For better or for worse, both terms are now widely used, and our task is to continue to try to imbue them with theoretical and substantive meaning reflecting the dramatic changes that have been taking place in all the major capitalist economies since about the late 1960s.

What we can say about these industries is that they often tend to disintegrate into transactions-intensive complexes of many small producers forming dense and multifaceted production agglomerations. In this regard, they seem to represent a throwback to nineteenth-century craft industries, though in fact they are characterized by many features (in terms of technologies, products, labor markets, and so on) that distinguish them from nineteenth-century precursors. The high-technology ensemble, in particular, is interpenetrated by large systems houses producing complex outputs for defense and space exploration purposes. This ensemble is thus commonly constituted as an interdependent blend of (a) large-scale assembly industries focused on internal economies of scope, and (b) disintegrated transactions-intensive industries marked by many small producers. Flexible production ensembles of all three major types are also often associated with two-tier occupational structures and labor markets, and in contrast to much fordist mass-production industry, they are subject to systems of labor relations that tend to facilitate the deployment and redeployment of labor, both in terms of absolute employment levels and in terms of the assignment of workers to different tasks within the firm (Atkinson 1985; Storper and Scott 1990). The economic geography of flexible production is also, on the whole, quite different from that of fordist mass production. Despite the existence of a number of areas where there is some spatial overlap between the two, much flexible manufacturing occurs in parts of Western Europe and North America (such as the Third Italy or the Sunbelt) where traditions of large-scale fordist-style industrialization are at best weakly developed.

The emerging economic hegemony of flexible production sectors has been accompanied and in part stimulated by a series of important changes in structures of governance and social coordination. In fordist mass production, there was a broad tendency for national governments to engage in macroeconomic steering and to provide extensive social-welfare systems whose net effect was to maintain high and generally expanding levels of social consumption. There were many variations on this modus operandi from country to country, but its general lineaments followed a fairly identifiable pattern, which is now commonly subsumed under the general label of *Keynesian welfare-statism*. During the 1970s, this political order of things fell under increasing attack from conservative critics, and the attacks became all the more successful as fordist mass production itself fell into crisis. Reaganism, Thatcherism, and analogous conservative political movements in continental Europe can in some degree be interpreted as the instruments by which the decisive breakup of the old order and the ushering in of the new were secured. The new order is one in which a variety of flexible production sectors have moved to the leading edges of capitalist development, and in which privatization, a fresh spirit of entrepreneurial capitalism, and an intensification of the winds of competition have come strongly to the fore.

The emergence of this putative new technological-organizational structure of production has been attended by a resurgence of spatially agglomerated production in many new industrial spaces combined with the increased globalization of economic relations mediated in large degree by the multinational corporation. This twofold developmental process has given rise to the international mosaic of regional economic systems referred to above, and many novel experiments in social and economic coordination at both the local and the global levels are now proceeding forward. On the one hand, these experiments (like the Ben Franklin Partnership in Pennsylvania, or the marketing associations of the Third Italy) seek to build new institutional frameworks around the idiosyncratic needs, cultures, and prospects of individual industrial districts. On the other hand (like the U.S.-Canada-Mexico free trade agreement, or the European Economic Community) they are also a response to the potential anarchy of a system of international economic relations that is always tending to elude the scrutiny and regulatory power of sovereign states.

REPRISE

Southern California has been swept up in these different economic and political trends, though in its own extremely distinctive manner. Its particular pathway to high-technology industrialization and regional development was initiated some time between the two world wars with the growth of the aircraft industry, and on this basis, after the late 1940s, it steadily developed as a major center of the aerospace-electronics industry in general. Throughout the era of fordist mass production it was seen as an exception, as an anomalous complex of regional and urban activity in comparison with what were then considered to be the paradigmatic cases of successful industrial development, i.e., the large manufacturing cities of the Northeast. Nowadays, with the steady ascent of flexible production organization, Southern California is often taken to be something like a new paradigm of local economic development, and its institutional bases, its evolutionary trajectory, and its internal locational dynamics have come to be seen as providing important general insights and clues about the unfolding of flexible production systems and about some of the political tasks that this brings forward (Marchand and Scott 1991; Soja 1989). At the same time, it must always be kept in mind that Southern California's manufacturing base has also been decisively shaped by its special role as the dominant provider of high-technology weaponry to the federal government of the United States during the last few decades, and by its many particularities of local history and culture. There are hence a multitude of unique features inscribed on the economic landscape of the region.

The chapters that follow seek to play upon the analytical tensions created by this forceful combination of the general and the particular in the history and geography of high-technology industrial growth in Southern California.

PART II

A Geographical and Historical Overview of the Southern Californian Technopolis

The Structure and Organization of High-Technology Industry in Southern California

A Brief Profile

I argued in the preceding chapter that we have now entered an era in which postfordist production sectors constitute the leading edges of capitalist economic growth and development. Southern California's high-technology industrial ensemble is a major and yet in many respects an idiosyncratic case of this phenomenon. Here, I shall show how high-technology industry grew in the region over the 1960s, 1970s, and 1980s. I shall then demonstrate how the ensemble is made up of a distinctive combination of small *flexibly specialized* producers and large *systems houses*, and I shall describe how these two segments of the local economy interrelate with each other so as to form a single and multifaceted industrial complex.

HIGH-TECHNOLOGY INDUSTRIAL DEVELOPMENT IN SOUTHERN CALIFORNIA DURING THE 1970S AND 1980S

GROWTH AND CHANGE

One of the problems that we immediately face in any examination of the recent historical record of high-technology industrial development in Southern California is the periodic redefinition of the official Standard Industrial Classification (SIC). The effect of this is to make it extremely difficult to obtain runs of consistent data on industrial activity

TABLE 3.1   EMPLOYMENT AND NUMBER OF
ESTABLISHMENTS IN HIGH-TECHNOLOGY
INDUSTRY BY SECTOR, SOUTHERN
CALIFORNIA, 1964

		Employment	Establishments
19	Ordnance & accessories	>68,440	43
357	Office, computing & accounting machines	8,751	60
366	Communications equipment	70,089	173
367	Electronic components and accessories	26,245	326
372	Aircraft & parts	>125,451	428
381	Engineering & scientific instruments	4,808	74
382	Measuring & controlling instruments	8,922	81
384	Medical instruments	3,213	136
Total		>315,919	1,321

SOURCE: U.S. Department of Commerce, Bureau of the Census, *County Business Patterns*.

over long periods of time. Tables 3.1, 3.2, and 1.5 provide three different definitions of high-technology industry in Southern California for the years 1964, 1974, and 1988 in terms of the Standard Industrial Classifications in force in each of those years (i.e., respectively, the classifications of 1957, 1972, and 1977). These definitions are of necessity extremely provisional, but they are probably the best approximations that can be made, at the two- and three-digit SIC levels, to the main high-technology industrial complex of the region for the specified years. The three definitions diverge from one another in important respects, and strictly speaking, data given in terms of one cannot be compared to data given in terms of another. Fortunately, however, many of the changes made in the Standard Industrial Classifications over the years have involved much readjustment *within* the given definitions of high-technology industry (especially in the change from the 1972 to the 1987 classifications) so that in aggregate the data assembled in tables 3.1, 3.2, and 1.5 are roughly comparable. Until 1972,

TABLE 3.2   EMPLOYMENT AND NUMBER OF
ESTABLISHMENTS IN HIGH-TECHNOLOGY
INDUSTRY BY SECTOR, SOUTHERN
CALIFORNIA, 1974

	Employment	Establishments
357 Office, computing & accounting machines	32,800	154
366 Communications equipment	63,913	310
367 Electronic components & accessories	32,128	516
372 Aircraft & parts	90,464	300
376 Guided missiles, space vehicles, & parts	63,171	34
381 Engineering & scientific instruments	3,792	84
382 Measuring & controlling instruments	16,478	228
384 Medical instruments	12,723	256
Total	315,469	1,882

SOURCE: U.S. Department of Commerce, Bureau of the Census, *County Business Patterns*.

guided missiles were included in SIC 19 (ordnance and accessories); and for the case of Southern California, indeed, SIC 19 is overwhelmingly dominated by the guided missile sector. SIC 19 was abolished in the 1972 Standard Industrial Classification, and guided missile manufacturers were reassigned to SIC 372 (guided missiles, space vehicles, and parts).

Tables 3.1 to 3.5 plus table 1.5 give us a strong sense of the changing pattern of high-technology industrialization in Southern California for the period since the early 1960s. The ways in which some of the data given in these tables were estimated need to be elucidated. For reasons of confidentiality, the source from which the data were taken (i.e., *County Business Patterns*) occasionally deletes information for certain sectors in particular counties. In such cases, I have made estimates, wherever possible, of the missing values from the frequency distributions of establishment sizes provided by the source. Unfortunately, the largest size-class defined by the source is open ended, and for the 1964

TABLE 3.3   EMPLOYMENT AND NUMBER OF
ESTABLISHMENTS IN HIGH-TECHNOLOGY
INDUSTRY BY COUNTY, SOUTHERN
CALIFORNIA, 1964

	Employment	Establishments
Los Angeles	249,837	1,090
Orange	48,237	111
Riverside	2,840	14
San Bernardino	>10	4
San Diego	>12,923	79
Santa Barbara	778	13
Ventura	>1,294	10
Total	>315,919	1,321

SOURCE: U.S. Department of Commerce, Bureau of the Census, *County Business Patterns.*

TABLE 3.4   EMPLOYMENT AND NUMBER OF
ESTABLISHMENTS IN HIGH-TECHNOLOGY
INDUSTRY BY COUNTY, SOUTHERN
CALIFORNIA, 1976

	Employment	Establishments
Los Angeles	202,396	1,123
Orange	60,544	402
Riverside	3,816	27
San Bernardino	3,162	40
San Diego	31,660	193
Santa Barbara	6,852	43
Ventura	7,039	54
Total	315,469	1,882

SOURCE: U.S. Department of Commerce, Bureau of the Census, *County Business Patterns.*

TABLE 3.5   EMPLOYMENT AND NUMBER OF
ESTABLISHMENTS IN HIGH-TECHNOLOGY
INDUSTRY BY COUNTY, SOUTHERN
CALIFORNIA, 1988

	Employment	Establishments
Los Angeles	265,306	1,311
Orange	103,370	780
Riverside	8,378	67
San Bernardino	9,528	88
San Diego	55,535	466
Santa Barbara	11,625	82
Ventura	16,155	162
Total	469,897	2,956

SOURCE: U.S. Department of Commerce, Bureau of the Census, *County Business Patterns*.

data (tables 3.1 and 3.3) this sometimes makes it impossible to estimate employment. As a result, some of the statistics given in tables 3.1
and 3.3 represent only loose lower bounds on employment levels. In
later years, *County Business Patterns* presents data in a way that makes
it possible to estimate suppressed employment figures even when there
are establishments in the largest and open-ended size-class. The method
for doing this is described in appendix A. Thus, when data for the
years 1976 and 1988 are presented (in tables 3.2, 3.4, 3.5, and 1.5)
they are either direct measures or point estimates.

The data indicate that high-technology industrial employment in
Southern California has grown strongly, if erratically, over the last
three decades. The year 1976 comes toward the end of the crisis
period of the mid-1970s, and hence the data shown in tables 3.2 and
3.4 represent an abnormally depressed economic situation. Even so,
high-technology industry outperformed almost all mass-production
sectors in both the United States and Southern California by a wide
margin at this time. More remarkable than the growth of employment
has been the growth in the number of high-technology *establishments*
in the region. This number more than doubled over the period from

1964 to 1988, suggesting, as we shall remark in more detail below, that average establishment size has been declining over the years.

At the same time, the pace of high-technology industrial development in the region has varied greatly from county to county. In Los Angeles County, which in quantitative terms dominates the whole region, high-technology industrial employment has been stable or declining over the last few decades (though numbers of establishments have increased modestly). By contrast, Orange and San Diego counties have expanded at a remarkable rate. In very recent years, the most peripheral and least developed counties—Riverside, San Bernardino, Santa Barbara, and Ventura—have started to grow very rapidly, and while this growth is relative to a small base we can observe some of the incipient phases of new high-technology industrial district formation occurring in these cases.

THE SHIFTING FREQUENCY DISTRIBUTION OF ESTABLISHMENT SIZES

In addition to the general patterns of growth and change described above, high-technology industry in Southern California has been undergoing a series of long-run changes in the frequency distribution of establishment sizes.

For present purposes, a rough twofold categorization of high-technology industrial establishments in Southern California is proposed. On the one side we have small and medium-sized establishments employing fewer than 500 workers; on the other side we have a group of large establishments that employ 500 workers or more. This line of demarcation is debatable of course, though as will be seen, it serves our objectives well, and most important, it coincides with the boundary of one of the major establishment-size categories defined by *County Business Patterns*, which is the source of the data used in this analysis.

Total employment in these two categories of high-technology industrial establishments was computed by the method described in appendix A. In 1988, small and medium-size high-technology establishments employed a total of 144,489 workers; and large high-technology establishments employed 325,372. Thus the large-establishment segment is 2.25 times larger in terms of total employment than the small. The small to medium-sized segment, however, is much larger in terms of total number of establishments, for it has an

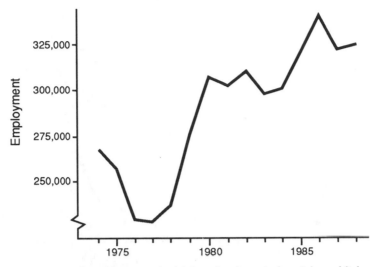

Figure 3.1. Total employment in high-technology industrial establishments with 500 or more workers in Southern California, 1974–1988. (See appendix A for data source.)

overwhelming 95.4 percent of the total. Moreover, over the period from 1974 to 1988, aggregate employment in small to medium-sized high-technology establishments in the region grew by 67.1 percent, whereas aggregate employment in the large-establishment segment grew by a comparatively modest 31.5 percent; concomitantly, employment in the small- to medium-sized–establishment sector increased in relative terms from 24.4 percent of all high-technology employment to 30.8 percent over the same period. Figures 3.1 and 3.2 trace out trends in absolute and relative employment for the large-establishment segment on a year-by-year basis, and figure 3.3 shows trends in (a) the number of large establishments as a percentage of all high-technology establishments in the region, and (b) the average size of high-technology establishments. The figures drive home the point that whereas absolute employment in the large-establishment segment of the high-technology industrial ensemble increased over much of the 1970s and 1980s, the segment is steadily losing ground in comparative terms to small and medium-sized establishments.

Figures 3.1, 3.2, and 3.3 also suggest that there are definite cyclical fluctuations in the overall relative downtrend observable in the large-establishment segment, with unusually strong expansions of employment in years when aggregate employment rises and unusually strong

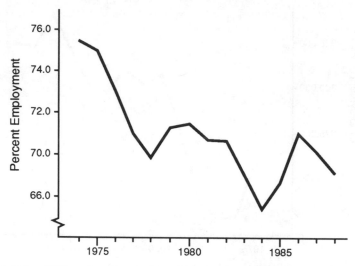

Figure 3.2. High-technology industry in Southern California, 1974–1988: Percentage of employment in establishments with 500 or more workers.

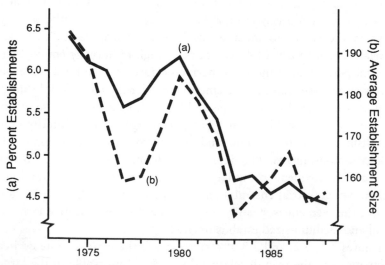

Figure 3.3. High-technology industry in Southern California, 1974–1988: Percentage of establishments with 500 or more workers, and average size of establishment.

decreases in years when it falls. Note, however, that the method used to estimate employment in large establishments has some propensity to magnify the amplitude of these ups and downs (see appendix A for details). The propensity is probably limited in its total effects, but we should nonetheless approach the revealed fluctuations with considerable circumspection. With this reservation in mind, temporal variations in employment in the large-establishment segment may be analyzed in terms of a logistic regression equation in which P_t (the proportion of high-technology employment in Southern California concentrated in establishments with 500 or more workers) is expressed as a function of t (time) and E_t (total regional employment in high-technology industry). The computed equation is

$$P_t = 1/[1 + \exp(0.964 + 0.071t - 0.000005E_t)]$$
$$\quad\quad\quad (0.010)\quad (0.000001)$$

which, with an R^2 of 0.81 and degrees of freedom of 12, is significant at the .01 level; the coefficients attached to the independent variables are significant at the same level.

As conjectured, the equation suggests that there is a clearly declining trend in P_t as a function of time and that this trend is punctuated by upturns and downturns in periods of rising and falling employment, respectively. To the degree that we can invest confidence in P_t as a real measure of temporal trends (see appendix A) it is evident that large establishments disproportionately take on additional workers in good times, and disproportionately lay off workers in bad times. This conjecture runs counter to the argument of Berger and Piore (1980) who claim that the large-establishment segment as a whole retains a relatively stable level of employment across the economic cycle, and that it is the small-establishment segment that absorbs the main fluctuations in aggregate employment. It is conceivable that Berger and Piore's claims may hold more widely true in mass-production systems, but further investigation of this point is needed.

If the large-establishment segment is of declining relative significance in the high-technology industrial complex of Southern California, it remains, as we have seen, of major and even growing importance in absolute terms. Two additional points must now be made. First, if we look at individual high-technology industrial sectors in Southern California, a couple of them evince a small but unambiguous relative *increase* in aggregate employment in large establishments. These sectors are SIC 366 (communications equipment) where employment in large establishments went from 75.0 percent of the sectoral total to 80.5 percent between 1974 and 1987, and SIC 376 (guided missiles, space vehicles, and parts) where employment in large establishments went from 94.7 percent to 97.4 percent. In both of these sectors, systems houses are especially well developed as a function of the massive internal economies of scope that accrue to the production of elaborate military and space technologies. Second, the large high-technology manufacturing establishments of Southern California are almost all subsidiary units of multiestablishment and multinational corporations, and if individual plants (and firms) may be downsizing, their economic and political power nevertheless remains enormous, and is indeed almost certainly increasing.

Some commentators (e.g., Brusco 1986, 1990; Trigilia 1990) have claimed that Marshallian industrial districts are made up only of small firms and establishments. The data presented above make it evident that large establishments are an important and relatively durable element of Southern California's high-technology industrial districts. These districts, moreover, are composed for the most part of a functionally adaptable blend of flexibly specialized producers and systems houses.

FLEXIBLE SPECIALIZATION AND SYSTEMS-HOUSE FORMS OF HIGH-TECHNOLOGY INDUSTRIAL PRODUCTION

Available published statistics do not allow us to distinguish between flexibly specialized producers and systems houses, as such, within the high-technology industrial ensemble of Southern California. However, most of the small producers are presumably flexible specialists of one variety or another, and many of the largest electronics, aircraft, and space equipment manufacturers can certainly be seen as being systems houses. The question before us is, how do these two segments of the local economy behave and interact, and how do they contribute (or not contribute) to the perpetuation and growth of industrial districts?

FLEXIBLE SPECIALIZATION

In conformity with the powerful line of argument first laid out by Piore and Sabel (1984), many scholars have sought to ground analysis of current technological-institutional structures of production in the idea of "flexible specialization." The idea is generally considered to apply with special force to firms that produce small batches of output in constantly changing product and process configurations, and it stands in direct opposition to the notion of mass production, i.e., a form of industry characterized by standardized outputs made in extremely long runs. Flexibly specialized firms are thus able to engage in high levels of product differentiation, customization, and semicustomization, and they often turn necessity into a virtue by transforming their endemic instability into an opportunity for constant technological upgrading and design innovation.

Because flexible specialization usually entails a breakdown of internal economies of scale and scope in the production process, it tends to be associated with small or medium-sized and vertically disintegrated units of production. These units then typically become caught up in dense linkage networks through which they are able to tap into significant external economies of scale and scope. With the resurgence of flexible specialization in modern capitalism, therefore, has come a pervasive tendency to reagglomerate economic activity. Sabel (1989) has argued, too, in favor of the view that a convergence between large firms and industrial districts may be occurring, in which the former increasingly externalize many kinds of production activities and are subsequently reorganized within wider transactional networks. We have observed above that in the high-technology industrial districts of Southern California a definite downsizing of production units has been systematically occurring. And this observation is consistent with the wider findings of analysts such as Acs and Audretsch (1990), Loveman and Sengenberger (1990), and Birch (1987), who have shown that significant decreases have occurred in establishment and firm sizes (in manufacturing and services) in the major capitalist economies since the 1970s. This tendency stands in marked contrast to an earlier period over much of this century in which rising concentration seems to have been the rule (Prais 1976).

SYSTEMS-HOUSE PRODUCTION

Despite the latter remarks, large production units remain—and will no doubt continue to remain—an extremely important element of the economic landscape of North America, both inside and outside of industrial districts. In the high-technology industrial districts of Southern California today, large production units flourish in particular abundance in the guise of systems houses. Specifically, the term "systems house" is used here to designate any industrial establishment that (a) has massive internal economies of scope, very often flowing from a design-intensive or R&D-intensive production process, that (b) therefore has a variegated internal structure and employs large numbers of workers, and (c) manufactures complex outputs in small batches, very often (but not necessarily) over a lengthy production period. At any one time, a given systems house may be engaged in several different production programs run largely in isolation from one another, but with certain managerial, purchasing, technical, etc., functions in common. Output specifications may change radically from one program to the next. Sometimes it may take months or even years to complete one production cycle (as in the case, for example, of the Space Platform currently under construction by McDonnell Douglas Astronautics, or the Space Shuttle produced by Rockwell Space Systems Division).

Systems-house producers are, as it were, latent flexible specialists that have been unable to escape from the force of internal economies of scope. That is, in the absence of the various synergies holding their many and differentiated internal parts together, they would presumably fragment into networks of smaller, more specialized producers with greater ease of entry into and exit from different product markets. Moreover, just as flexibly specialized firms were present in the period of fordist mass production (though rarely at the leading edges), so too were systems houses in the form, for example, of major motion picture studios, big publishing houses (but not printing works), shipyards, and so on; and if they are perhaps most commonly found in technology-intensive sectors today, they are by no means restricted to high-technology industry but are also found in a wide variety of other manufacturing and service sectors.

FLEXIBLE SPECIALIZATION SYSTEMS HOUSES, AND POSTFORDISM

Together, the flexibly specialized and systems-house segments of Southern California's high-technology economy constitute a peculiar kind of postfordist industrial system. Both of them represent opposite poles of a continuum of technological and organizational possibilities, and at the same time, both stand in marked opposition to mass production. A suggested tripartite ordering of these forms of manufacturing activity is laid out in figure 3.4 where fundamental archetypes are

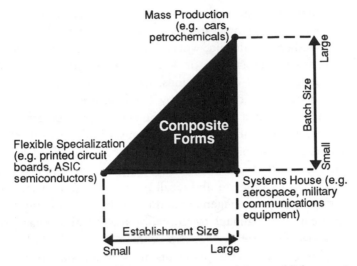

Figure 3.4. Types of production units arranged by establishment size and batch size.

arrayed according to characteristic establishment size and batch size. These two dimensions of variation of course stand in as proxies for other variables such as levels of product standardization, routinization of production processes, length of production cycle, and so on. To be sure, any given production unit may not in reality conform precisely to one of the three archetypes, and composite forms can be identified, as for example, in the case of specialized car manufacturers that combine elements of all three and would hence tend to be located somewhere in the interior of the triangle shown in figure 3.4.

Notwithstanding their evident differences from flexibly specialized producers, systems houses are assuredly an authentic element of the postfordist flexible economy. They make much use of flexible equipment in the form of computerized and robotized machines, they focus on the production of small batches of varied products that may go through many design changes as they are in process, and they drive forward large segments of the rest of the flexible economy, for even though they may be marked by intense internal economies of scope, they invariably consume a wide range of diverse, variable, and often unpredictable inputs (whereas in mass-production industries the trend is toward standardization and streamlining of inputs as far as possible). Systems houses, in brief, are typically interconnected via intricate transactional networks with large numbers of flexibly specialized producers. For the same reason, they are very often found in dense flexible-production agglomerations. In the high-technology systems houses of Southern California, workers are frequently unionized, with the International Association of Machinists and the United Auto Workers the dominant organizations. Workers employed in smaller units of production in the region, by contrast, are rarely unionized. Paradoxically—but as a reflection of the genesis of Southern California's high-technology industrial systems houses in the period from the 1930s to the 1950s—union contracts tend to be rather "fordist" in nature. These contracts typically lay much emphasis on detailed job descriptions, seniority in layoff and recall procedures, and a strict line of demarcation between management and labor. In many establishments, attempts are now being made to reorganize the old labor-relations system and above all to set up workers' teams with rotating job responsibilities, though the latter experiments are still in a state of flux. In a number of recent interviews with representatives of management, it was also found that high-technology systems houses in Southern California rarely put just-in-time methods of input-output organization into practice, probably because of the variability and unpredictability of the production schedules that they face.

LOCATION AND LINKAGE STRUCTURES IN SOUTHERN CALIFORNIA'S HIGH-TECHNOLOGY INDUSTRIAL DISTRICTS: A PRELIMINARY VIEW

Figure 3.5 displays the locational pattern of large high-technology manufacturing establishments in Southern California in 1990. For ease of drafting the figure, only the ninety-three high-technology establishments in the region with employment of 1,000 or more workers are shown. Many of these establishments have head offices in Southern California, but perhaps the majority (e.g., Ampex, General Dynamics, Interstate Electronics, Kyocera, McDonnell Douglas, etc.) have head offices elsewhere, including other countries. Also indicated in figure 3.5 are isolines denoting levels of accessibility to all aerospace-electronics establishments (986 of them) in the region for which addresses could be readily obtained. Most of the latter establishments consist of small and disintegrated production units. Accessibility at any given location to the set of 986 aerospace-electronics establishments is defined as $\sum d_j^{-1}$ where d_j is the distance from that location to the jth aerospace-electronics establishment. The isolines plotted in

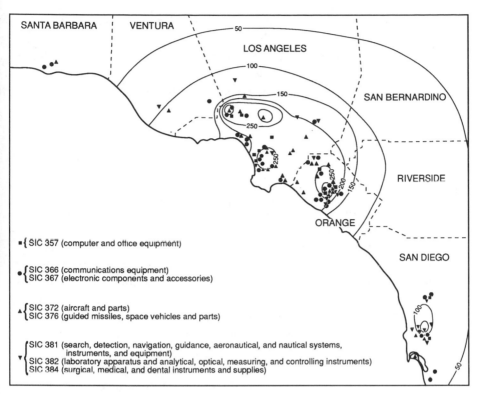

SANTA BARBARA | VENTURA
LOS ANGELES
SAN BERNARDINO
RIVERSIDE
ORANGE
SAN DIEGO

■{ SIC 357 (computer and office equipment)

●{SIC 366 (communications equipment)
 {SIC 367 (electronic components and accessories)

▲{SIC 372 (aircraft and parts)
 {SIC 376 (guided missiles, space vehicles and parts)

 {SIC 381 (search, detection, navigation, guidance, aeronautical, and nautical systems,
▼{   instruments, and equipment)
 {SIC 382 (laboratory apparatus and analytical, optical, measuring, and controlling instruments)
 {SIC 384 (surgical, medical, and dental instruments and supplies)

Figure 3.5. Southern California high-technology industrial establishments with 1,000 or more workers. SIC codes conform to the 1987 Standard Industrial Classification. Isolines designating accessibility levels to all aerospace-electronics producers in the region are shown. (Data from California Manufacturers' Association, *California Manufacturers' Register*, Newport Beach, Database Publishing Co., 1990.)

figure 3.5 sharply delineate four of the major high-technology industrial districts of Southern California, i.e., (a) the San Fernando Valley area to the northwest of central Los Angeles, (b) the El Segundo-Hawthorne-Inglewood area to the southwest of central Los Angeles, (c) northern Orange County, and (d) the San Diego area.

The striking feature of figure 3.5 is the fact that large establishments concentrate for the most part in and around the major high-technology industrial districts. Contrary to what we might expect on the basis of presuppositions about the location of land-intensive economic activities, large establishments are for the most part *not* to be found on the cheapest land toward the far periphery of the entire urban system; nor, certainly, are they to be found at the center of the entire metropolitan system; rather, they cluster to a significant degree at intermediate locations where local levels of accessibility to suppliers are comparatively high. The locational association between large establishments and the main high-technology industrial districts suggests that there is a spatial and functional symbiosis between these establishments and the rest of the production system. Despite the internal economies of scope that characterize large systems houses, they typically have massive and multifaceted demands for externally supplied material inputs and subcontract services. We know that some of these inputs come from far beyond the confines of Southern California. We also know that there is a remarkable intraregional network of economic transactions in the region focused on large producers.

The latter point can be dramatically exemplified with data on subcontracting patterns for NASA prime contractors. In fiscal year 1989, there were five major NASA prime contractors in Southern California who individually awarded more than $1 million in subcontracts to first-tier subcontractors (NASA 1989). The five prime contractors were the California Institute of Technology, General Dynamics, McDonnell Douglas, Rockwell International, and TRW. These five institutions held twenty different NASA prime-contract awards at eight different locations in Southern California in 1989. In total, they gave out 4,787 first-tier subcontracts worth $10,000 or more each. Of these, 2,698 (56.4 percent) were awarded to Southern Californian producers, and they constituted 38 percent of the aggregate $1,540 million given out. The fact that significantly more than half of the contracts awarded went to local firms, and that these contracts also represented much less than half of the total dollar amount subcontracted out, signifies that intraregional short-distance linkages are biased towards smaller transactions. Out of the total of 4,787 first-tier subcontracts nationwide, 648 second-tier subcontracts worth more than $10,000 each were awarded in turn. In this second subcontracting tier, 208 contracts (31.1 percent) were given out to Southern Californian producers and they represented 49.2 percent of the aggregate value of all second-tier subcontracts. Many of the 208 second-tier subcontracts awarded to Southern Californian producers originated from outside the region and thus they comprise a blend of long-distance and short-distance linkages.

Large aerospace-electronics establishments in Southern California thus have major impacts through their procurement practices on local economic growth and development. These impacts eventually filter down through the region's transactional networks to the very smallest subcontractors and service suppliers. Unlike mass-production industries, which have often had an inimical effect on industrial districts by initiating a dynamic of horizontal and vertical integration combined with decentralization of routinized branch plants, the systems houses of Southern California have consistently played a very positive role in helping to sustain the wider local industrial base. The fact that they are gradually shrinking in size and importance over the course of time suggests that they may be continuing to play an important role through the spinoff and externalization of particular functions. However, since the late 1980s, they have been much affected by severe cutbacks in federal defense expenditures that have resulted in significant layoffs and plant closures, with disastrous consequences for lower tiers of subcontractors in the region.

CONCLUSION

I have demonstrated that industrial districts may consist of varying combinations of both large and small establishments, and that large producers are often quite instrumental in inducing and sustaining agglomeration. In some cases, no doubt, the advent of large establishments may lead to the deliquescence of a formerly viable industrial district. In other cases, as with high-technology industry in Southern California, large establishments frequently function as mainsprings of development and growth over long periods of time.

One important point that emerges from the discussion in both this chapter and the previous one is that industrial districts can be conceptualized at a high level of abstraction, and that this conceptualization can be fruitfully applied to a wide variety of historical and geographical cases. This claim in no way dismisses the importance of additional finely delineated analyses that are sensitive to the peculiarities of history and geography or to the effects that such peculiarities always have on the form and functions of individual places (cf. Amin and Robins 1990). However, it does aver that there are common underlying dynamics and processes that allow us to approach these diverse individual instances of industrial districts with a unified theoretical language.

The high-technology industrial districts of Southern California are a potent illustration of the general definition of industrial districts offered in chapter 2, just as they are marked by many important features that are purely local and episodic in character. They also dramatically exemplify the constructive role that large systems houses may play in flexible high-technology production agglomerations, and the ways in which both large and small producers can coexist in mutual functional and spatial interdependence over long periods of time.

CHAPTER 4

Southern California's Pathway to High-Technology Industrial Development, 1920–1960

There is going to be a Detroit of the aircraft industry.
Why not here in Los Angeles?

E. J. Clapp (1926)

How, we may ask, was Southern California's extraordinarily dense and advanced high-technology industrial system initiated? How did the process of industrialization unfold over time, and how did it come to be expressed in so multifarious a complex of activities?

The original inception of high-technology industry in Southern California goes back to the 1920s and 1930s, when the aircraft industry first took root in the region. During World War II, enormous expansion of the aircraft industry occurred, and the first stirrings of missile and military electronics production took place. Over the next fifteen years or so the aerospace-electronics complex in the region emerged as *the* main focus of high-technology industry in the country, and it came to function as a great growth machine driven forward by lavish Department of Defense procurements on the one hand and an expanding and internally generated stock of agglomeration economies on the other hand (Clark 1981; Markusen and Bloch 1985; Steiner 1961). These agglomeration economies reside preeminently in the localized production networks and labor markets that have steadily been put into place in the region over the last several decades.

THE GENESIS OF SOUTHERN CALIFORNIA'S HIGH-TECHNOLOGY INDUSTRIAL COMPLEX

The empirical circumstances attending the birth of the aircraft industry in Southern California in the 1920s and 1930s represent a complicated story and one that has hitherto not been well understood. Fortunately, the story has recently been recounted in great historical detail by Lotchin (1992) in his book *Fortress California, 1910–1961*, and what follows runs, in part, parallel to his account.

In the very earliest phases of any industry's growth, it is often the case that many widely scattered places are more or less equally likely to emerge as locational foci of the industry. This state of affairs certainly seems to have been a feature of the aircraft industry, which in the 1920s functioned at a variety of locations throughout the United States. Its establishment and eventual rise to dominance in Southern California seem to have been due, in the first instance, to a combination of several fortuitous circumstances, and then, in the second instance, to the systematic development of extensive agglomeration economies as the industry moved into its formative stages and began to attain critical mass. Among the circumstances that helped to initiate aircraft production in Southern California were the early flowering of a culture of amateur aviation in the region, and the presence of a number of early aircraft industry pioneers such as Martin, the Loughead Brothers, Douglas, Ryan, and Northrop. There was, in addition, a tightly knit power elite which over the first few decades of the twentieth century was intent on fostering local economic growth and which commanded the financial means to have a significant practical impact. Thus, in 1920, a group of Los Angeles businessmen led by Harry Chandler, the publisher of the *Los Angeles Times*, raised $15,000 to help start Donald Douglas in the business of aircraft manufacture. The local military establishment also contributed to the growth of the infant industry by its demands for a variety of experimental planes. Finally, until the mid-1930s, the open shop rules that prevailed throughout Southern California represented a major advantage that helped the burgeoning aircraft industry in its earliest years of development (Cunningham 1951; Hatfield 1973; Lotchin 1992; Markusen et al. 1991; Markusen and Yudken 1992; Schoneberger 1984).

Some authors have claimed that the abundant sunshine, mild winters (permitting outdoor construction of aircraft), and the all-around excellent flying weather of Southern California were also decisive factors in the local development of the industry (e.g., Hammond 1941). This claim seems rather unconvincing, however, given the much greater early success of the industry in the northeast of the country where these alleged advantages were conspicuously absent. Indeed, in the 1920s and much of the 1930s, Southern California was actually a

TABLE 4.1   MAJOR AIRCRAFT-PRODUCING
STATES, 1925–1937

	1925		1931		1937	
State	Establish-ments	Wage earners	Establish-ments	Wage earners	Establish-ments	Wage earners
California	4	203	10	n.a.	24	11,520
Connecticut	1	n.a.	5	625	3	n.a.
Kansas	2	n.a.	8	185	5	510
Michigan	2	n.a.	9	777	3	n.a.
New York	15	890	19	2,161	17	4,206
Ohio	5	616	10	1,071	13	502
Pennsylvania	2	n.a.	8	n.a.	7	632
Total U.S.	44	2,701	101	9,870	92	24,003

SOURCE: U.S. Department of Commerce, Bureau of the Census, *Biennial Census of Manufactures.*

(n.a. = not available)

minor center of the industry, with only some 10 percent of the country's aircraft manufacturing capacity. The data presented in table 4.1 indicate that over the 1920s and down to the early 1930s the industry was largely concentrated in the Manufacturing Belt (in New York and Ohio above all), with the western part of the United States lagging well behind. Then, over the 1930s, California (i.e., Southern California for the major part) steadily outstripped all other states in terms of both aircraft production establishments and especially employment. By 1937, California had 26.1 percent of the nation's establishments and 48 percent of total wage earners in the aircraft industry.

Among the earliest aircraft firms to settle in the region were the Douglas Aircraft Company and the Lockheed Aircraft Company. Both were founded in the 1920s, the former in Santa Monica, the latter in Burbank, with Douglas also setting up a branch plant at El Segundo in 1932. Another important early firm, Ryan Aeronautical, was established in San Diego in 1931. This was followed by a spate of successful new firms over the 1930s. Thus, in 1935, the Consolidated Aircraft Corporation (later Consolidated-Vultee and then General Dynamics Convair) made its appearance in San Diego. In the same year, North American Aviation (later Rockwell North American) moved to Ingle-

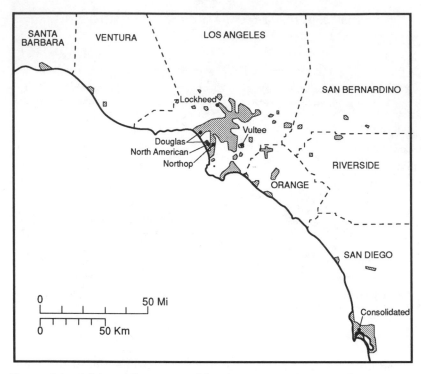

Figure 4.1. Major airframe assembly plants in Southern California in the 1930s. The urbanized areas at the time are shaded.

wood from the northeast of the country. Vultee Aircraft Inc. (which merged with Consolidated in 1943) was set up in Downey in 1936. In 1938–39, John Northrop, who had earlier worked for both Douglas and Lockheed, founded Northrop Aircraft Inc. in Hawthorne. And in 1941 Douglas established yet another branch plant—at Long Beach— that eventually became the firm's main production unit. All of these aircraft manufacturing establishments were located in what were then the fringes of the built-up area of the region, where land was relatively cheap and where adjacent airstrips were available (see fig. 4.1). All were engaged predominantly in final airframe assembly, with engines imported from the northeast of the country where engine manufacture was (as it is today) locationally concentrated. By the late 1930s, after considerable and often bitter confrontations between management and labor, most of the big assembly plants in the region (with the major exception of Northrop) had been effectively unionized (Allen and Schneider 1956).

Notwithstanding the evident growth of the industry in Southern California over the late 1930s, the region might well have remained a minor outlier relative to the U.S. aircraft industry as a whole, had not a number of critical technological breakthroughs occurred. Two such breakthroughs merit special mention. One was Lockheed's creation of the L-10 Electra aircraft in 1933, and the other—of surpassing significance—was the development by Douglas of the DC-3 aircraft in 1935 (Miller and Sawers 1968; Phillips 1971). These two aircraft offered superior standards of speed and efficiency, and they rapidly became the preferred craft in the rapidly growing airline industry. In 1933, according to Phillips (1971), Lockheed products accounted for only some 10.6 percent of all new aircraft added to U.S. domestic fleets, and Douglas products accounted for just 1.2 percent. These percentages had risen to 32.8 percent and 59 percent, respectively, by 1935 thanks to the L-10 and the DC-3; and by 1937 the equivalent values were 11.1 percent and 87 percent, i.e., virtually the totality of all new orders.

Whatever the peculiar and complicated conditions that attended the original foundation of Southern California's main aircraft assembly plants, the turning point of the region's fortunes and its emergence as *the* dominant center of the industry (and eventually of the entire aerospace-electronics industry) dates especially from this period of technological advance and growth in the late 1930s. Even so, we can still not project forward from these events (i.e., the initial founding acts and the first major round of technology-driven expansion) to the subsequent developmental pattern of the complex. This subsequent pattern is one of great intricacy involving as it does the shifting military needs and policies of the U.S. government, rapid technological change, and the active diversification of the complex. But one important factor dating from these early years certainly helped to maintain the region's leading status. As the aircraft industry expanded, so there came into being in the surrounding area a network of dependent subcontract shops and parts suppliers, and a widening pool of specialized and habituated labor. One directory of manufacturing firms in the Los Angeles area in 1939 lists six major aircraft assembly plants together with thirty aircraft accessories and parts suppliers and three aeronautical instruments manufacturers (Los Angeles County Chamber of Commerce 1939). Many other types of industrial establishments listed in the same directory under such headings as machine shops or metal working shops must also have been linked both directly and indirectly to the growing aircraft industry in the region. The external economies that were almost certainly generated in this way no doubt helped to enhance the region's comparative advantages in aircraft production, thereby raising productivity levels and contributing to the emergence of a functionally interrelated system of agglomerated production activities.

CONSOLIDATION AND EARLY DIVERSIFICATION OF SOUTHERN CALIFORNIA'S HIGH-TECHNOLOGY INDUSTRIAL BASE, 1940–1950

With the outbreak of World War II, the aircraft industry in Southern California made a major leap forward, as assembly plants were pushed to expand their production of military aircraft to the limits of their capacity. Employment in the industry in Los Angeles jumped from 15,000 in 1939 to 190,700 in 1943 at the peak of wartime production (see table 4.2). This expansion was facilitated by a large intake of female employees into the industry, and by the fine-tuning of assembly procedures. For a brief time during the war, the aircraft industry came close to becoming a classic mass-production industry, with Vultee in Downey actually installing a powered assembly line (Rae, 1968). However, with the turn to small batch production of evermore complex individual aircraft in the postwar years, this tendency has been permanently reversed. The wartime expansion of aircraft production was also underpinned by a vast expansion of outsourcing networks, with significant elements of these networks concentrated in the local area (Day 1956; Harlan 1956). In fact, in the nation as a whole, subcontracting in the industry increased from 10 percent of all work performed to 38 percent between 1940 and 1944 (Cunningham 1951; Lilley et al. 1946). This increase in subcontracting tended to reinforce the overall growth of Southern California's aircraft manufacturing agglomeration, for reasons that have been amply articulated by Day (1956: 209–210):

> From the prime contractor's point of view, ease of liaison and the possibility of an increase in personal control are the most important advantages arising from close proximity. . . . The greater ease of control tends to keep the location of the smaller subcontract firms close to the main plant. The numerous small outside manufacturers with their relatively tiny orders require proportionately greater attention from the prime contractor when compared with the same purchase dollars spent for a single major subcontract item. Thus, the small subcontracts and ordinary shop overload work

TABLE 4.2   EMPLOYMENT IN AIRCRAFT
ASSEMBLY IN LOS ANGELES, 1939–1950

Year	Employment in aircraft	Aircraft as % of all Los Angeles employment
1939	15,000	11.5
1940	34,800	21.0
1941	74,200	33.0
1942	129,100	39.0
1943	190,700	40.0
1944	152,400	36.5
1945	95,700	30.0
1946	50,700	21.0
1947	48,400	20.0
1948	44,600	20.0
1949	65,000	17.1
1950	70,500	17.0

SOURCE: Wilburn (1971).

are, in the majority of cases, placed in companies in the same urban area as the prime contractor and seldom outside a 300- to 400-mile radius.

Large establishments as well as small were caught up in this local network of subcontracting activity and parts production, and among the more important of these were Garrett, AiResearch, and Hughes Aircraft in Los Angeles and Rohr in San Diego (Austin 1965; Chapin 1966; Schoneberger and Scholl 1985). In this fashion, the geographical bases of the aircraft industry as a dense, localized production complex in Southern California were progressively secured.

Simultaneously, the region was incipiently on the point of flowering as a major locus of missile and defense electronics production. Already, in 1929, the Guggenheim Aeronautical Laboratory (renamed the Jet Propulsion Laboratory in 1943) had been founded at the California Institute of Technology in Pasadena, with Theodore Von Karman as its director. Over the subsequent decades, the laboratory came to play an increasingly important role in the development of rocket technology and in the training of skilled personnel. In 1942, Von Karman and his associates founded Aerojet Engineering Corporation (later Aerojet General) in Azusa, just east of Los Angeles, on the basis of an Air Force contract to develop jet-assisted take-off rockets (Hoyt 1971; Malina 1964). Douglas Aircraft, too, was an early participant in rocket technology with its Roc I guided bomb developed over 1940–1941 (Ingells 1979; Maynard 1962). Roc II followed in 1944. In 1943, Lockheed was given a contract by the Army to develop a jet fighter aircraft (i.e., the F-80 Shooting Star). The Marquardt Company was founded in Van Nuys in 1944 and began development of ramjet engines. Douglas started work on the Corporal E missile in 1944, and this was developed further by the Firestone Defense Products Division, which produced the WAC Corporal missile in the same year. The Firestone plant had been set up in Los Angeles four years earlier to manufacture tank treads and aircraft tires. The year 1945 marked a great intensification of work on missile development and production. On the basis of its earlier experiences in rocketry, Douglas undertook to produce the Nike Ajax surface-to-air missile in 1945 and the Sparrow II in 1950. In 1947, Hughes Aircraft secured an Air Force contract for guided air-to-air missile development that resulted in the Falcon missile in the early 1950s; and in 1945 Consolidated-Vultee initiated an R&D program that would eventually lead to the Atlas Intercontinental Ballistic Missile. Also in 1945, Consolidated-Vultee produced the Lark surface-to-air missile, and Ryan Aeronautical began work on the Firebird. North American, in its turn, started work on the Navaho missile for the Navy in 1946. The record thus tersely recited is testimony to the extraordinary extensiveness of rocket and missile development in Southern California, even as early as the period of the World War II.

A roughly parallel development of electronics can be sketched out. Prior to the 1940s, Southern California had only a weakly developed electrical/electronics industry. Kidner and Neff (1945a, 1945b, 1946) indicate that in the various subsectors making up the electrical machinery industry of Los Angeles in 1939, employment was only a modest 2,202 to 2,387 workers (see table 4.3) and compared to the United States as a whole (and especially the metropolitan areas of the northeastern seaboard), Southern California was rather poorly endowed with electrical industries (cf. Hall and Preston 1988; Hund 1959; Warner 1989). Even its communications equipment and radio-manufacturing industries were of minor importance, though these were later to expand and diversify in remarkable ways. In spite of the underdeveloped state of the prewar electronics industry in Southern

TABLE 4.3   SUBSECTORS OF THE ELECTRICAL
MACHINERY INDUSTRY IN LOS ANGELES,
1939

	Employment	Percent of U.S.
Batteries, storage & primary	346	2.30
Communications equipment	132	0.00
Electrical appliances	172	0.86
Electrical measuring instruments	<12	<0.17
Electrical products n.e.c.	21	0.35
Generating, distribution, & industrial apparatus	873	1.24
Insulated wire & cable	<173	<1.10
Radios, radio tubes & phonographs	532	1.22
Wiring devices & supplies	62	0.43
X-ray & therapeutic apparatus	64	3.27
Total	2,202–2,387	

SOURCE: Kidner and Neff (1945a, 1945b).

California, a few local firms founded at this time survived through the 1940s and ultimately participated in the postwar electronics boom. Among them were Collins Radio, Gilfillan, and Hoffman Radio. Bendix and Lear also had branch plants in the region producing aircraft radio equipment. In addition, a number of prewar aircraft firms—most notably Hughes Aircraft—later diversified into electronics.

In 1942, one of these early electronics firms, namely Gilfillan (now ITT Gilfillan), developed a ground control approach (GCA) radar system in cooperation with engineers at MIT. The GCA system was used to assist aircraft landing in bad weather. It was widely applied in the later years of the war, and played a major role in the Berlin airlift. After 1945, Hughes Aircraft started to take a major lead as a significant innovator in military electronics. The firm had originally been established by Howard Hughes in Burbank in 1932 as a service facility for his air-racing activities. After a move to Glendale, the firm was permanently established in Culver City in 1941. Here, the firm worked on flexible feed chutes for aircraft machine guns, and developed—under federal contract—the prototype HK-1 flying boat and the XF11 reconnaissance plane. In 1945, the firm hired both Simon Ramo and Dean

Wooldridge who quickly built up an advanced electronics capacity, and in 1948 the firm won an $8 million contract to construct radar weapons control units for the Lockheed F-94 (Barlett and Steele 1979; Hughes Aircraft Company 1986). Ramo himself has written of this era of Hughes Aircraft:

> It came to house the largest concentration of technical college graduates, including the greatest number of Ph.D.s in any single industrial facility of that period except for the Bell Telephone Laboratories in New Jersey. (Ramo 1988: 36)

By 1952, Hughes Aircraft was employing over 15,000 workers, 1,000 of whom were scientists; and by the end of the 1950s, the firm was responsible for some 20 percent of the electronics business of the entire state of California (Arnold et al. 1960).

During the 1940s, the educational and research infrastructure of the region was also changing rapidly, and facilities for the training of advanced engineering and scientific workers were now expanding apace. The role of the Jet Propulsion Laboratory at the California Institute of Technology has already been mentioned. At the University of California, Los Angeles, a College of Engineering was established in 1941 with an emphasis on aeronautical engineering. In 1942, Northrop opened an Aeronautical Institute (later Northrop University) to train its own engineers. At the University of Southern California, an engineering program focusing on aeronautics was inaugurated in the late 1940s, and at the same time, the university's electrical engineering program was greatly strengthened (cf. Bloch 1987). In 1946, Project RAND was set up with federal money as a department of Douglas Aircraft, and it was given a mandate to inquire into the feasibility of intercontinental nonsurface warfare (RAND Corporation 1963). Out of this project the RAND Corporation was born in 1948 as an independent not-for-profit organization funded by the Air Force. This event presaged a remarkable efflorescence of military-industrial research institutions that were to grow up within the region over the subsequent ten or fifteen years.

GROWTH OF THE COMPLEX, 1950–1960

DEFENSE SPENDING AND INDUSTRIAL GROWTH IN SOUTHERN CALIFORNIA

As the above discussion makes evident, Southern California during the war years was a hive of experimental projects and technological explorations underpinned by the military activities of the federal government. All of this activity was soon to blossom into a great network of productive activity and innovation as Southern California's high-technology industrial base expanded in the postwar years. That said, the ending of World War II ushered in a period of deep economic depression in Southern California. By 1948, employment in the aircraft industry had fallen to 44,600—a decline of 76.6 percent compared to the peak employment of the industry during the war, and the decline made itself felt even more widely than this by reason of the direct and indirect connections of the industry to the rest of the local economy. In 1949, a total of 178,000 workers were unemployed in Los Angeles, giving an overall rate of unemployment of 13.6 percent (Clayton 1962; Collier and Perry 1953). This period of economic decline, however, was soon to be dramatically broken as the Korean War broke out in June 1950, and as the long Cold War set in (Urbanomics 1969).

These events helped to secure Southern California's rise to preeminence as the nation's major producing region for defense equipment. During World War II, despite the extraordinary expansion of the aircraft industry, California as a whole was third after New York and Michigan in total federal military contract awards (Peck and Scherer 1962). By 1953, it had attained first place with some 15.4 percent of all Department of Defense prime contract awards. The state has kept its lead ever since, averaging about 20 percent of prime contract awards over the period from the 1950s to the 1980s, with Southern California accounting for some 70 percent to 80 percent of this total (Bloch 1987; Clayton 1967).

Table 4.4 shows Department of Defense prime contract awards in the state over the 1950s. There was a marked peak in awards during the Korean War, followed by a sharp downturn in 1954–1957. In the aftermath of the Soviet Union's successful launching of Sputnik in October 1957, prime contract awards began to turn up again, and they then in effect grew generally if irregularly down to the late 1980s. Special tabulations of unpublished Department of Defense data for 1960 made by Isard and Ganschow (1963) allow us to penetrate beneath the aggregate prime contract award figures for the state and to assess the pattern of awards for the seven counties of Southern California (see table 4.5). As the table shows, Southern California as a whole accounted for 71.1 percent of all prime contract awards in the state in 1960, and Los Angeles county alone accounted for 54 percent. Indeed, Los Angeles was the leading recipient of prime contracts out

TABLE 4.4   DEPARTMENT OF DEFENSE PRIME
CONTRACT AWARDS, 1951–1960

Year	Prime contract awards current dollars (000,000)		Prime contract awards constant 1960 dollars (000,000)		California as % of U.S.
	U.S.	California	U.S.	California	
1951	30,212	3,988	35,050	4,627	13.2
1952	38,344	4,908	41,070	5,257	12.8
1953	27,026	4,162	29,345	4,519	15.4
1954	10,623	2,762	11,508	2,992	26.0
1955	13,336	2,814	14,415	3,041	21.1
1956	16,473	3,311	17,235	3,464	20.1
1957	17,989	3,382	18,298	3,440	18.8
1958	20,832	4,485	20,898	4,472	21.4
1959	23,902	5,283	23,927	5,289	22.1
1960	22,462	4,839	22,462	4,839	21.5

SOURCE: Department of Defense, Office of the Secretary, *Prime Contract Awards by State*.

of all SMSAs in the country in 1960, with New York a distant second. To be sure, Los Angeles's lead was in part a reflection of its role as a location for the head offices of a high proportion of the country's defense contractors, and much of the prime contract money received would eventually have found its way via subcontracting relations to establishments in other regions. Nevertheless, the existence of a dense and growing network of subcontractors in the Los Angeles area serving the aerospace-electronics industry also probably ensured that a significant proportion of the money remained in the area. As Karaska (1967) has suggested, moreover, there was certainly a large return flow to Southern California of subcontract orders from aerospace firms located in other parts of the country, and this phenomenon would much enhance local defense-dependent employment.

This great outpouring of Department of Defense money into the industrial apparatus of Southern California stimulated considerable expansion of manufacturing employment and population over the 1950s. Collier and Perry (1953) suggest that direct defense employment accounted for 13 percent of the *total* labor force of Los Angeles

TABLE 4.5   AWARDS OF PRIME MILITARY
CONTRACTS IN THE SEVEN COUNTIES OF
SOUTHERN CALIFORNIA IN 1960

County	Prime contract awards ($000,000) awards	As a % of total state awards	As a % of total national
Los Angeles	2,633	54.0	12.5
Orange	80	1.7	0.0
Riverside	11	0.0	0.0
San Bernardino	29	0.6	0.1
San Diego	629	12.9	3.0
Santa Barbara	60	1.2	0.3
Ventura	22	0.5	0.1
Total	3,467	71.1	16.5

SOURCE: Isard and Ganschow (1963).

in the early 1950s, with the aircraft industry having a direct and indirect multiplier effect of 2.74. According to Clayton (1962), defense spending accounted for about 1 in 4 of all *manufacturing* workers in the region by the late 1950s. Tiebout (1966) calculated for the early 1960s that the direct, indirect, and induced effects of defense spending in the Los Angeles-Long Beach SMSA accounted for 43.5 percent of total employment.

THE STATISTICAL RECORD OF GROWTH

Four major industrial sectors would seem to embody most of the high-technology industrial activity in the region in the immediate postwar years, and employment changes in these sectors no doubt fairly faithfully reflect the impacts of defense spending on the Southern Californian economy. The four sectors are (in the terms of the 1957 Standard Industrial Classification) SIC 19 (ordnance and accessories), SIC 366 (communications equipment), SIC 367 (electronic components), and SIC 372 (aircraft and parts). Unfortunately, the 1957 Standard Industrial Classification entailed significant redefinition of SIC 366; and at the same time, SIC 367 was defined as an entirely new sector. Hence, continuous and consistent time-series data for the two electronics sectors are not available for the time period under consideration here.

TABLE 4.6   EMPLOYMENT IN THE
AEROSPACE-ELECTRONICS COMPLEX OF
SOUTHERN CALIFORNIA, 1947–1962

Year	SIC 19: Ordnance & accessories	SIC 366: Communications equipment	SIC 367: Electronic components	SIC 372: Aircraft & parts
1947	327	n.a.	n.a.	78,208
1949	94	n.a.	n.a.	79,793
1951	33	10,153	n.a.	135,686
1953	6,199	35,099	n.a.	211,660
1956	14,368	31,863[a]	n.a.[b]	237,391
1959	51,710	26,422	11,306	203,839
1962	51,453	59,209	23,808	170,251

SOURCE: U.S. Department of Commerce, Bureau of the Census, *County Business Patterns*.
[a] Definitional change in SIC 366 after 1957.
[b] SIC 367 defined only after 1957.

With this latter difficulty in mind, table 4.6 shows employment in the four principal high-technology sectors in Southern California over the period from 1947 to 1962. The table indicates the great expansion and diversification of the defense-oriented industrial system after World War II. The outputs of the system now consist not just of aircraft but also of missiles, communications equipment (i.e., avionics, guidance and control apparatus, and military communications systems), and electronic components (Arnold et al. 1960). The data given in table 4.6 show that after the outbreak of the Korean War, the aircraft and parts sector expanded with particular vigor (with a major switch from propellor to jet-propulsion technology occurring around the same time) (Bright 1978). The aircraft industry then declined again in the second half of the 1950s, in part because of decreasing Department of Defense expenditures, and in part because of the increasing substitution of missiles for aircraft in national defense. Concomitantly, the ordnance and accessories sector grew rapidly after the mid-1950s as intermediate-range ballistic missiles (IRBMs) and inter-continental ballistic missiles (ICBMs) were brought prominently into production. Employment in both SIC 366 and SIC 367 soared as more and more

TABLE 4.7   POPULATION IN THE SEVEN
COUNTIES OF SOUTHERN CALIFORNIA 1940,
1950, AND 1960

County	Population		
	1940	1950	1960
Los Angeles	2,785,643	4,151,687	6,038,771
Orange	130,760	216,224	703,925
Riverside	105,524	170,046	306,191
San Bernardino	161,108	281,642	503,591
San Diego	289,348	556,808	1,033,011
Santa Barbara	70,555	98,220	168,962
Ventura	69,685	114,647	199,138
Total	3,612,623	5,589,274	8,953,589

SOURCE: U.S. Department of Commerce, Bureau of the Census, *Census of Population.*

contrived electronic equipment was developed for applications in air-craft and missiles and their associated ground control systems.

The growth of the defense industries also helped to spur massive population growth in the region, and indeed Ikle (1960) has shown that in-migration to Los Angeles over the period from 1940 to 1959 is closely and positively correlated with changes in employment in the aircraft industry. In 1940, the population of the region stood at 3.61 million. Twenty years later, it had grown by 148 percent to 8.95 million (see table 4.7). In absolute terms, most of this growth was concentrated in Los Angeles county, the high-technology industrial heartland of the region, which added 3.25 million people between 1940 and 1960. However, two other major foci of high-technology industry in the region, San Diego County and (after 1950) Orange County, also grew apace (Lund 1959). Not all of this population growth can be uniquely ascribed to the direct and indirect effects of defense spending, of course, though if the evidence cited earlier on the multiplier effects of defense spending is correct, population would certainly have expanded much less rapidly had such spending been curtailed.

What were the detailed spatial and sectoral components of this industrial growth? How did particular firms develop and grow over this period? How was the regional industrial system constituted as an interdependent network of producers and supporting services? And what kinds of institutional arrangements underpinned the whole system and helped to drive it forward?

SECTORAL PATTERNS OF GROWTH, 1950–1960

As the aerospace-electronics industrial complex of Southern California became more deeply entrenched in the region in the 1950s, it came typically to consist of large systems houses surrounded by dense networks of smaller establishments providing various kinds of specialized material inputs and services. Final product configurations in this industrial complex were extremely variable, as reflected in the proliferation of specialized niches in military markets, where, even as production proceeds, radical and frequent design changes are often called for. The data laid out in tables 4.8 and 4.9 show some of the main types of aircraft and missiles produced in Southern California in the 1940s and 1950s, and condensed as the data may be, they give a strong sense of the dramatically shifting character of defense production work in the region. This sense is heightened if we also take into account the large numbers of experimental and prototype aircraft produced (and which are not registered in table 4.8). Even civilian aircraft production—at Convair, Douglas and Lockheed—experienced many shifts and turns over the 1950s.

THE AIRCRAFT AND PARTS SECTOR

In the 1950s, the major aircraft assemblers in Southern California were Convair (which was absorbed into General Dynamics in 1953), Douglas, Lockheed, North American Aviation, and Northrop. To a remarkable degree, these manufacturers were still producing aircraft at their original prewar locations.

Rae (1968) reports that the size of these assembly plants in 1948 ranged from 4,900 workers for Northrop to 18,522 for North American. Then, as now, there were significant internal economies of scale and scope in aircraft assembly, making large production units the norm. That said, these establishments also put out large quantities of work, and so they were functionally dependent on an extensive network of direct and indirect input suppliers. At this time, the Los

TABLE 4.8   MAJOR AIRCRAFT-PRODUCTION
PROGRAMS UNDERTAKEN BY SOUTHERN
CALIFORNIAN MANUFACTURERS, 1940–
1960[a]

Model	Production dates	Quantity produced
Consolidated Aircraft Corporation/Consolidated-Vultee/Convair		
PB2Y	1940–41	200
Liberator B24-A to -M	1941–46	11,388
Dominator B32	1943–45	115
B36-A to -H	1947–52	325
Convair 240	1947–58	571
Convair 340	1951–60	209
Delta Dagger F102-A	1955–58	873
TF102-A	1955–58	63
Convair 440	1955–63	186
Hustler B58 /-A	1956–62	200
Convair 880	1958–61	65
Douglas Aircraft Company		
Dauntless SBD-1 to -6	1939–44	5,321
Havoc A20 to a20K-DO	1939–44	6,278
DB-7B & 7C	1941–42	829
Skytrain C47-A to -F	1941–44	8,172
Invader A26-DE to A26F	1941–45	2,454
DC-4	1941–46	79
Skymaster C54 to C54M-DO	1941–49	952
Flying Fortress B17F to G	1942–43	2,495
Liberator B24-D to -J	1942–43	954
DC-6	1944–51	538
Skyraider AD-1 to -7	1945–56	3,155
Skyknight F3D-1 to -3	1946–48	265
Globemaster II C124 /-C	1948–53	448
Skyray F4D-1 to -2	1948–54	421
DC-7	1950–56	336
Skywarrior A3D-1 to -2T	1950–60	282
C118 /-A	1951–52	100
B47B to -D	1951–53	274
Skyhawk A4D-1 to -5	1952–62	1,548
DC-8	1955–62	165

TABLE 4.8   (*cont.*)

Model	Production dates	Quantity produced
Lockheed Aircraft Company		
Hudson	1940–43	2,654
Lodestar	1940–43	625
Lightning P-38	1940–45	9,923
Ventura/Harpoon	1941–45	3,028
Flying Fortress B-17	1942–45	2,750
Constellation	1943–51	233
Shooting Star	1943–51	1,732
Neptune P2V	1944–62	1,051
T-33	1948–59	5,691
F-94	1949–54	854
U-2	1950–60	114
Super Constellation	1951–59	579
Stratojet B-47	1953–57	394
Hercules C-130	1954–	1,604[b]
Starfighter F-104	1955–67	741
Seastar T2V-1	1956–58	150
Electra L-188	1958–62	170
Orion P-3	1959–	522[b]
North American Aviation		
Harvard II Series	1939–41	1,275
Mustang I to IA	1940–41	770
B25-C	1940–41	863
P51 Series	1940–45	15,586
B25 Series	1941–44	6,390
Liberator B24-G	1942–45	430
F82 Series	1944–46	250
Sabre F86 Series	1944–58	5,579
T28 Series	1948–63	1,457
Super Sabre F100 Series	1949–59	1,935
T39 Series	1959–62	185
Northrop Corporation		
V-72	1940–43	400
Black Widow P-61-A -G	1941–46	735
Scorpion F-89A -J	1946–59	1,435
Talon T-38 /-A	1956–60	207

Model	Production dates	Quantity produced
Ryan Aeronautical Company		
Navion A/B	1939–43	1,238
Recruit PT-22	1940–42	1,048
PT-21	1940–45	100
NR-1	1940–45	100
Fireball FR-1	1943–46	66
Vultee Aircraft Company		
Valiant BT-13 -15	1939–44	11,537
Vanguard P-66	1940–41	144
A-31 /-A	1940–44	597
Vengeance A-35 /-A to -B	1940–44	931

SOURCE: Anderson (1976), Angelucci (1980), Francillon (1982), Hatfield Collection (1943), Jones (1968, 1975), Maynard (1962), Munson (1972), Swanborough (1973), Taylor (1980).

[a] Aircraft produced in quantities of fewer than fifty are not shown.

[b] Aircraft still in production as of 1989; production figure includes all output to 1980.

Angeles Chamber of Commerce (1950) in its directory of local manufacturing firms listed 349 firms under the rubric of "aircraft parts and accessories." This figure is certainly an underestimate of all the local firms with direct and indirect ties to the aircraft industry and we should add to it firms in such sectors as machining, casting, plastics molding, and electronics, among others. The Select Committee on Small Business (1956) reports that in 1954 twenty-one aircraft manufacturers nationwide did business with 34,623 different firms, of which California alone accounted for 10,314, or 29.8 percent.

Thus constituted as an agglomerated network of producers (and concomitantly as a focus of external economies), the aircraft industry in the region maintained its leading role, with some 30 percent of the nation's employment in SIC 372. For the most part, the industry produced military aircraft (see table 4.8). Lockheed, however, also produced Constellations and Superconstellations for civilian markets, and Douglas produced large quantities of civilian aircraft in the DC series, with the jet-powered DC-8 coming into production in the late 1950s. Also in 1955 Convair started work on its ill-fated 880 jet airliner. In addition, in the mid-1950s, Hughes Aircraft in Culver City began to manufacture helicopters on a significant scale.

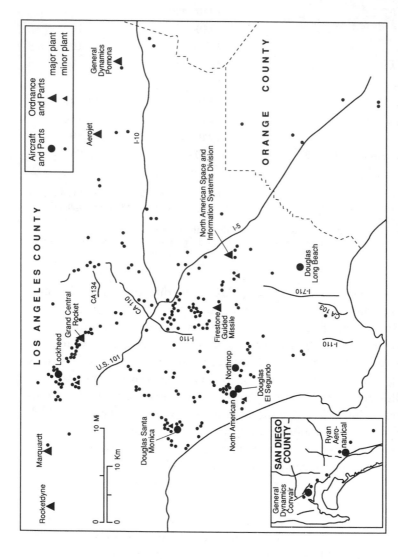

Figure 4.2. Locations of aircraft, ordnance, and parts manufacturers, Southern California, 1955. San Diego shown in inset. Freeways are shown as of 1955. (Data from California Manufacturers' Association.)

TABLE 4.9 MAJOR GUIDED MISSILE- AND ROCKET-PRODUCTION PROGRAMS UNDERTAKEN BY SOUTHERN CALIFORNIAN PRIME CONTRACTORS, 1940–1960

Prime contractor	Start agency	Program date	Contract
Douglas Aircraft	Roc I	1940	Army
Douglas Aircraft	Roc II	1944	Army
Douglas Aircraft	Corporal E	1944	Army
Firestone Tire & Rubber	Corporal	1944	Army
Consolidated-Vultee	Lark (XSAM-N-2)	1945	Navy
Ryan Aeronautical	Firebird	1945	USAF
North American Aviation	Navaho	1946	USAF
Hughes Aircraft	Falcon	1947	USAF
Douglas Aircraft	Honest John	1951	Army
Douglas Aircraft	Sparrow II	1950	Navy
Convair (General Dynamics)	Terrier	1953	Navy
Convair (General Dynamics)	Atlas	1954	USAF
Northrop	Snark	1954	USAF
Douglas Aircraft	Genie	1955	USAF
North American	Hound Dog	1955	USAF
Ramo Wooldridge/Douglas Aircraft	Thor	1955	USAF
Ramo Wooldridge	Titan I	1955	USAF
Jet Propulsion Labs/Sperry	Sergeant	1955	Army
Naval Operations Test Center China Lake	Zuni	1956	Navy
Aeronutronic Systems	Shillelagh	1958	Army
Convair (General Dynamics)	Redeye	1959	Army

SOURCE: Aircraft Industries Association of America (1957); American Aviation Magazine (1956); Birtles and Beaver (1985); Ordway and Wakeford (1960); Ulanoff (1959).

Figure 4.2 shows the locations of 232 individual aircraft and parts producers in the region in the mid-1950s. This figure is based on address data taken from the *California Manufacturers Register* for 1955. The main assembly plants together with surrounding cohorts of parts producers cluster tightly together in Los Angeles County in three main areas, i.e., the inner-city area of Los Angeles, the eastern San Fernando Valley (especially around Burbank-Glendale), and in the western Los Angeles basin (especially in Santa Monica and the El Segundo-Hawthorne area). There was also at this time a small outlier of the industry in San Diego, focused on Convair. The bases of this geographic pattern were laid down in the 1930s when the locations of most of the large aircraft assembly plants were established. Even today the pattern is surprisingly little changed, though the severe restructuring of the aircraft industry in the late 1980s is now beginning to have a tangible effect on the intraregional geography of the industry.

THE MISSILE PRODUCERS

Missiles are assembled out of the same basic subsystems as aircraft, namely, an airframe, a power plant, and a guidance and control mechanism. Accordingly, as missiles started to become an essential element of the defense arsenal, the aircraft manufacturers were especially well placed to move rapidly into this expanding market, and they did so with great success over the 1940s and 1950s. By 1961, the top five aircraft producers in the United States as a whole accounted for 68.3 percent of all missile production (Simonson 1964). Aircraft manufacturers also had the advantage of long familiarity with the inner complexities of the Department of Defense, the monopsonistic market for missiles. To be sure, a number of specialized missile manufacturers had already made their appearance in Southern California before the 1950s. As indicated earlier, these were Aerojet-General, Marquardt, and the Firestone Guided Missile Division. In addition, Grand Central Rocket was founded in 1955 as a rocket propellant and engine producer, though six years later it was absorbed by Lockheed. A few electronics firms such as Hughes Aircraft and (after 1953) Ramo Wooldridge were also involved as prime contractors with missile production. However, it was the aircraft firms that entered most forcefully into this now burgeoning sector of production, and by the mid-1950s, most of the large aircraft assemblers had established active missile divisions.

As early as 1950, Douglas Aircraft established a Missile Division within the firm's Santa Monica plant. In 1962 the Missile Division became the Missile and Space Systems Division, which in 1964 moved to Huntington Beach (where it was subsequently renamed McDonnell

Douglas Space Systems). Lockheed set up its Missile Systems Division in Van Nuys in 1954, though the division moved a year later to Sunnyvale in the Bay Area (Yenne 1987). Also in 1954, shortly after the "Teapot Committee" headed by John Von Neumann had recommended construction of an ICBM with an H-bomb warhead, General Dynamics established its Convair Astronautics Division in San Diego, where the Atlas ICBM was constructed (see table 4.9); in the same year, the firm also set up its Pomona Division, where the Terrier missile was manufactured for the Navy. In 1955, North American Aviation opened both its Space and Information Systems Division in Downey (manufacturing Hound Dog missiles), and its great Rocketdyne Division in Canoga Park where the engines for the first Atlas, Thor, and Jupiter systems were produced. Finally, the Ford Motor Company created its Aeronutronic Systems Division in Glendale in 1956 where work on the Shillelagh missile began; and in 1960, the establishment moved to Newport Beach where in 1976 it was renamed Ford Aerospace and Communications Corporation.

The locations of ordnance (i.e., missile) manufacturers and parts suppliers in Southern California in the middle of the 1950s are shown in figure 4.2. At this time, there were only some twelve such establishments in the region, though they were for the most part extremely large in size. Their geographic distribution is much like that of aircraft and parts establishments, with some of the more recently founded plants at that time (such as General Dynamics-Pomona and Rocketdyne) occupying relatively peripheral locations. By the mid-1950s, the major missile producers in the region had also become caught up in a dense local network of interindustrial linkages. Thus, a missile market directory of the period informs us that within the confines of Southern California, there were eight missile prime contractors connected to eleven major subcontractors who in turn were connected to 175 subcontractors providing electronic guidance, tracking, telemetering, and checkout equipment (American Aviation Publications 1958). Almost all of these producers were located in Los Angeles County, with the residue mainly in Orange and San Diego counties.

ELECTRONICS

With the increasing use of electronic technologies in both aircraft and missiles, there was an enormous and sudden expansion of Southern California's electronics industry over the 1950s. In a survey made by

Arnold et al. (1960), it was found that 76.3 percent of the sales of a sample of sixty-two electronics firms in Los Angeles were directed to military end uses. According to one report, the entire state had 14,858 employees in electronics in June 1950, and one year later the number had grown to 26,504, over 75 percent of whom were located in Southern California (California State Chamber of Commerce 1952). This growth was due to the opening of new electronics divisions by aircraft and missile producers, and more importantly to the emergence of large numbers of specialized independent electronics manufacturers.

The first aerospace company to establish an electronics division in the region was Northrop with its Anaheim Division (later Nortronics) inaugurated in 1951. The Anaheim Division was the earliest major systems house in Orange County. North American Aviation set up Autonetics in Downey in 1955 alongside its Space and Information Systems Division. Lockheed Electronics was established in Burbank in 1960. Many of the aircraft and missile producers in the region also developed significant in-house electronics production capacity over the 1950s.

More important, a series of independent defense electronics manufacturers grew up within the region, a few of which dated from the prewar years (see above), but most of which have their origins in the 1950s. Thus, in addition to such older firms as Bendix, Collins, Gilfillan, Hoffman Radio, Hughes Aircraft, and Lear, during the 1950s such important producers as Hallamore, Interstate Electronics, Litton Industries, Ramo Wooldridge, RCA Missile and Surface Radar Division, Robertshaw-Fulton, and Teledyne along with a growing mass of smaller components manufacturers made their appearance within the industrial fabric of the region (Lamden and Pemberton 1962; Mettler 1982; O'Green 1988). In addition, Hughes established both its Ground Systems Division in Fullerton in 1957 and another electronics plant in El Segundo in 1958. Ramo Wooldridge came into being as a spinoff from Hughes Aircraft because of internal disputes occasioned by Howard Hughes's management failures. Tex Thornton left Hughes for the same reason, and promptly began to develop Litton Industries (Barlett and Steele 1979). Ramo and Wooldridge set up business in Inglewood where the firm (via its Space Technology Laboratory) was given the task by the Air Force of acting as systems manager for the Atlas ICBM, i.e., coordinating the entire development and production process (but not actually engaging in direct manufacturing activities; these were the responsibility of Convair Astronautics as prime contractor). Within a year, employment in Ramo Wooldridge had risen to 3,269 (Hoyt 1971), and by 1957 the firm was overseeing 220 prime contractors and thousands of subcontractors (Mettler 1982). In 1958, the firm merged with Thompson Products of Cleveland to become Thompson Ramo Wooldridge (later, TRW). Because Thompson Ramo Wooldridge was the systems manager on the Air Force ICBM program, it was not allowed to bid as prime contractor on other Air Force projects. In response to this problem, the Space Technology Laboratory was split off from the firm in 1958 as a wholly owned subsidiary, and in 1960 it became the federally owned Aerospace Corporation in Inglewood (Witze 1965). Thompson Ramo Wooldridge was now free to bid on other Air Force projects, and it did so in succeeding years with considerable success.

Figure 4.3 is a map of 470 electronics establishments in the greater Los Angeles area in the middle of the 1950s. The locations of these establishments correspond to address data given by the Los Angeles Chamber of Commerce (1955). The map reveals a locational pattern of establishments marked by a fairly strong presence in the inner city of Los Angeles—where most of the electronics producers of the 1930s were situated (cf. Pegrum 1963)—complemented by three main decentralized clusters. One of these lies to the northeast in Pasadena; another spreads out to the northwest along the San Fernando Valley (Izzard 1961; Security First National Bank 1960); and yet another extends to the west and southwest to Santa Monica and the El Segundo-Hawthorne area. This pattern corresponds markedly to the one shown for aircraft and parts manufacturers in figure 4.2. Note that there is little sign in figure 4.3 of the extensive decentralization of electronics producers that eventually occurs into the western sections of the San Fernando Valley and into northern Orange County, where two great high-technology industrial districts make their definite historical appearance over the 1960s and 1970s.

INSTITUTIONAL-INFRASTRUCTURAL COMPLEMENTS OF THE SOUTHERN CALIFORNIAN AEROSPACE-ELECTRONICS COMPLEX IN THE 1950s

Within the high-technology industrial complex of Southern California, there also developed a grid of private and public defense research laboratories of various kinds. The earliest of these, as we have seen, were the Jet Propulsion Laboratories and the RAND Corporation. In

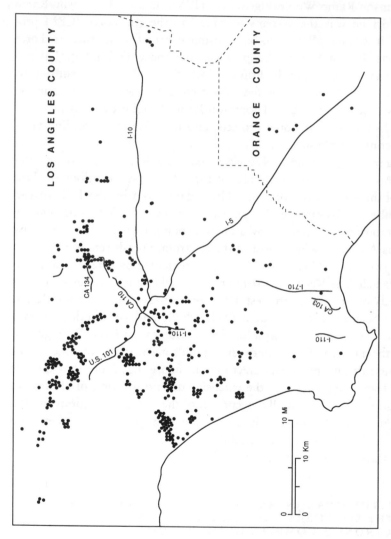

Figure 4.3. Locations of electronics establishments in the greater Los Angeles area, 1955. Freeways are shown as of 1955. (Data from Los Angeles Chamber of Commerce.)

addition, the Santa Barabara Research Center was started in 1952 by an ex-employee of Hughes. The Center was purchased by Hughes Aircraft in 1956, and then rapidly came to prominence in the infrared electronics field (Hughes Aircraft Company 1986). In 1960, Hughes acquired a further research laboratory, one that had been started in Malibu in 1958 by Potter Electric Company (Hamilton 1962). The laboratory was renamed the Hughes Malibu Research Center and it developed as a major center of laser research. In 1956, the System Development Corporation (dedicated to the performance of R&D for the Air Force) emerged out of the RAND Corporation. And as mentioned earlier, the Aerospace Corporation was set up in 1960 in order to carry out general integration of Air Force space and missile programs. Lastly, General Motors created its Defense Research Laboratories (later Delco Systems Operations) in Santa Barbara in 1960 where work proceeded on marine acoustics and electronics for aerospace applications.

An event of major significance for the overall growth and development of the Southern Californian aerospace-electronics complex was the Air Force's establishment of the Western Development Division (WDD) of the Air Research and Development Command. The WDD was set up in Inglewood in 1954 (just after Atlas had received top Air Force priority) and was immediately assigned the responsibility of acting as the main Air Force liaison body with manufacturers involved in developing the Atlas ICBM. Under the then newly developed weapons system management procedure, prime contractors supervised the work of subcontractors and integrated all subsystems into the final product, whereas before the 1950s the armed services were directly responsible for procurement, and the prime contractors simply assembled the final product (Harlan 1956; Kucera 1974; Peck and Scherer 1962; Stekler 1965). Even so, considerable governmental coordination of manufacturers' operations was required under the new weapons system procedure, and the presence of the WDD in the region was a reflection of the intense local transactional networks that this task called forth. By the end of 1954, the WDD was also responsible for the Titan missile, and then in 1955 for the Thor IRBM (Air Force Systems Command n.d.). In 1957, the WDD was redesignated the Air Force Ballistic Missile Division, and through a series of complex mutations, it survives to this day in the form of the Space Systems Division.

This strong military presence in the region was, and is, complemented by a large number of military bases used variously for aircraft and weapons testing and missile launches. Among the more important of these bases are Camp Pendleton Marine Corps Base, China Lake Naval Weapons Center, Cooke AFB (after 1958, Vandenberg AFB), Edwards AFB, March AFB, Miramar Naval Air Station, North Island Naval Air Station, Norton AFB, and Point Mugu Naval Test Range.

To this extensive system of activities and institutions underpinning the high-technology production networks of Southern California, we must add not just the major internationally reputed universities (as already indicated), but also an exceptionally dense cluster of smaller colleges and schools producing large numbers of trained technical workers. In-migration added greatly to the existing pool of skilled workers over the 1950s. At the same time the vast expansion of urban infrastructure (especially the freeway system and a greatly extended suburban fringe) in Southern California throughout the decade contributed to the overall growth of the region and helped to consolidate its role as a major high-technology industrial complex.

THE WAY FORWARD

By the end of the 1950s, the aerospace-electronics complex of Southern California had been firmly set in place, and the region was now by far the largest high-technology industrial region in the world, a status that it maintains to the present day. With the launching of Sputnik in 1957, and the formation of NASA in 1958, U.S. efforts to reach space intensified greatly. Southern California's aerospace-electronics producers participated in a major way in these efforts, leading to further diversification of the complex over the 1960s into space vehicle and equipment production. An early manifestation of this tendency was the collaboration between the Jet Propulsion Laboratory, Ramo Wooldridge, and the Army Ballistic Missiles Agency to launch in January 1958 the first U.S. satellite (i.e., *Explorer*) to orbit the earth (Hagen 1964). A year later, in 1959, Rocketdyne's Redstone engine was used to power the first manned space flights in NASA's Project Mercury (Bland 1964).

Two further important trends were in evidence in the region's pathway to high-technology industrialization as its formative period was coming to an end. The first was that the endemic undergrowth of small subcontract shops and input suppliers providing specialized (often customized) services to high-technology producers had now expanded to really major proportions. These smaller firms were engaged in the manufacture of such outputs as printed circuit boards, transistors, electronics assembly services, molded plastics, and aluminum foundry products. The second trend involved the steady bifurcation of high-technology labor markets, with a well-paid managerial, scientific, and technical stratum at the top, and a poorly paid unskilled stratum at the bottom. The lower stratum was and is primarily composed of Hispanic and Asian immigrants (including large numbers of women), and after the mid-1950s these immigrants were actively absorbed into the burgeoning sweatshop segment of the high-technology industrial complex.

By the late 1950s, political leaders in other regions of the United States were becoming aware of Southern California's expanding high-technology industrial capacity and its favored position in Department of Defense prime contract awards. In May 1959 Senators Jacob K. Javits and Kenneth B. Keating, both of New York, attempted to undercut this state of affairs with their Armed Services Competitive Procurement Act, which sought to reduce Department of Defense spending in California while increasing it in other states (Clayton 1962; Committee on Armed Services 1959; Schiesl 1984). California's congressional delegation, however, succeeded in persuading the Armed Services Committee to annul the bill, and Southern California's position as the nation's premier aerospace-electronics manufacturing region was thus ensured. This success no doubt reflected in part the political power and skills of the California delegation; but it also certainly reflected the circumstance that Southern California (like parts of the Bay Area) had by this time become a massive locus of production and labor-market activity engendering such potent agglomeration economies that it was now virtually impossible to reorganize the spatial bases of defense contracting except at unacceptably high cost.

Southern California has continued to the present day to develop and grow on the basis of its high-technology industrial networks formed over the period from 1940 to 1960. Other parts of the United States (e.g., Texas, Colorado, New England, New York, and elsewhere) have also participated vigorously in defense contracting, but since the mid-1950s, none has done so as insistently or as successfully as Southern California.

PART III

Analyses of the Core High-Technology Industrial Complex

CHAPTER 5

The Aircraft and Parts Industry

Thus far we have examined the theoretical, geographical and historical framework of high-technology industrial development in general in Southern California. We shall now begin the task of probing into the detailed workings of specific high-technology sectors within the region, and in the next three chapters we look in turn at three major sectors: aircraft and parts, missiles and space equipment, and electronics. These three sectors represent the essential core of the region's high-technology industrial complex.

The discussion that follows is based in part on detailed fieldwork and questionnaire surveys, and—in the interests of scrupulousness—it will be necessary at times to move aside from the main narrative in order to comment on various problems encountered in collecting the data and weighing the evidence.

A DESCRIPTIVE OVERVIEW OF THE AIRCRAFT AND PARTS INDUSTRY

THE INDUSTRY IN NATIONAL CONTEXT

Figure 5.1 depicts aggregate employment trends in SIC 372 (aircraft and parts) for the whole of the United States from 1950 to 1990. Fortunately, the definition of SIC 372 has remained stable over this entire period of time, and so the employment data graphed in figure 5.1 can be read as one continuous series. Also shown in figure 5.1 are total Department of Defense dollar outlays on aircraft over the same

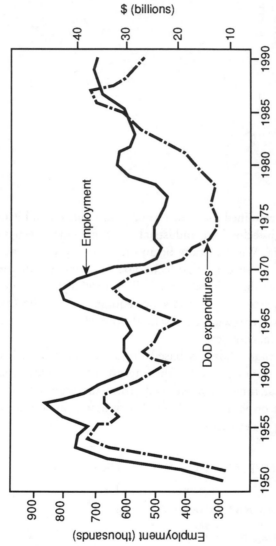

Figure 5.1. U.S. employment in SIC 372 (aircraft and parts) and Department of Defense expenditures (in constant 1990 dollars) for aircraft products and services. (Data from U.S. Department of Labor, Bureau of Labor Statistics, *Employment, Hours and Earnings, United States 1909–90*, Bulletin 2370; and Aerospace Industries Association of America, Inc., *Aerospace Facts and Figures*, Washington, D.C., Aerospace Research Center, Economic Data Service.)

period. The temporal variation in these outlays is clearly mirrored in changes in employment (Clayton 1967; Peck and Scherer 1962; Schiesl 1984). We may note the rising activity coincident upon the Korean War in the early 1950s and the Vietnam War buildup in the late 1960s. Then, in the early 1970s to mid-1970s, a pervasive slowdown in military spending occurred accompanied by the onset of recession in the aircraft industry (State of California 1981). After the late 1970s, the combined effects of civil airline deregulation (in 1978) and expanding Department of Defense procurements resulted in an upswing in employment over much of the 1980s. Since 1987, cutbacks in Department of Defense spending on aircraft are once more beginning to result in employment declines, especially in Southern California.

These ups and downs of the industry are superimposed upon what appears to be a long-term downtrend in employment in SIC 372 from the mid-1950s onwards. This downtrend is in part a reflection of periodic economic crises in the industry, and in part it is a reflection of a long-term process of technological and organizational restructuring. In actual fact, when we look at value of output, the industry appears considerably more healthy than when we just consider employment. Thus, the total value of output from SIC 372 increased by 77.2 percent from $43.6 billion in 1968 (a peak year for employment) to $77.3 billion in 1987, where all monetary values are given in constant 1987 dollars. These statistics are testimony to the ever-increasing complexity of modern aircraft, and this complexity shows up in turn in relative increases in skilled white-collar managerial, scientific, and technical workers in the industry. From 1968 to 1990 when total U.S. employment in SIC 372 decreased from 820,700 employees to 706,0000 employees, the percentage of nonproduction workers in the labor force increased from 40.3 percent to 51.6 percent. These intertwined developments (i.e., general employment decline combined with rising technical sophistication and value of output) have been intensified both by the substitution of guided missiles for aircraft in Department of Defense procurements (Gansler 1980) and labor-saving technological change in the industry. In 1989, military aircraft accounted for 63.7 percent of all aircraft industry sales in the United States.

THE INDUSTRY IN SOUTHERN CALIFORNIA

The trends that we have observed in the industry at the national level are mirrored in similar trends within Southern California, which has accounted fairly consistently over the postwar period for about 20 percent to 30 percent of total U.S. employment in SIC 372.

Table 5.1 provides an immediate glimpse of the incidence of the industry in the seven counties of Southern California for the years 1956, 1972, and 1985. Throughout the entire postwar period, employment in SIC 372 in Southern California has been overwhelmingly located in Los Angeles County with San Diego County a distant second. However, both of these primary centers of the industry in the region have experienced much decentralization of employment over recent decades, both to other parts of the region and to other parts of the country.

Figure 4.2, in the previous chapter, shows the location of the industry in Southern California in 1955, and the dominance of Los Angeles County is clearly evident. On closer inspection, the mass of establishments in Los Angeles County disaggregates into three major locational foci, the first close to the city center, the second coinciding with the Burbank-Glendale area to the north, and the third in the west-central area of Los Angeles stretching from Santa Monica and Culver City through Inglewood to El Segundo and Hawthorne. In the mid-1950s, little evidence is to be found of decentralization of the industry, apart from a handful of establishments (small parts manufacturers for the most part) located in the northern half of Orange County.

By 1972, the aircraft and parts industry in Southern California (as in the nation at large) was in a state of some decline. The geographical distribution of the industry in the region is displayed in figure 5.2. Not a great deal seems to have changed in the distribution for 1972 compared with 1955, despite the passage of more than a decade and a half. The body of establishments close to the center of Los Angeles has thinned out and the San Diego outlier has noticeably declined. A very modest acceleration of plant decentralization into Orange, Riverside, and San Bernardino counties is also visible, reflecting the expansion of the urbanized area into these counties.

By 1988, a number of changes in the locational structure of aircraft-assembly plants and parts makers in Southern California is apparent though they are still fairly modest (see fig. 5.3). Some continued erosion of the main nucleus of establishments in Los Angeles County is evident, especially in the west-central area. Los Angeles, nonetheless, remains by far the predominant focus of the industry in Southern California. Additionally, large numbers of small subcontractors now occupy a very evident locational niche in the northern half of Orange County. These subcontractors are linked in part to the thriving

TABLE 5.1 NUMBER OF ESTABLISHMENTS AND EMPLOYMENT IN SIC 372 (AIRCRAFT AND PARTS) FOR SELECTED YEARS IN THE SEVEN COUNTIES OF SOUTHERN CALIFORNIA

	1956		1972		1985	
	Establishments	Employment	Establishments	Employment	Establishments	Employment
Los Angeles	487	196,691	243	103,069	219	92,970
Orange	10	226	22	3,537	56	3,859
Riverside	3	n.a.	3	n.a.	8	2,500–4,999
San Bernardino	0	0	6	n.a.	8	2,500–4,999
San Diego	25	39,724	18	7,543	31	13,728
Santa Barbara	0	0	0	0	5	250–499
Ventura	0	0	4	1,895	11	500–999
Southern California	525	>236,641	296	>116,044	338	116,307–122,053

SOURCE: U.S. Department of Commerce, Bureau of the Census, *County Business Patterns*.
(n.a. = not available)

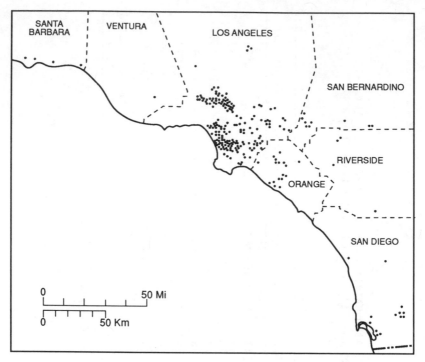

Figure 5.2.   The aircraft and parts industry (SIC 372) in Southern California, 1972. One dot equals one manufacturing establishment.

high-technology industrial complex that has also grown apace in Orange County since the 1960s.

Over the entire postwar period, the aircraft industry in Southern California has been persistently focused on a set of key central locations occupied by major producers (see fig. 5.4). Many of these locations, as already noted, have remained unchanged since the industry was first implanted in the region in the 1920s and 1930s, and such major modern aircraft assemblers as McDonnell Douglas, Northrop, Rockwell North American and General Dynamics Convair still occupy plants that can be traced back to the 1930s and 1940s. Moreover, as the industry has evolved, an elaborate network of labor markets and linkage relationships has been built up, further binding major producers to their established locations. In comparison with the functional and spatial restructuring of many traditional manufacturing sectors in the U.S. economy that has gone on over the period since the late 1960s

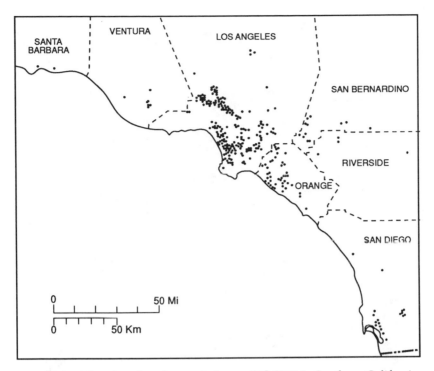

Figure 5.3.   The aircraft and parts industry (SIC 372) in Southern California, 1988. One dot equals one manufacturing establishment.

(in industries such as cars, machinery, electrical appliances, and so on), the aircraft and parts industry in Southern California has been distinctive for its extraordinary locational stability. That said, pressures currently acting on the industry are likely to produce some dramatic restructuring over the 1990s. In the early 1990s, the major Lockheed plant at Burbank closed down and much of its assembly work was transferred to Georgia. In addition, massive layoffs have occurred throughout the aerospace industry in Southern California since 1987 as a consequence of Department of Defense cutbacks.

In order to examine the functional and locational dynamics of the industry in more detail, we need now to consider some of the peculiarities of the local labor markets and interestablishment linkage structures that have taken shape around the industry in Southern California over the last few decades.

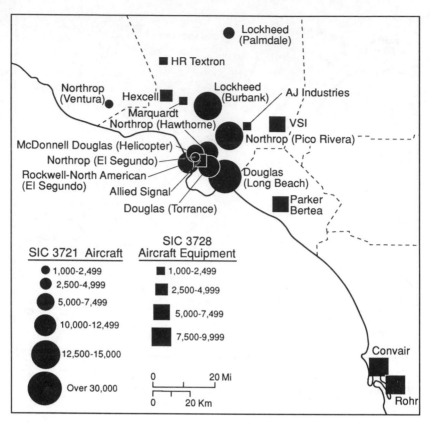

Figure 5.4.   Establishments with 1,000 or more workers in SIC 3721 (aircraft) and SIC 3728 (aircraft equipment not elsewhere classified). (Data from various industrial directories.)

LOCAL LABOR MARKETS

LABOR PROCESS AND LABOR RELATIONS

The core of the modern aircraft industry in Southern California is made up of large final assembly plants or systems houses linked to a wide variety of parts and subassembly manufacturers. In these assembly plants, aircraft are gradually put together along a series of workstations at each of which crews of skilled and semiskilled production workers (sheet metal workers, riveters, metal bonders, lathe operators, boring mill operators, plumbers, painters, upholsterers, and so on) perform designated tasks. These are usually completed over a period of a few days, after which the semifinished airframe is then moved downline to the next workstation.

The crews that work at different stages on the airframe are for the most part rather different from the quasi–self-managing teams that have emerged in many production sectors as the notion of "responsible autonomy" in industrial relations has gained acceptance (as in neofordist car plants, for example). In a few cases the team concept has been introduced into the Southern Californian aircraft industry, but this is still far from being a general *modus operandi*. Each worker's activity in any given crew is typically governed by an explicit job description, and rotation between jobs is the exception rather than the rule. Supervision and managerial control of production work tend to be tightly organized, and worker seniority remains the basis for layoff and recall decisions virtually everywhere in the industry. Despite these "fordist" elements in the prevailing labor-relations system, workers are on the whole more skilled than was (and is) the case with workers on the classical fordist assembly line in mass-production industries. In addition to the many blue-collar workers employed in the aircraft industry, large cadres of technicians, engineers, and scientists are also employed and are present in great numbers throughout the Southern Californian labor market.

Workers in most of the large aircraft assembly plants in Southern California are unionized, though parts-producing plants are in general free from union organization. At the present time, two major unions account for the majority of blue-collar workers in the main assembly plants, namely, the International Association of Machinists and Aerospace Workers (IAM), which is present in several of the Lockheed plants as well as McDonnell Douglas (Torrance) and General Dynamics Convair, and the United Automobile, Aerospace, and Agricultural Implement Workers of America (UAW), which is present in McDonnell Douglas (Long Beach), McDonnell Douglas Helicopters, and Rockwell North American (at El Segundo, Palmdale, and Downey). For its part, Northrop has successfully resisted unionization, and it handles worker-management relations through its internal Employee Relations Department. Various professional guilds also exist for the purposes of collective representation of the interests of technicians, engineers and scientists in the industry. The Engineers and Scientists Guild represents professional employees at Lockheed, and the Southern California Professional Engineering Association represents similar workers at McDonnell Douglas. Both of these guilds are recognized by the National Labor Relations Board as legitimate collective-bargaining units.

THE SPATIAL STRUCTURE OF LOCAL LABOR MARKETS

We now turn to an analysis of local labor markets, focusing above all on the spatial relations between workers' residences and job locations.

In order to investigate this issue, major aircraft assembly plants were invited to provide simple counts of the number of people they employ by the zip code of employees' places of residence. A positive response to this invitation was received from Lockheed (which provided data on its Burbank, Palmdale, and Rye Canyon plants), McDonnell Douglas (Long Beach, Carson, and Torrance plants), and Rockwell North American (El Segundo and Palmdale plants). Collectively, these eight plants accounted for 56,676 employees, or about half of the total employment in SIC 372 in Southern California in 1988. Maps of the local labor markets surrounding the eight establishments are presented in figures 5.5, 5.6, and 5.7. For ease of exposition, data for different establishments belonging to the same firm are combined together in a single map.

Scrutiny of figures 5.5, 5.6, and 5.7 suggests that the spatial configuration of these local labor markets has been shaped by a powerful gravitational effect focused on individual places of employment. Indeed, each local labor market seems to have been pulled tightly inward to its own central hub, and there is surprisingly little spatial overlap between different labor-market areas in different sections of the metropolis. This island-like character of local labor markets within the same metropolitan area is all the more unexpected in view of the gigantic proportions of some of the core workplaces (e.g., 30,110 employees at McDonnell Douglas Long Beach, and 12,015 at Lockheed Burbank in 1988).

These casual observations may be formalized with the aid of a multinomial logit model. In this model, the probability (p_{ij}) that the ith employee works at the jth establishment is expressed as a positive func-

Figure 5.6 (*opposite*). Residential locations of workers employed by Lockheed plants at Burbank, Palmdale, and Rye Canyon. Major freeways are shown. Each dot represents thirty workers. (Permission of Lockheed to publish this information is gratefully acknowledged.)

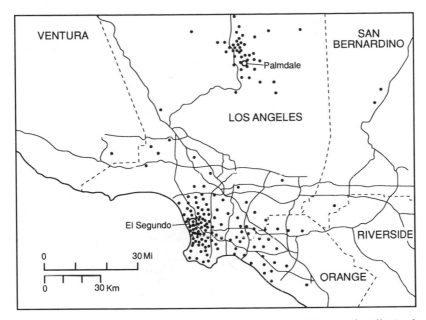

Figure 5.5. Residential locations of workers employed by Rockwell North American plants at El Segundo and Burbank. Major freeways are shown. Each dot represents thirty workers. (Permission of Rockwell North American to publish this information is gratefully acknowledged.)

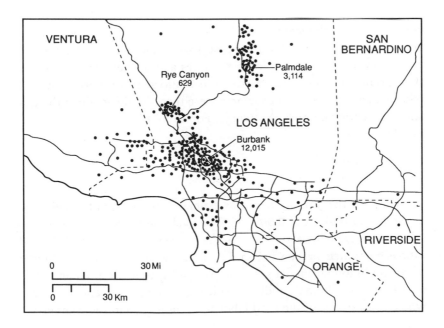

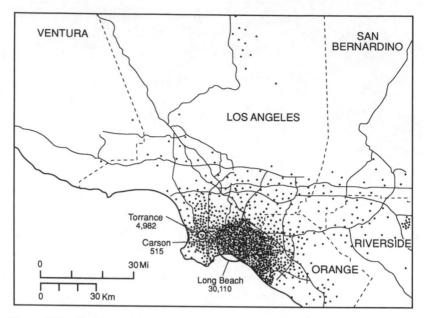

Figure 5.7. Residential locations of workers employed by McDonnell Douglas plants at Long Beach, Carson, and Torrance. Each dot represents thirty workers. The number attached to each establishment name represents total employment at that plant. (Permission of McDonnell Douglas to publish this information is gratefully acknowledged.)

tion of total employment (E_j) at j, and as an inverse function of the distance (D_{ij}) between i and j. Distances were calculated as the number of miles between given employment places and the geometric center of appropriate zip code areas in Southern California. All workers with a residence in any given zip code area were then simply assigned the distance value for that area as a whole. For all 56,676 workers, the computed model is

$$p_{ij} = \frac{\exp{(\alpha E_j / D_{ij})}}{\sum_j \exp{(\alpha E_j / D_{ij})}}.$$

The value of the parameter α was estimated by maximum likelihood methods and is given as 0.000766. The likelihood ratio, ρ^2, is equal to 0.90, which is highly significant. In the present instance, the likelihood ratio is computed as the value of $1 - (L^*/L)$, where L^* is log likelihood of the multinomial model given above, and L is the log likelihood of an alternative minimal model in which p_{ij} is simply set equal to E_j / T, where T is the size of the total labor force employed in the eight estab-

TABLE 5.2   ANNULAR STRUCTURE OF
AIRCRAFT WORKERS' RESIDENCES AROUND
PLACE OF EMPLOYMENT: DENSITY PER
SQUARE MILE

Ring no.	Distance band around workplace (miles)	Establishments[a]							
		1	2	3	4	5	6	7	8
1	0–5	82.8	13.8	0.6	27.6	9.0	1.6	11.4	5.0
2	5–10	30.7	6.1	0.8	9.6	1.5	0.4	5.7	0.2
3	10–15	18.9	2.3	0.3	5.6	1.3	0.5	1.6	2.2
4	15–20	6.4	1.0	0.2	2.9	0.5	0.1	1.0	0.0
5	20–25	2.5	0.6	0.1	2.5	0.1	0.1	0.6	0.0
6	25–30	0.9	0.2	0.0	0.3	0.1	0.1	0.5	0.0
7	30–35	0.8	0.1	0.0	0.8	0.1	0.0	0.2	0.0
8	35–40	0.4	0.1	0.0	0.3	0.0	0.0	0.1	0.0
9	40–45	0.2	0.1	0.0	0.3	0.0	0.0	0.0	0.0
10	45–50	0.2	0.0	0.0	0.0	0.0	0.0	0.1	0.0

[a] 1: McDonnell Douglas (Long Beach), 2: McDonnell Douglas (Torrance), 3: McDonnell Douglas (Carson), 4: Lockheed (Burbank), 5: Lockheed (Palmdale), 6: Lockheed (Rye Canyon), 7: Rockwell North American (El Segundo), 8: Rockwell North American (Palmdale).

lishments. The latter model would provide an accurate description of the given data if local labor markets for the eight establishments were perfectly fluid over the whole metropolitan area.

The magnitude of the likelihood ratio confirms the notion that the local labor markets of these eight producers are indeed very tightly defined in their geographical organization by establishment size and journey-to-work distances. Moreover, while establishments that are close together clearly share in overlapping local labor-market areas (see fig. 5.7), those that are farther apart appear to be much less in competition with one another, at least in the short run.

This point about the evident disconnectedness of local labor markets in different sections of the metropolis may be driven home by consideration of tables 5.2 and 5.3, which provide information on the spatial distribution of workers' residences in concentric zones centered

TABLE 5.3   ANNULAR STRUCTURE OF
AIRCRAFT WORKERS' RESIDENCES AROUND
PLACE OF EMPLOYMENT: PROPORTION OF
LABOR FORCE IN EACH RING

		Establishments[a]							
Ring no.	Distance band around workplace (miles)	1	2	3	4	5	6	7	8
1	0–5	0.22	0.22	0.08	0.18	0.33	0.19	0.18	0.26
2	5–10	0.24	0.29	0.34	0.19	0.17	0.13	0.28	0.03
3	10–15	0.25	0.18	0.21	0.18	0.24	0.29	0.13	0.59
4	15–20	0.12	0.11	0.19	0.13	0.13	0.10	0.11	0.01
5	20–25	0.06	0.09	0.08	0.15	0.01	0.07	0.09	0.00
6	25–30	0.03	0.04	0.04	0.02	0.03	0.08	0.08	0.01
7	30–35	0.02	0.01	0.01	0.07	0.03	0.06	0.05	0.02
8	35–40	0.01	0.01	0.02	0.02	0.02	0.07	0.03	0.02
9	40–45	0.01	0.02	0.01	0.04	0.01	0.01	0.01	0.01
10	45–50	0.01	0.01	0.01	0.00	0.01	0.00	0.02	0.00
11	>50	0.03	0.02	0.01	0.02	0.02	0.00	0.02	0.00

[a]1: McDonnell Douglas (Long Beach), 2: McDonnell Douglas (Torrance), 3: McDonnell Douglas (Carson), 4: Lockheed (Burbank), 5: Lockheed (Palmdale), 6: Lockheed (Rye Canyon), 7: Rockwell North American (El Segundo), 8: Rockwell North American (Palmdale).

on each workplace and inscribed at five-mile intervals. Both tables suggest that the local labor market for any establishment rarely extends much beyond about fifteen or twenty miles in radius from the establishment. In particular, table 5.3 shows that more than 50 percent of each establishment's labor force resides within fifteen miles of the place of work, and in most cases, more than 75 percent resides within twenty miles. The three major employers in our labor-market data set (i.e., Lockheed [Burbank], McDonnell Douglas [Long Beach], and Rockwell North American [El Segundo]) are all at least fourteen miles from one another, which suggests, perhaps, that large plants have at least some tendency to occupy locations where they can build and dominate a stable local labor-market territory beyond the range of effective short-run competition on the part of other major employers.

The same process may also help to explain in part the formation of multiple industrial districts of the same type within a single region (as in the case of the Southern Californian aircraft and parts industry), for beyond a certain size limit, diseconomies of scale may well begin to set in. It seems to be the case, too, that workers are to some degree locked by their place of residence into a particular local labor-market area within the metropolis. If so, do they, when unemployed, restrict their job search to firms within the same local labor-market area, or do they search over a much wider area for alternative employment? If the latter is the case, is there some critical distance (or isochrone) such that they will prefer to shift their residential location rather than endure an extended journey to work? And are there significant differences in these regards between different socioeconomic groups? We shall return to these questions in chapters 8 and 9.

INDUSTRIAL ORGANIZATION AND INTERESTABLISHMENT LINKAGES

The aircraft and parts industry in Southern California today forms an extensive complex of activities, interlinked with one another but also connected to a wider circle of establishments in such industries as nonferrous foundry work, machinery, electronics, instruments, and missiles and space vehicles. As such, there are powerful multiplier effects that flow from the industry (and especially from those segments of the industry that are maintained by military expenditures) into other sectors of the local economy (Bolton 1966; Steiner 1961; Tiebout 1966). All of this interconnection within and between industrial sectors in the region gives rise to a significant stock of agglomeration economies that helps to maintain the economic vigor of the industry. This aspect of the industrial geography of the region is extremely rich and multifarious. To bring the problem within manageable bounds, we shall focus in what follows on the present-day intrasectoral linkages of SIC 372 in Southern California.

INTERESTABLISHMENT LINKAGE DATA

In order to examine linkage patterns in the aircraft and parts industry of Southern California, a mail questionnaire survey of establishments was implemented over the summer of 1988. The questionnaire was sent out to a total of 986 establishments in Southern California, comprising (a) the 299 establishments shown in figure 5.3, whose addresses are drawn from the 1988 edition of the *California Manufacturers Register*, plus (b) a further 687 establishments whose addresses were extracted from a variety of other directories, and most importantly from diverse yellow pages telephone directories. *County Business Patterns* for 1988 records a total of 347 establishments in SIC 372 in Southern California, so it is clear that most of the 986 establishments that were sent a questionnaire would turn out to be engaged in forms of business other than aircraft and parts manufacturing. Unfortunately, the data sources did not always provide enough information to allow effective screening of establishments at an early stage. In fact, out of a total set of 114 questionnaires returned, twenty-one (or 18.8 percent) were from establishments in other SIC categories (mainly wholesaling). In addition, forty-five (39.3 percent) were returned by the post office because the addressee was no longer at the indicated address, two (1.8 percent) came back with the notation that the recipients would not participate in the survey, and just forty-six (40.6 percent) were sent back (filled out in varying degrees of completeness) by bona fide aircraft and parts manufacturers. The final response of forty-six questionnaires is decidedly low, even when we take account of the number of establishments that have gone out of business and those that were erroneously included in the initial list of addresses. No doubt the low response rate can at least in part be attributed to the fact that many of the questions posed were directed toward confidential and proprietary matters. Fortunately, a one-sample Kolmogorov-Smirnov test indicates that the frequency distribution of questionnaire respondents by size class is not significantly different from the expected distribution as recorded in *County Business Patterns* for 1988 (see table 5.4). Despite the correspondence between the sample and the population, we must still remain alert to the possibility of other biases in the questionnaire data, and we must thus approach our conclusions with due reserve.

GENERAL LINKAGE STRUCTURES

As indicated, the questionnaire that was sent out to individual establishments was designed to elicit information on forms of interplant transactions. For each establishment, data were collected on activities

TABLE 5.4   FREQUENCY DISTRIBUTION OF
QUESTIONNAIRE RESPONDENTS IN SOUTHERN
CALIFORNIA BY EMPLOYMENT SIZE CLASS
COMPARED WITH EQUIVALENT DATA FROM
COUNTY BUSINESS PATTERNS

Establishment size class, employees	Respondents, percentage frequency	*County Business Patterns*, percentage frequency
1–4	6.7	17.9
5–9	15.5	13.8
10–19	11.1	16.4
20–49	33.3	17.9
50–99	15.5	10.7
100–249	6.7	9.2
250–499	6.7	5.8
500–999	2.2	5.8
1,000+	2.2	4.0
Number of establishments	45	347

such as sales and marketing, purchasing, subcontracting, modes of transacting, and so on. These data were gathered in order to evaluate the expectation that there exists within any localized industrial complex a critical network of interestablishment transactions helping to hold the complex together as a spatial agglomeration. In particular, as suggested earlier, this critical network may be expected to be primarily composed of rapidly changing and small-scale transactions linking local producers to a mass of small specialized plants providing critical service and subcontracting functions on a custom and semicustom basis. Larger, more standardized and more regular linkages will tend to be directed over longer distances because their associated transactions costs will generally be much lower per unit of interaction. If true, these conjectures imply that small plants will be apt to sell more of their output locally than large plants, and that these local sales will consist of comparatively nonstandardized products.

This problem was broached in the first instance by means of a simple logistic-regression model, which seeks to define the proportion (C_i) of the ith establishment's customers located in Southern California as a function of (a) the establishment's total sales (S_i), and (b) the proportion (T_i) of the establishment's sales that consists of work subcontracted in from other firms. The variable S_i tests for the hypothesized scale effect; it is expressed in logarithmic form in the final model because of the disproportionate spread in the sales figures for small and large establishments. The variable T_i is a rough proxy measure of the standardization/variability dimension in linkage structures; it may be contrasted with off-the-shelf sales where output is made to general catalogue specifications. As we shall see, the effects of T_i on linkage patterns (and hence location) are in large degree derived from the intense levels of face-to-face communication that are called for in the subcontracting relation.

The computed logistic-regression model is given as:[1]

$$C_i = 1/[1 + 0.0236 \exp(1.4484 \log S_i - 0.0311 T_i)],$$
$$\quad\quad\quad (0.4525) \quad\quad (0.0084)$$

$$R^2 = 0.45; \text{ d.f.} = 2,38; F = 15.08.$$

The standard errors of the regression coefficients are shown in parentheses on the line immediately underneath the equation. The regression as a whole and both of the regression coefficients are statistically significant at the 0.01 level. This is an especially encouraging performance because the data on which the model is based refer not to aggregations of observations (such as census areas) but to individual observations (i.e., establishments), which are usually more susceptible to extreme value problems. For this reason, the modest R^2 of 0.45 must be seen as being rather convincing (though recall that the sample is biased toward medium-sized establishments). The model tells us that firms with larger sales volumes and/or more standardized outputs are more likely to sell to a wide circle of customers beyond Southern California; conversely, firms that are smaller and/or more dependent on variable subcontract work are more likely to restrict their sales activity to Southern California.

A second means of evaluating the relationship between linkage structure and establishment size draws from information elicited on

---

1. To estimate the model by regression methods, it is rearranged in the form: $\log(C_i^{-1} - 1) = \alpha + \beta_1 \log S_i + \beta_2 T_i$, where α, β_1 and β_2 are the numerical parameters. However, in cases where C_i is equal to either zero or unity, computational difficulties are encountered. In order to avoid these difficulties, the following practical rule was applied: (a) if $C_i = 0$, C_i is set equal to $C_i + \epsilon$, and (b) if $C_i = 1$, C_i is set equal to $C_i - \epsilon$, where ϵ is any arbitrarily small constant. In the present instance, ϵ is set equal to 0.000001.

TABLE 5.5   POOLED DATA FOR TOP THREE
SUPPLIERS OF QUESTIONNAIRE RESPONDENTS

		Size of respondent (annual sales)		All respondents
		<$2,250,000	>$2,250,000	
a.	Total respondents providing usable information	22	17	39
b.	Total number of suppliers reported	62	51	113
c.	Suppliers with known locations	53	43	96
d.	Suppliers located in Southern California	51	28	79
e.	d as a percentage of c.	96.2%*	56.1%*	82.3%

* The percentages for the two groups were found to be significantly different at the 99 percent level using a difference-of-proportions test.

questionnaire respondents' specific purchasing and contracting arrangements. Establishments were asked to designate their three largest suppliers of inputs (whether standard materials or subcontracted work) over the previous twelve months (table 5.5). In response to this question, a total of thirty-nine establishments reported information on 113 suppliers. Of these, it was possible to determine the locations of ninety-six, and seventy-nine (82.3 percent) of them were found to be located in Southern California. Figure 5.8 delineates the locations of these seventy-nine suppliers, along with the locations of reporting establishments, and it is very evident from this figure that there is a close locational symbiosis between the two sets of establishments. The data set forth in table 5.5 provide further insights into the nature of this symbiosis. Notice that in the table, respondents are grouped into one of two size categories, i.e., those with gross annual sales of less than $2.25 million, and those with gross annual sales greater than $2.25 million, where the figure of $2.25 million represents the median gross annual sales volume of all respondents. A total of twenty-two small respondents reported on fifty-three suppliers with known locations, of which fifty-one (96.2 percent) are in Southern California; and seventeen large respondents reported on forty-three suppliers with known locations, of which twenty-eight (65.1 percent) are in the

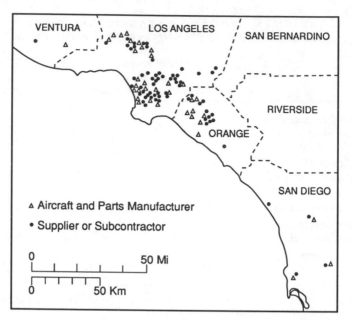

Figure 5.8. A sample of thirty-six aircraft and parts manufacturing establishments and their suppliers and subcontractors in Southern California.

region. The statistically significantly higher incidence of short-distance
linkages among smaller establishments confirms their disproportionately strong connections to the local industrial complex.

Questionnaire respondents were further asked to list those customers (if any) with whom they had multiyear contracts. The results,
broken down as before into two groups based on volume of annual
sales, are presented in table 5.6. Of the forty-six aircraft- and parts-
manufacturing establishments that completed and returned a questionnaire, thirty-one (67.4 percent) indicated that they had a multiyear
contract with one or more customers. Only 56 percent of respondents with annual sales of less than $2.25 million had such arrange-
ments, whereas 81 percent of respondents with annual sales greater
than $2.25 million reported having multiyear contracts. This finding is
consistent with the notion that smaller producers tend to have less
stable external transactional relations than larger producers. When the
location of respondents' customers is taken into account, a yet more
revealing pattern emerges. Respondents with annual sales of less than
$2.25 million maintained 88.5 percent of their multiyear contracts
with *local* customers; establishments with annual sales of more than

TABLE 5.6 POOLED DATA FOR MULTIYEAR
DELIVERY CONTRACTS OF QUESTIONNAIRE
RESPONDENTS

	Size of respondent (annual sales)		All respondents
	<$2,250,000	>$2,250,000	
a. Number of respondents	25	21	46
b. Number of respondents with multiyear delivery contracts	14	17	31
c. b as a percentage of a	56.0%*	81.0%*	67.4%*
d. aggregate number of multiyear contracts indicated	26	51	76
e. Number of multiyear contracts with firms in Southern California	23	25	48
f. e as a percentage of d	88.5%*	49.0%*	63.2%

*The percentages for the two groups were found to be significantly different at the 99 percent level using a difference-of-proportions test.

$2.25 million had multiyear contracts with a more far-flung set of customers, only 49 percent of whom are located in Southern California. Once more, then, it turns out that small establishments are markedly more connected to the local complex than are large. These remarks reinforce the proposition that the aircraft and parts industrial complex in Southern California is to a very significant degree caught up in a dense local web of finely woven transactions-intensive linkages.

MODES AND TYPES OF INDUSTRIAL INTERLINKAGE

The above analyses are fortified by additional data collected in the questionnaire on different modes of transacting within the aircraft and parts industrial complex of Southern California.

Respondents were asked to estimate what percentage of the total time leading up to a sale of output is on average spent in different modes of communication. The modes are (a) telex or fax, (b) tele-

TABLE 5.7   PERCENTAGE OF TIME ON
AVERAGE ALLOCATED TO DIFFERENT MODES
OF TRANSACTING IN THE NEGOTIATIONS
LEADING UP TO A SALE OF OUTPUT OR
SUBCONTRACTED WORK

Mode	Off-the-shelf sale (n = 23)	Sale of subcontract work (n = 38)
Telex/fax	9.5	7.6
Telephone	54.5	46.1
Mail	21.8	21.1
Face-to-face contact	12.0	22.8

phone, (c) mail, and (d) face-to-face contact. Respondents were also requested to provide this estimate separately for (a) an off-the-shelf sale, and (b) a sale of subcontract work. The results of this phase of the survey reveal patterns confirming the general thrust of the earlier theoretical analysis (see table 5.7). For an off-the-shelf sale, telephone and mail are the two most intensively used modes of transacting, with face-to-face contact a distant third. For a sale of subcontract work, where the need for close contact and consultation between the contracting parties is comparatively high, telephone and face-to-face contact are the most preferred modes of transacting. Symptomatically, the use of telex or fax communication modes is particularly low when subcontracting linkages are at issue.

The other point to remark upon in regard to table 5.7 is that out of a total of forty-four establishments, only twenty-three (52.3 percent) acknowledged that they sold off-the-shelf items, whereas thirty-eight (86.4 percent) claimed that at least part of their business came from work subcontracted to them. Subcontracting was found to be particularly important for establishments with annual sales of less that $2.25 million. For such establishments, subcontracting comprises 79.2 percent of their sales. For establishments with annual sales of more than $2.25 million, subcontracting work accounts for 36.2 percent of their sales—a much lower figure, though one that is still high in absolute terms. This high incidence of subcontracting arrangements, in conjunction with the finding that much of the transacting leading up to a subcontract involves expensive face-to-face communication, helps to account for the intense levels of locational agglomeration observable within the industry in Southern California (see Harlan 1956). Of course, many of the larger establishments in the complex have significant nationwide and worldwide linkages. However, both large and small establishments are also intertwined with one another in a dense localized network of small-scale and comparatively nonstandardized transactional activities. This phenomenon is expressed in the mutual locational attraction that aircraft assembly and parts manufacturing establishments evidently exert upon one another.

THE ROLE OF LARGE PRODUCERS WITHIN THE SOUTHERN CALIFORNIAN AIRCRAFT AND PARTS INDUSTRY

In addition to the above investigations, an effort was made to assess the effects of the major aircraft assembly plants in the region on the structure of interestablishment linkages. It must be pointed out once more that these plants operate intensely over a global level of activity. What, though, is their precise relationship to the Southern California complex?

To answer this question, much useful information was gleaned from questionnaire respondents about their sales to eleven major aircraft assemblers in Southern California, i.e., General Dynamics Convair (San Diego), Lockheed (Burbank), Lockheed (Palmdale), McDonnell Douglas (Long Beach), McDonnell Douglas (Torrance), McDonnell Douglas Helicopter Company (Culver City), Northrop (Hawthorne), Northrop (El Segundo), Northrop (Palmdale), Northrop (Pico Rivera), and Rockwell North American (El Segundo). As it happens, only one of these eleven establishments returned a completed questionnaire, and this establishment has been deleted from the analysis that follows. Two main pieces of information now need to be discussed.

First, questionnaire respondents were asked to specify the value of their annual sales to each of these eleven major producers. Respondents' sales to the major producers as a percent of total revenues were then calculated. Table 5.8 sets out the main summary statistics relating to this operation. For each of two size categories of respondents, table 5.8 shows (a) mean percentage sales to major producers, with the mean for size-category k defined as $100 \sum_j (\sum_j S_{ij})/S_i^*)/n_k$ and (b) aggregate sales to the eleven major producers as a percentage of the

TABLE 5.8   PERCENT OF QUESTIONNAIRE
RESPONDENTS' TOTAL SALES DIRECTED TO
ELEVEN MAJOR AIRCRAFT PRODUCERS IN
SOUTHERN CALIFORNIA

	Size of respondent (annual sales)	
	<$2,250,000 (n = 25)	>$2,250,000 (n = 19)
Average of individual percentages[a]	14.88	11.56
Percentage for aggregated data[a]	17.01	7.40

[a] For definitions see text.

aggregate of respondents' gross annual sales [i.e., $100 (\sum_i \sum_j S_{ij}) / \sum_i S_i^*$)]

where S_{ij} is the sales of the ith respondent to the jth major producer, S_i^* is the gross sales of the ith respondent, and n_k is the number of respondents in the kth size category. It had been expected to find sales patterns indicative of a clearly defined linkage hierarchy, with small establishments much less strongly linked—in proportional terms— than large establishments to the major producers (Sheard 1983). This kind of hierarchy is sometimes described as manifesting an "alpine" structure (an organizational form that is often taken to be especially characteristic of mass-production systems). Contrary to expectations, the data presented in table 5.8 indicate that, in comparison to large establishments, small establishments tend to sell a much greater proportion of their output to the leading producers in the region. What is particularly striking here is the magnitude of small establishments' involvement with the leading producers, for 15 percent to 17 percent on average of their annual sales are accounted for in this way. We should note that this sales activity probably constitutes only a small proportion of the total purchases made by the leading eleven producers. Nevertheless, such activity is evidence that interfirm linkages cut across whatever hierarchical structures may also exist, and that the leading producers have some direct dependency on the dense networks of small producers that ramify throughout the region. In this context it should also be observed that little evidence was found among the aircraft and parts producers of Southern California of just-in-time delivery agreements between different establishments. In fact, 65.9 percent of forty-four respondents indicated that they had no such agreements whatever.

Second, respondents were also asked to provide data that might enable us to gain some understanding of the informational intensity of their transactional relations with the eleven leading producers. Respondents were queried on face-to-face contact intensity in terms of (a) the number of times over the previous twelve months that their establishment had been visited by a representative of one of the leading producers, and (b) the number of times over the previous twelve months that an employee belonging to their establishment had visited one of the leading producers. These figures were then used to compute both average visits per establishment and the average number of visits to and from the eleven major producers per $10,000 of sales. The results of these computations are arrayed in table 5.9, where, again, establishments are classified by size category. The data show that small establishments, as expected, generate fewer visits than large establishments. When we examine visits per $10,000 of sales, however, small establishments are three times more likely than large to make visits to or receive visits from the leading producers. When we recalculate average visits made and received by weighting the data for each establishment by gross sales we find that small establishments are more likely by a factor of four or five to one to make or receive visits than large. It is thus apparent that small establishments have a much greater propensity (per unit of output) than large to engage in face-to-face contact with representatives of the eleven leading producers. Moreover, the communication between them is very much a two-way street, for representatives of the leading producers are just as likely to visit smaller establishments as the latter are to visit one of the major eleven.

In these ways the transactions-intensive nature of the aircraft and parts manufacturing complex of Southern California is yet further revealed. Most important, the small establishment segment of the complex appears to constitute a finely grained infrastructure of subcontractors providing specialized and critical services to the whole local system of production. This phenomenon reinforces the agglomeration economies that are so strongly evident in the Southern Californian aircraft and parts industrial complex. Even major producers, whose main transactional activity extends far beyond the boundaries of Southern California, seem to be dependent in detailed but critical ways on these same agglomeration economies.

TABLE 5.9 VISITS BETWEEN QUESTIONNAIRE RESPONDENTS AND ELEVEN MAJOR PRODUCERS IN SOUTHERN CALIFORNIA

	Size of respondent (annual sales)					
	<$2,250,000			>$2,250,000		
	Visits to major producer	Visits from major producer	Total	Visits to major producer	Visits from major producer	Total
Average visits per establishment	22.3	20.4	42.7	32.7	29.6	62.3
Average visits per $10,000 sales to major producers	2.1	2.1	4.2	0.7	0.6	1.3
Average visits per $10,000 sales to major producers weighted by gross sales	1.9	1.7	3.6	0.4	0.3	0.7

CONTINUITY AND CHANGE

I have made an effort to shed some light on the multifaceted puzzle of the aircraft and parts industry in Southern California by showing in a very preliminary way how it evolved in the postwar decades, how local labor markets form and are sustained around individual large producers, and how the pattern of intraregional and interestablishment linkages in the industry is organized. The aircraft and parts industry has evolved spatially and temporally in ways that contrast sharply with the patterns of evolution that have characterized both mass-production and craft-industrial activity in the United States. Unlike mass production, the aircraft and parts industry has until recently been largely immune from the traumatic forms of restructuring, rationalization, and deindustrialization that swept across the United States over the 1970s and 1980s (though the immediate future of the industry is now in considerable question). Unlike craft-industrial activity (such as clothing, furniture, or leather goods) the aircraft and parts industry has been a focus of great technological innovation and change focused on giant systems houses, with its outputs becoming steadily more complex over the course of time. Thus the industry has been marked by continual internal transformation, but also by an uncommon geographical stability during most of its existence. Certainly, there has been a steady local decentralization of the industry within Southern California, and many sorts of routine manufacturing processes in the industry have been moved to other parts of the nation and the globe over the last couple of decades. By and large, however, the region's aircraft and parts manufacturing complex weathered remarkably well the ups and downs of the postwar years, and even today its central R&D and prototype-development functions in the region are likely to remain active despite the recent loss of significant portions of the industry's final assembly operations.

The analysis above provides a number of clues as to the sources of this resilience over most of the postwar period and helps us toward a prognostication of possible future trends. Three main points must now be made. First, over the years, the industry has grown in association with dense pools of highly specialized blue-collar and white-collar labor. These labor pools are geographically arranged in ways that make them extremely accessible to producers, and they represent significant positive external economies. Second, as demonstrated, the industry has immediate access within the Southern Californian complex to a wide variety of specialized input and service providers, yielding a further harvest of external economies. In particular, even though the industry is closely linked to wider national and international markets, the local infrastructure of small producers and subcontractors is undoubtedly a critical element of its functional organization. Third and last, the very presence of these dense webs of external economies in the region is at least in part one of the sources of the industry's notable innovative capacities. The presence of such large numbers of highly qualified personnel in a single region and the well-developed social division of labor (with, as its corollary, intense transactional interchanges between establishments) provide the basic conditions under which continual mutual learning and productive forms of interestablishment cooperation are possible. The effects of these processes mount cumulatively and help to endow the industry with a significant competitive edge. To this competitive edge must be added the major technological and R&D breakthroughs in both civilian and military aircraft production that have characterized the Southern Californian industry since the 1930s, from the Douglas DC-3 and its various descendants through Lockheed's F-104 fighter aircraft (the Starfighter) in the 1950s and 1960s, to Northrop's B2 ("Stealth") bomber today (Miller and Sawers 1968).

That said, it seems that there is currently a twofold danger looming over the industry and the region, and that this danger is sufficiently serious and sufficiently damaging in its implications that it calls for concerted public attention at the local, state, and national levels. On the one hand, military aircraft production is subject to the marked vagaries of defense contracting, and this means that the economy of Southern California is exposed to considerable risk. Since the late 1980s, this theoretical risk has been manifest in tangible job loss throughout the region's high-technology industrial ensemble. On the other hand, civilian aircraft production (and much of the parts-manufacturing sector too) is now facing rapidly increasing competitive pressures on world markets. The recent success of the European Airbus, and the current Japanese effort (orchestrated by MITI) to develop a supersonic transport plane some time in the 1990s are forewarnings that Southern California's competitive edge is now under mounting threat (Seitz and Steele 1985). The urgent need is for effective contingency plans to take up slack as federal defense procurements now begin to taper off, and for policies that help to maintain the technological and commercial primacy of the aircraft and parts industry in Southern California and the United States as a whole. These issues insistently clamor for attention. In the absence of more active and coherent industrial policies, the aircraft and parts industry may well one day suffer the fate that has already befallen cars, steel, and significant segments of the semiconductor industry in the United States. The consequences for Southern California of such a turn of events would be nothing less than disastrous.

CHAPTER 6

The Missile and Space Industry

The Southern Californian Nexus in National Context

INTRODUCTION

The missile and space industry is today one of the mainstays of the entire U.S. military-industrial complex. It employs only about 1 percent of the nation's total manufacturing labor force, but its economic and political significance far outweighs its simple direct employment capacity, and it has been an important source of technological innovations throughout the postwar decades. Much of the industry is scattered geographically across the United States, but it is dominated by the enormous aerospace agglomeration of Southern California, which accounts for about one-third of the industry's total productive capacity. Here, I shall approach the growth and development of Southern California's missile and space production nexus on the basis of an examination of the industry in the United States as a whole, and in this manner I shall attempt to construct a synoptic overview of the industry's locational propensities.

POSTWAR DEVELOPMENTS IN SOUTHERN CALIFORNIA AND THE UNITED STATES

We have seen in chapter 4 how Southern California developed as a center of missile production as early as the 1940s, and how it then flourished over the 1950s as the dominant focus of the industry within

117

the country as a whole. We now need to set this story in its wider national setting.

Immediately after World War II, a number of German rocket scientists (headed by Wernher von Braun) were brought to the United States under the aegis of Operation Paperclip. This program was controlled by the U.S. Army and resulted in the development of a center of aerospace production activity in Huntsville, Alabama, in competition with the emerging Southern Californian industry. The Ordnance Department of the Army operated under an arsenal system so that much of its weaponry, including new rocket technologies, was developed in its own plants (Hall 1988). The German rocket scientists were incorporated into this system at the Redstone Arsenal in Huntsville (Bright 1978; Parson 1962). The Air Force, by contrast, relied almost exclusively on a stable of private contractors for its main defense procurements, and many of the most important of these contractors were located in Southern California (Bilstein 1974, 1980; Hall 1988; Kucera 1974). Furthermore, by the mid-1950s, the Air Force had gained a decisive advantage over the Army in the matter of missile development and overall control of the nation's missile defenses (Bright 1978). This then helped to boost the growth of the Air Force's numerous contractors (and their dependent subcontractors) in Southern California, while impeding the ability of the Redstone Arsenal to grow as an equivalent center of aerospace production activities (Armacost 1969; Hall 1988).

One of the important factors underlying this ascendancy of the Air Force was the report of the Teapot Committee (set up in 1953 by Trevor Gardner, Special Assistant for R&D in the Department of Defense), which called for the initiation of a national ICBM program. Among the members of the committee were John von Neumann, Simon Ramo, and Dean Wooldridge—the two latter individuals both employees of Hughes Aircraft at the time—and ten other representatives of academia, the aircraft industry, and the military (Neufeld 1990). The committee's report recommended a six-year program to develop an ICBM capable of delivering nuclear ordnance over intercontinental distances. To this end, the Atlas program—which had been run by Convair in San Diego since World War II—was resuscitated. The program had been funded by the Army Air Force during the war, and was then kept going in a small way by Convair alone until 1951. In 1952, the Air Force renewed funding on the ballistic version of the

Atlas, and in May 1954, thanks to the Teapot Committee's recommendations, Atlas was given top priority. In July of the same year, Gardner created the Western Development Division (WDD) of the Air Research and Development Command (ARDC) at Inglewood, California, with procurement authority for the Atlas program. By this time, Ramo and Wooldridge had resigned from Hughes Aircraft and had founded the Ramo-Wooldridge Corporation (later TRW) in south Los Angeles. Although Convair was designated as the prime contractor for Atlas, Ramo-Wooldridge was selected to manage the overall R&D and integration of the program in January 1955 (Neufeld 1990).

Work on a second ICBM program was recommended by the Air Force Scientific Advisory Committee in 1955. The Martin Company was selected and signed a contract to design and develop the Titan at its new plant in Denver, Colorado (Neufeld 1990). A host of smaller programs was also now beginning to proliferate in response to shifting perceptions of needs within the military (Simonson 1964). The recommendation by the Air Force to build the Titan included the suggestion that a tactical ballistic missile also be developed. This move brought the Army and the Air Force once more into direct competition, but again the Air Force gained the upper hand and started planning for development of the Thor IRBM. Douglas Aircraft, which in 1950 had established a Missile Division in its Santa Monica plant, signed a contract in December 1955 to build Thor under the umbrella of the WDD.

In 1955, too, a move was made within the Air Force to set up a missile facility at Holloman Air Development Center in New Mexico. However, by the end of the year, the WDD in Southern California had effectively established itself as *the* major weapons development center in the United States with a family of high-priority missile projects, including the Atlas, Titan, and Thor (Armacost 1969; Neufeld 1990), and the consolidation of the Southern Californian complex was now secured. In July 1957, Vandenburg Air Force Base was established in the region for the training of missile crews and the development and testing of intercontinental ballistic missiles (Caidin 1959). Of the more than twenty-five missile projects in development, production, or service in 1955, fourteen were run by contractors located in Southern California (*Aviation Week* 1956). Convair was now actively developing the Atlas ICBM and was actually producing the Terrier SAM; the firm also was engaged in R&D for a more advanced Terrier and the new Tartar missile. Douglas Aircraft was in full production with the Sparrow, Nike, and Honest John and was just beginning development of the Thor IRBM and the Little John tactical missile. Hughes was engaged in production of its Falcon air-to-air missile. North American's Navaho missile, in development since 1947, engendered significant technical expertise within the company but never entered production. The Northrop Snark strategic missile was both in production and in the early stages of deployment. The JPL/Firestone Corporal Missile continued in production and service use (see appendix B).

THE RISE OF THE MODERN MISSILE AND SPACE INDUSTRY

By the late 1950s, then, a significant missile-manufacturing capacity had been installed in both the United States and Southern California. Despite these advances, the launch of Sputnik by the USSR on October 4, 1957, engendered the perception that the U.S. space program was in need of serious rethinking. Fear of a missile gap spurred congressional action for a unified agency to oversee and coordinate the nation's aerospace projects. Thus in 1958 the National Aeronautics and Space Administration (NASA) was created by the federal government. In addition, much of the interservice rivalry that had characterized the missile program in the 1950s was brought under control, and in 1959 the Air Force was given full responsibility for all military space programs, a state of affairs that has continued to the present day (Baker 1978).

The U.S. missile and space industry now entered its most rapid period of development, and the 1960s saw a great unfolding not just of missile programs but also of space exploration projects (Mercury, Gemini, Mariner, and Ranger) culminating in the manned lunar landing (Apollo 11) in July 1969 (Nicks 1985; Osman 1983; Wilson 1982; see also appendix C). This phase of development of the industry was fueled by continually expanding federal outlays on missile and space equipment, and Southern California, building on the immense agglomeration of aerospace production activities that had steadily been put into place in the region since the late 1930s, continued to absorb the lion's share of these outlays. In the rest of the country, there was a widely dispersed phalanx of missile and space equipment producers, but it was always overshadowed by the great concentration of manufacturers in Southern California.

GROWTH AND ORGANIZATION OF THE MODERN U.S. MISSILE AND SPACE INDUSTRY

RECENT EMPLOYMENT CHANGES

For present purposes, the modern missile and space industry is defined in terms of the Standard Industrial Classification (SIC) as SIC 376, i.e., guided missiles, space vehicles, and parts. SIC 376 breaks down into three four-digit sectors, namely, SIC 3761 (guided missiles and space vehicles), SIC 3764 (space propulsion units and parts), and SIC 3769 (space vehicle equipment not elsewhere classified).

Governmental statistics on aggregate national employment in the U.S. missile and space industry are available on a yearly basis from 1972, when SIC 376 was first defined as a distinctive category in the Standard Industrial Classification. National employment statistics for the three four-digit sectors that make up SIC 376 are arrayed in table 6.1 for the years 1972–1987, inclusive. Throughout the 1960s, the industry grew at a rapid pace, but over the 1970s employment declined, and then over the 1980s expanded steadily again (with the exception of the downturn of 1982). As is to be expected, these trends mirror spending patterns by the two major purchasers of aerospace products, namely, the Department of Defense (DOD) and NASA (see table 6.2). Most especially, the extended downturn of the 1970s can be ascribed to the severe budgetary crises of the federal government during these years, and the upturn of the mid-1980s to the very assertive defense policies of the Reagan administration. At the present time, with defense budgets in the United States declining once again, employment in SIC 376 is also starting to drop (cf. *Aviation Week and Space Technology* 1989; Southern California Association of Governments, 1989).

Thus, employment changes in the industry are geared largely to changes in governmental procurements, with additional modulations induced by processes of technological change. There has been much investment in labor-saving equipment in the industry over the last couple of decades, and especially in numerically controlled and robotized manufacturing systems for machining, welding, and assembly. This investment has presumably slowed down overall rates of employment growth, though contrary to the claims of a recent government report (U.S. Department of Labor 1986) its impact on the relative proportions of blue-collar and white-collar labor in the industry has not been great. In 1972, blue-collar workers accounted for 39.7 percent of the total workforce in SIC 376, and in 1987 they accounted for 38.3 per-

TABLE 6.1   TOTAL EMPLOYMENT IN SICS
3761, 3764, 3769 FOR THE UNITED STATES,
1972–1987[a]

Year	SIC 3761 Guided missiles and space vehicles	SIC 3764 Space-propulsion units and parts	SIC 3769 Space-vehicle equipment, n.e.c.
1972	118,400	20,800	20,900
1973	117,300	22,500	20,200
1974	116,900	21,000	16,500
1975	110,800	20,500	16,300
1976	106,200	19,000	16,500
1977	94,000	18,600	7,200
1978	93,800	20,100	8,200
1979	104,600	22,200	9,500
1980	106,500	25,500	8,700
1981	106,500	26,700	17,900
1982	99,600	25,300	21,400
1983	110,700	27,600	24,400
1984	120,900	28,200	26,700
1985	154,300	29,800	33,700
1986	174,200	31,400	22,100
1987	166,700	31,800	15,100

[a] SOURCE: U.S. Department of Commerce, Bureau of the Census, *Census of Manufactures*, 1987.

cent. Over the same period of time, productivity (value added per worker) grew in real terms by just over 50 percent.

THE ORGANIZATION OF THE INDUSTRY

One of the important characteristics of the missile and space sector is that it is dominated by large systems houses embedded in dense networks of smaller flexibly specialized establishments that provide them with innumerable physical inputs and subcontract services. The latter establishments are to be found in sectors like aerospace parts production, plastics molding, aluminum foundry work, machining, electronic components, instruments, and so on. The industry, then, consists of a

TABLE 6.2   DEPARTMENT OF DEFENSE
EXPENDITURES ON MISSILES AND NASA
OUTLAYS ON AEROSPACE PRODUCTS AND
SERVICES, 1972–1990[a]

| | DOD expenditures on missiles | | NASA outlays | |
| | Millions of dollars | | Millions of dollars | |
	Current	Constant	Current	Constant
1972	3,009	6,632	3,372	7,432
1973	3,023	6,372	3,270	6,892
1974	2,981	5,964	3,181	6,364
1975	2,889	5,265	3,181	5,797
1976	2,296	3,942	3,548	6,092
1977	2,781	4,469	3,840	6,171
1978	3,096	4,698	3,859	5,856
1979	3,786	5,263	4,064	5,649
1980	4,434	5,550	4,712	5,898
1981	5,809	6,528	5,278	5,931
1982	6,782	6,963	5,926	6,084
1983	7,795	7,692	6,556	6,470
1984	9,527	9,062	6,939	6,600
1985	10,749	10,229	7,081	6,738
1986	11,730	10,990	7,215	6,760
1987	11,473	11,089	7,442	7,193
1988	11,676	11,676	8,926	8,926
1989	13,370	12,858	10,427	10,028
1990	13,757	12,778	12,360	11,480

[a] SOURCE: Aerospace Industries Association of America, *Aerospace Facts and Figures 89/90.*

shifting transactions-intensive complex of systems houses and dependent flexibly specialized producers in functionally adjacent sectors.
The frequency distributions of establishments by size in each of the
three four-digit SIC categories that make up SIC 376 are shown in
table 6.3. These data are consistent with the notion of the industry as
a combination of large systems houses and smaller specialized produc-

TABLE 6.3   FREQUENCY DISTRIBUTIONS OF
ESTABLISHMENTS BY EMPLOYMENT IN SICS
3761, 3764, AND 3769 FOR THE UNITED
STATES, 1987[a]

	SIC 3761 Guided missiles and space vehicles		SIC 3764 Space-propulsion units and parts		SIC 3769 Space-vehicle equipment, n.e.c.	
	Establishments		Establishments		Establishments	
	Number	*Percent*	*Number*	*Percent*	*Number*	*Percent*
Number of employees						
1–9	1	2.5	4	11.4	14	21.2
10–19	1	2.5	3	8.6	9	13.6
20–49	3	7.5	8	22.9	13	19.7
50–99	1	2.5	3	8.6	9	13.6
100–249	2	5.0	3	8.6	10	15.2
250–499	1	2.5	3	8.6	5	7.6
500–999	2	5.0	4	11.4	4	6.1
1,000–2,499	8	20.0	3	8.6	0	0.0
2,500+	21	52.5	4	11.4	2	3.0
Total	40	100.0	35	100.0	66	100.0

[a] SOURCE: U.S. Department of Commerce, Bureau of the Census, *Census of Manufactures*, 1987.

ers, for in final assembly work (i.e., SIC 3761) average establishment size is 4167.5 whereas in parts production (SIC 3769) average employment is only 228.8.

Within the complex, labor markets are typically segmented. The central systems houses employ for the most part highly paid white-collar and blue-collar workers (the latter engaged mainly in skilled assembly and machining). Toward the functional margins of the complex we find establishments that employ large numbers of unskilled, low-wage immigrant and female workers, very often under sweatshop conditions. This phenomenon of segmentation is especially marked within the Southern Californian complex.

LOCATIONAL STRUCTURE OF THE INDUSTRY

The contemporary locational pattern of the U.S. missile and space industry is summarized in figures 6.1 and 6.2, which identify individual plants by four-digit SIC category. The pattern is made up of many plants distributed across the country (but with an evident locational bias towards the Sunbelt) with an overwhelmingly dominant agglomeration in Southern California. As is apparent from a scrutiny of figure 6.3, many of these manufacturing locations are closely associated with DOD testing facilities, NASA installations, and other military establishments. Such a relationship is conspicuous in the case of the Southern Californian agglomeration, as well as in the cases of smaller agglomerations in (a) the San Francisco Bay Area (associated with the Air Force Station at Sunnyvale and the NASA-Ames Research facility at Moffett Field), (b) Phoenix (associated with four major test facilities in southern Arizona), (c) Denver-Colorado Springs (associated with the U.S. Air Force Space Command and the North American Air Defense Command at Cheyenne Mountain), (d) Huntsville (Marshall Space Flight Center and the Redstone Arsenal), (e) Cape Canaveral (with its major launch facility), and (f) the Washington, D.C. region, which is not only where the Pentagon is located, but is also the site of major NASA and DOD installations (NASA 1990). The presence of two major rocket-propulsion manufacturers in Utah adjacent to three DOD testing facilities is also worthy of note. The locational attraction exerted by these installations resides largely in their demands for work such as R&D, final assembly, repair, and proving of missiles and aerospace equipment (cf. Ball 1962). However, these particular spatial relations are far from being dominant or primary. Many major missile and space manufacturers are located at great distances from major defense-space ground installations, and it may be argued, in particular, that the main Southern Californian agglomeration can only be satisfactorily accounted for in terms of a wider conception of industrial organization and location.

THE SOUTHERN CALIFORNIAN MISSILE AND SPACE INDUSTRIAL AGGLOMERATION

Table 6.4 lays out data from *County Business Patterns* on total employment and number of establishments for SIC 376 in Southern Cali-

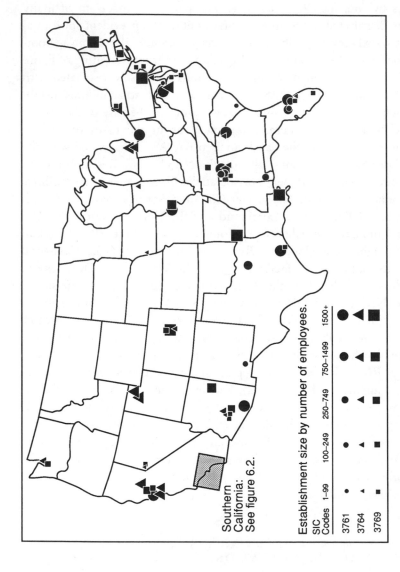

Southern
California:
See figure 6.2.

Establishment size by number of employees.

SIC Codes	1–99	100–249	250–749	750–1499	1500+
3761	•	●	●	●	●
3764	◂	◂	◂	◀	◀
3769	▪	■	■	■	■

Figure 6.1.   The location of the U.S. missile and space industry, 1987. (Data from *County Business Patterns*, U.S. Department of the Census, 1987.)

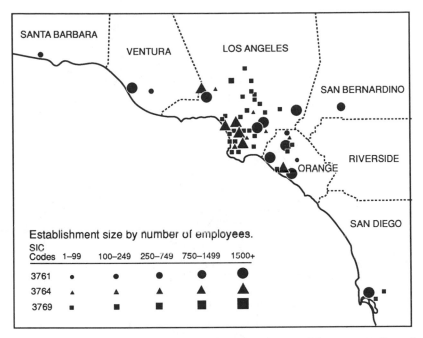

Figure 6.2. The locational structure of the Southern Californian missile and space industry. (Data from *California Manufacturers' Register*, 1989, and *Interavia ABC Aerospace Directory*, 1989.)

fornia and Los Angeles over the period from 1974 to 1988.[1] In 1988, Southern California accounted for 40.5 percent of total national employment in SIC 376, and Los Angeles accounted for 66.6 percent of the Southern Californian total. The pattern of change in the industry in Southern California and Los Angeles over the last two decades runs parallel to the national trend, with marked declines of employment in the late 1970s, and rapid growth over the 1980s (State of California Commission on State Finance 1990).

The growth of the aerospace-electronics complex in Southern California over the postwar decades owes much to its own internal dynamic of development, which has continually brought forth a rich assortment of agglomeration economies. These agglomeration economies reside in (a) the dense networks of specialized input providers

1. Note that, unlike the *Census of Manufactures* (which is the source of table 6.1), *County Business Patterns* (which is the source of table 6.4) does not provide data for SIC 376 before 1974.

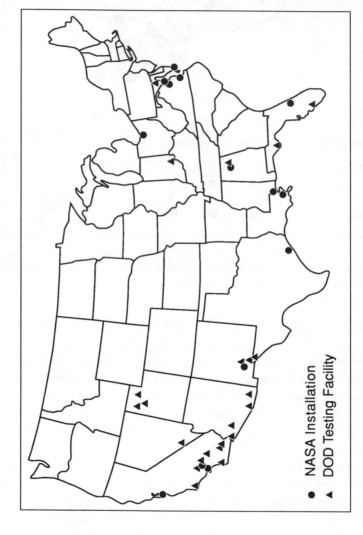

Figure 6.3. DOD test facilities and NASA installations. (Data from NASA *Pocket Statistics,* 1990, and *National Atlas of the U.S.A.,* 1970.)

- ● NASA Installation
- ▲ DOD Testing Facility

TABLE 6.4 EMPLOYMENT AND NUMBER OF
ESTABLISHMENTS IN SIC 376 (GUIDED
MISSILES, SPACE VEHICLES, AND PARTS) IN
THE U.S., SOUTHERN CALIFORNIA, AND LOS
ANGELES, 1974–1988[a]

	United States		Southern California		Los Angeles	
	Em-ployment	Estab-lishments	Em-ployment	Estab-lishments	Em-ployment	Estab-lishments
1974	141,804	129	67,956	42	44,476	22
1975	146,172	113	67,297	35	46,498	19
1976	139,781	110	63,171	34	44,589	18
1977	124,582	107	60,996	37	45,764	21
1978	128,587	107	63,445	39	47,399	23
1979	128,048	100	60,930	36	47,297	23
1980	136,243	107	58,789	39	45,243	24
1981	144,747	104	63,262	40	49,709	25
1982	164,791	103	59,824	37	46,449	22
1983	176,694	113	65,012	43	51,637	28
1984	172,377	109	68,402	40	55,027	26
1985	182,994	111	72,836	41	55,711	27
1986	195,768	118	72,241	43	53,866	28
1987	195,512	124	75,243	41	56,318	28
1988	219,623	153	88,910	47	59,235	31

[a] SOURCE: U.S. Department of Commerce, Bureau of the Census, *County Business Patterns*. Employment data for Southern California are computed by summing data for seven counties. Where employment data for individual counties are suppressed for reasons of confidentiality, estimates are made by taking the medians of the interval data provided by the source.

and subcontractors within the region; (b) the presence of a major pool of skilled aerospace workers (both blue-collar and white-collar); hence, at the time of the *1980 Census of Population*, 32 percent of the 28,282 aerospace engineers in the United States were located in the seven counties of Southern California; and (c) a local infrastructure of research and aerospace management organizations (together with the DOD and NASA installations noted earlier). We also need to acknowledge the impacts of federal defense and space expenditures on Southern Californian manufacturers, and the role of these expenditures in sustaining the entire aerospace-electronics com-

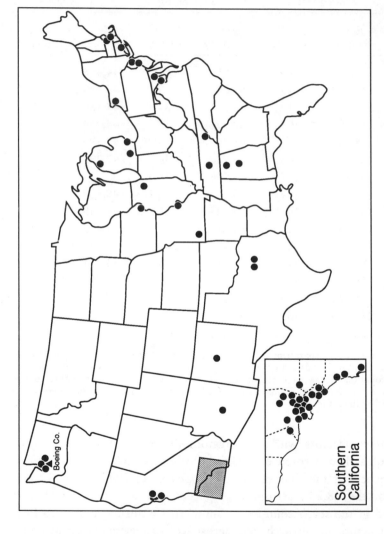

Figure 6.4. First-tier subcontractors of Boeing Company for the Saturn V program. (Data from Bilstein 1980.)

plex (Cochran 1988; Gibson and Merz 1971). Such expenditures are not strictly speaking an agglomeration economy—if anything their focus on Southern California is an effect of agglomeration and not a cause—but they have been essential in driving forward the development of the entire system in the postwar decades.

The overall dominance of the Southern Californian agglomeration within the U.S. missile and space industry may be further emphasized by reference to figures 6.4 to 6.7. These figures identify the locations of first-tier subcontractors for five major prime contractors on the Saturn V project over the years 1960 to 1969. In all cases, the concentration of subcontractors in Southern California is evident, even when the prime contractor (Boeing or IBM) is located in another region. The figures also indicate that prime contractors located in Southern California put out work to subcontractors in other regions, often at great distances from Southern California, and this feature underlines the point that in modern industrial systems, dense constellations of intra-agglomeration linkages are invariably complemented by other linkages to the rest of the world.

Essentially the same insistent role of the Southern Californian agglomeration is revealed by appendices B and C. For the missile, launch vehicle and booster rocket programs over the period 1950 to 1990 mentioned in appendix B, 45.3 percent of prime contractors are located in Southern California. For the space vehicle programs designated in appendix C, over 70 percent of all prime contractors are located in Southern California.

CONCLUSION

Two main points constitute the conclusion to this chapter. They run parallel to the conclusions of chapter 5.

In the first place, the missile and space industry has hitherto flourished under generally rising DOD and NASA expenditures for missiles and space equipment. This state of affairs is now changing radically. Under conditions of international *détente*, DOD procurements are currently declining and will certainly continue to do so over the coming years, possibly by very significant amounts, depending on the changing international situation and the magnitude of the federal budget deficit. This anticipated decline will have many repercussions on the industry, and, because of the industry's multiplier effects on the rest of the Southern Californian economy it will also have a negative

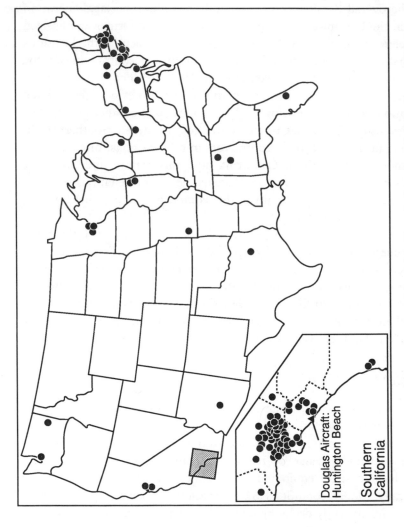

Figure 6.5. First-tier subcontractors of Douglas Aircraft Company for the Saturn V program S-IV and S-IVB. (Data from Bilstein 1980.)

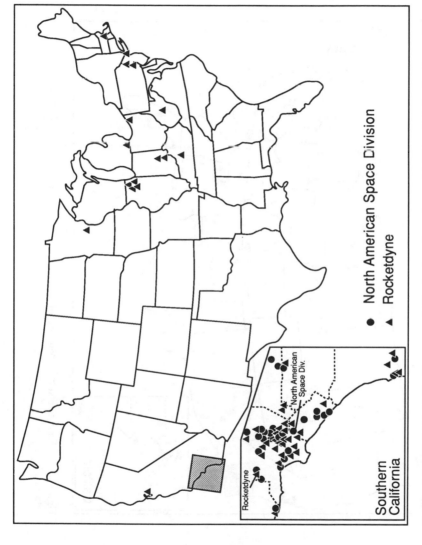

● North American Space Division

▲ Rocketdyne

Southern California

Figure 6.6. First-tier subcontractors of North American Space Division and Rocketdyne. (Data from Bilstein 1980.)

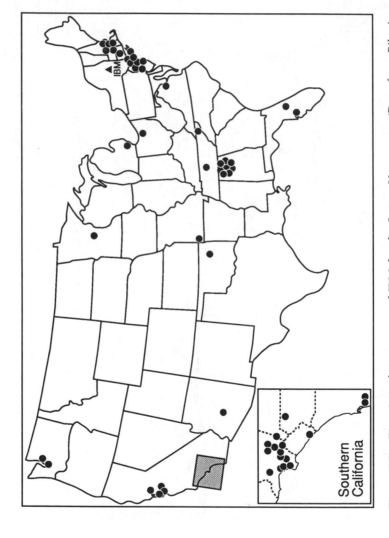

Figure 6.7. First-tier subcontractors of IBM for the Saturn V program. (Data from Bilstein 1980.)

Southern California

impact on a host of local input providers (Southern California Association of Governments 1989). In addition, NASA is currently under considerable pressure, with the overall space program being widely questioned in Congress and in the press (cf. Covault 1988; Ride Commission Report 1987). It is therefore unlikely that projected DOD expenditure declines will be compensated for by rising NASA expenditures, especially in a situation where large federal budget deficits continue to prevail.

In the second place, much of the U.S. missile and space industry has in the past been sheltered from foreign competition, both because of the preferential purchasing of domestically made products by federal agencies, and because of the past failure of foreign manufacturers to match U.S. quality standards (Stevenson 1990). This situation, too, is likely to change drastically, particularly as civilian markets expand; and Japan, Europe (especially after 1992), and even Brazil, China, and Russia may be expected to enter more forcefully into international markets for aerospace products in the future (Harr and Kohli 1990; OECD 1985; Subcommittee on Economic Stabilization 1989).

In this combination of circumstances, it seems likely that the U.S. missile and space industry will be under considerable threat over the coming years, and this threat looms over even its most viable core as represented by the Southern Californian agglomeration (Vartabedian 1990). Throughout the whole of its history, the industry has flourished as a highly regulated sector in the sense that production programs, technologies, R&D, skills, markets, and other critical attributes have been subject to considerable governmental control and influence. In the future, the industry will be much buffeted in the winds of the coming new competition (Stevenson 1990). The latter remark is reinforced by the observation that much of the competition is likely to come from countries that are successfully providing institutional infrastructures to bolster the market performance of their own producers. The policy imperative—as I shall argue at length in chapter 12—is in part to distill the lessons of the past successes (and failures) of the U.S. missile and space industry and to devise forms of public-private partnership capable of sustaining a technologically dynamic and price-competitive industry in the face of increasingly contested international markets.

CHAPTER 7

The Electronics Industry

Out of the historical roots described in chapter 4, there emerged in Southern California after about the mid-1950s one of the largest and most dynamic electronics manufacturing complexes in the United States, with a multifaceted focus on computers, military and space communications equipment and avionics, and a diversity of components from printed circuit boards to advanced semiconductor devices. The development of the industry has been much encouraged by federal defense spending, both in the form of direct procurements as well as indirectly via the industry's provision of crucial inputs to the aircraft, missile, and space sectors. There is now also a rapidly expanding segment of the electronics industry in the region that is focused on purely commercial markets.

GROWTH AND SPATIAL STRUCTURE

THE STATISTICAL RECORD

For the period from the late 1950s to 1987, the electronics industry is definable in terms of three three-digit SIC categories, namely, SIC 357 (office and computing machines), SIC 366 (communications equipment), and SIC 367 (electronic components and accessories). After 1987, a large proportion of SIC 366 was reassigned to SIC 381 (search and navigation equipment), and thus for more recent years, SIC 381 is

TABLE 7.1   NUMBER OF ESTABLISHMENTS
AND TOTAL EMPLOYMENT IN THE SOUTHERN
CALIFORNIAN ELECTRONICS INDUSTRY (SIC
357, SIC 366, SIC 367)

	Establishments		Employment	
	Total	Rate of change	Total	Rate of change
1959	316	—	43,517	—
1968	640	102.5%	125,006	187.3%
1977	1,116	74.4%	138,422	10.7%
1986	1,796	60.9%	233,230	68.5%

SOURCE: U.S. Department of Commerce, Bureau of the Census, *County Business Patterns*. The data shown represent aggregates for the seven counties of Southern California. Occasionally, *County Business Patterns* suppresses data for particular sectors in particular counties; where this is the case, employment has been estimated from interval data provided by the source.

added to the other three sectors to make up a composite electronics sector.

These definitions of the electronics industry admittedly leave much to be desired. However, the designated sectors are overwhelmingly focused on the high-technology segments of the industry; and for the period covering the 1960s, 1970s, and 1980s, more detailed four-digit categories provide at best only a discontinuous data series for the counties of Southern California. On the basis of a rough estimate, SICs 357, 366, and 367 accounted for some 90 percent to 95 percent of all electronics employment in the region in 1986. With 13.4 percent of the nation's total employment in these three sectors, Southern California ranks as one of the major centers of electronics production anywhere in the world.

Throughout the postwar period from the 1950s to the 1980s, the electronics industry of Southern California has grown continually in terms of employment and number of establishments, except for periodic downturns corresponding to economic recessions or cutbacks in federal defense spending. Table 7.1 shows the number of establishments and employment totals in the industry as a whole in Southern California from 1959 to 1986. Over this period of time, the definitions of the three SIC categories that make up the electronics industry for the purposes of this study remain internally consistent. The number

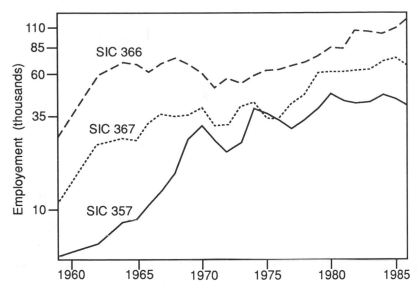

Figure 7.1. Employment in SIC 357 (office and computing machines), SIC 366 (communications equipment), and SIC 367 (electronic components and accessories) in Southern California, 1959–1986. (Data from U.S. Department of Commerce, Bureau of the Census, *County Business Patterns*. The data shown represent aggregates for the seven counties of Southern California. Occasionally, *County Business Patterns* suppresses data for particular sectors in particular counties; where this is the case, employment has been estimated from the interval data provided by the source.)

of establishments grew from 316 to 1,796 over the designated time period, and total employment grew from 43,517 to 233,230. Rates of growth have tended to decrease somewhat in recent years by comparison with rates that prevailed in the 1950s and 1960s, though even over much of the 1980s expansion remained remarkably vigorous.

In figure 7.1 this pattern of growth is broken down by sector. The industry's early growth in the 1950s is based primarily on the production of communications equipment (SIC 366), with electronic components and accessories (SIC 367) growing strongly in the 1960s, and with office and computing machines (SIC 357) moving briskly ahead after the late 1960s. Since the early 1970s, all three sectors have expanded rapidly more or less in parallel with one another. In combination with the aerospace industry, they form a complex of productive activities comprising a core of large systems houses locked into a network of innumerable smaller specialized producers and subcontractors. Systems-house manufacturing is especially strongly developed in the communications equipment sector, where outputs often consist of large-scale R&D-intensive one-of-a-kind or small-batch products for particular military or space programs.

THE CHANGING SPATIAL PATTERN

The industry's overall record of growth is superimposed upon a constantly shifting locational structure, involving above all the steady decentralization of the industry from Los Angeles, and its locational recomposition within a series of high-technology industrial districts in the outer cities of the region. Even so, as shown by table 7.2, Los Angeles County remains the regional hub of the electronics industry. Orange and San Diego counties come second and third in order. They are followed in turn by Ventura and Santa Barbara counties, which are beginning to evince strong signs of new high-technology industrial district formation. Riverside and San Bernardino counties have remained over the entire postwar period somewhat unreceptive to high-technology industrial development, possibly because of their older and more traditional industrial base anchored in steel, metalworking, and machinery manufacture. However, this base has declined rapidly in recent years, and definite signs of new high-technology industrial growth are now increasingly evident in these latter two counties. All of these shifting locational structures may be more clearly apprehended by reference to maps of individual establishments within the study region (figs. 4.3, 7.2 and 7.3).

In 1955, as revealed by figure 4.3, the electronics industry was largely confined to three major districts, one of which corresponds to the original locational base of the small prewar electrical industry close to the central business district of Los Angeles, with the other two more or less coinciding with the early geographical concentrations of the aircraft industry. The first of these lies to the west of the Los Angeles basin, stretching from Santa Monica in the north to El Segundo in the south; the second is situated in the Burbank-Glendale-North Hollywood area in the eastern San Fernando Valley.

Figure 7.2 shows that by 1972 the electronics industry in the central area of Los Angeles was beginning to thin out, though the two districts in Santa Monica-El Segundo and Burbank-Glendale-North Hollywood are still at this time important centers of the industry. Also, three major high-technology industrial districts in the outer cities of the region emerged over the 1960s and early 1970s, and

TABLE 7.2 NUMBER OF ESTABLISHMENTS AND EMPLOYMENT IN SIC 357 (OFFICE AND COMPUTING MACHINES), SIC 366 (COMMUNICATIONS EQUIPMENT), SIC 367 (ELECTRONIC COMPONENTS AND ACCESSORIES), AND SIC 381 (SEARCH AND NAVIGATION EQUIPMENT) IN SOUTHERN CALIFORNIA, BY COUNTY, 1988

	SIC 257		SIC 366		SIC 367		SIC 381	
	Estab-lishments	Em-ployment	Estab-lishments	Em-ployment	Estab-lishments	Em-ployment	Estab-lishments	Em-ployment
Los Angeles	114	11,320	73	8,441	414	28,542	68	38,461
Orange	124	13,621	16	1,306	269	18,401	34	29,396
Riverside	4	20–99	2	100–249	22	2,965	2	20–99
San Bernardino	6	108	7	356	28	583	1	100–249
San Diego	71	7,640	29	3,030	144	9,805	27	6,199
Santa Barbara	7	284	6	197	20	1,948	6	5,308
Ventura	14	649	8	1,000–2,499	62	3,110	9	1,843

SOURCE: U.S. Department of Commerce, Bureau of the Census, *County Business Patterns*.

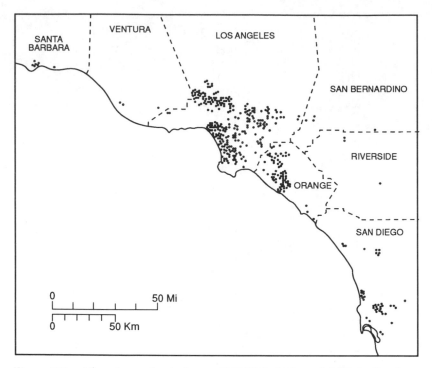

Figure 7.2. The electronics industry (SIC 357, 366, and 367) in Southern California, 1972. One dot equals one manufacturing establishment.

these attracted a large complement of electronics manufacturing establishments. These districts are located in Orange County (and above all in the area in and around Irvine), the westward extension of the San Fernando Valley cluster into Chatsworth-Canoga Park, and the northern suburbs of San Diego where a small but very active electronics complex focused on components and computers was beginning to take shape in the early 1970s.

Figure 7.3 shows the situation in 1988, which represents a continuation of the trends already noted in figure 7.2. The thinning out of electronics establishments in the central area of Los Angeles continues, and is even evident in a small way in the two inner districts of Santa Monica-El Segundo and Burbank-Glendale-North Hollywood. By contrast, the high-technology industrial areas in Orange County, Chatsworth-Canoga Park and San Diego have grown conspicuously in comparison with the pattern for 1972. There is also evidence of new industrial district formation in Santa Barbara and Ventura counties as

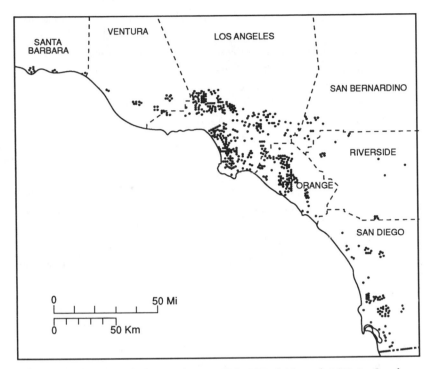

Figure 7.3. The electronics industry (SIC 357, 366, and 367) in Southern California, 1988. One dot equals one manufacturing establishment.

well as in the Irvine Spectrum development to the southeast of the main Irvine Business Complex.

With these preliminaries in mind, we now look in some detail at the employment and linkage structures of a sample of electronics manufacturers in Southern California. The data for this phase of the analysis were collected by means of a questionnaire survey, and before we proceed further a few comments are in order about the design of the survey.

SPECIFICATIONS OF A QUESTIONNAIRE SURVEY

The questionnaire survey of electronics manufacturers in Southern California was carried out in late 1988 and early 1989. The questionnaire form itself comprised four pages of detailed queries on such matters as production processes, outputs, sales volume, upstream and downstream linkages, subcontracting activities, and employment.

An attempt was made to send a questionnaire to all electronics producers in Southern California, including both single-establishment
firms and the individual establishments of multiestablishment firms.
The questionnaire was mailed to a total of 2,993 establishments
gleaned from a variety of directories, but principally from the yellow
pages telephone directories for the many different communities of
Southern California. Out of the total set of questionnaires dispatched,
a total of 110 were returned by respondents, of which however only
seventy-three (66.4 percent) turned out to be bona fide electronics
manufacturers. In addition, 290 questionnaires were returned by the
post office as undeliverable. If we assume that 2,703 questionnaires
were actually delivered and that 66.4 percent of these represent
genuine electronics manufacturing establishments, then the total response rate is 4.1 percent. This is an unusually low response, even for
this kind of survey, where response rates are more often in the general
area of 10 percent to 15 percent.

Part of the reason for the low rate no doubt lies in the circumstance
that the questionnaire was not only long and complex, but also asked
for much detailed proprietary information; part perhaps is due to the
large numbers of very small establishments in the electronics industry,
often run under sweatshop conditions and owned by immigrant entrepreneurs. In fact, as suggested by table 7.3, the size distribution of
sampled electronics manufacturers is significantly biased against small
establishments in comparison to the corresponding distribution of all
electronics manufacturers in the region. A Kolmogorov-Smirnov one-
sample test of the two distributions displayed in table 7.3 indicates
that they differ from one another at the 0.05 level of significance. Because of these manifest problems of the sample, the analysis that now
follows should be treated with some circumspection. Nonetheless, the
general results of the analysis seem reasonable enough, and they are
consistent with the general weight of evidence that is offered elsewhere
in this book.

EMPLOYMENT STRUCTURES

At the present time the electronics industry of Southern California
employs about a quarter-of-a-million workers, almost all of them in
nonunionized establishments. According to the sample survey, 24.7
percent of the workers in the industry are engaged in managerial and
R&D occupations, and 55.4 percent are engaged in manual produc-

TABLE 7.3 SIZE DISTRIBUTION OF SAMPLE
OF ELECTRONICS ESTABLISHMENTS
COMPARED WITH SIZE DISTRIBUTION OF THE
POPULATION OF ALL ELECTRONICS
ESTABLISHMENTS IN SOUTHERN CALIFORNIA

Employment size category	Sample establishments, 1988		Population of establishments, 1986	
	Number	Percent	Number	Percent
1–4	5	6.8	428	23.8
5–9	9	12.3	223	12.4
10–19	16	21.9	264	14.7
20–49	21	28.8	324	18.0
50–99	8	11.0	208	11.6
100–249	10	13.7	194	10.8
250–499	2	2.7	81	4.5
500–499	0	0.0	31	1.7
1,000+	2	2.7	43	2.4
Totals	73	100.0	1,796	100.0

SOURCE FOR POPULATION: U.S. Department of Commerce, Bureau of the Census, *County Business Patterns*. The data shown represent aggregates for SIC 357, SIC 366, and SIC 367, and the seven counties of Southern California.

tion work. Of the latter workers, more than half are members of minority ethnic or racial groups (table 7.4). At the same time, 43.7 percent of all production workers are female. These simple data suggest at once that local labor markets in the Southern Californian electronics industry tend to be split into rather distinctive upper and lower tiers with the lower tier formed dominantly by immigrants and women.

Over the last few decades large numbers of immigrants (often undocumented) have moved steadily into the Southern Californian electronics industry, and they now perform the majority of all assembly and fabrication work (cf. Fernandez-Kelly 1987). As shown by table 7.4, Hispanics represent the largest ethnic group in the industry, and they account for 29.3 percent of production worker jobs among sample establishments on a simple average basis. Asians (particularly Vietnamese) form the next major group, with 18.4 percent of production worker jobs, and this group is now expanding at a particularly rapid

TABLE 7.4   ETHNICITY, RACE, AND GENDER
IN EMPLOYMENT PATTERNS AMONG SAMPLE
ELECTRONICS ESTABLISHMENTS (N = 62)

| | Percentage of production workers | |
	Simple average	Weighted average
Asians	18.4	18.1
Hispanics	29.3	22.8
African-Americans	3.6	10.4
Females	43.7	41.1

rate. African-Americans constitute only a small minority (3.6 percent) of production workers. Observe that on a *weighted* average basis the percentage of Hispanics among production workers falls to 22.8 percent and the percentage of African-Americans rises to 10.4 percent, signifying that Hispanics are proportionally overrepresented in small establishments and African-Americans in large. This finding may possibly be an outcome of a certain preference by small employers for illegal immigrants (among whom Hispanics predominate) thus displacing many African-Americans except in the large establishment segment of the industry where greater concern for legality and affirmative action programs is more likely to prevail.

Two additional significant items of information were revealed by the questionnaire. One is that levels of part-time and temporary employment in the electronics industry are very small, for on average only 2.9 percent of all production workers at sample establishments are involved in part-time work, and only 3 percent are involved in temporary work. The other is that labor turnover among production workers is on the whole, and as expected, extremely high. Layoff and recall rates in excess of 25 percent a year are recorded respectively for 39.7 percent and 49.2 percent of sample establishments; and rates in excess of 50 percent are recorded respectively for 17.5 percent and 31.7 percent of establishments. These data reveal that there is a rapid rotation of production workers through the local job system. As Angel (1989) has suggested in a study of the semiconductor industry in Silicon Valley, high levels of turnover may also be expected to occur for many classes of scientific and technical workers in high-technology industrial districts. The phenomenon of high turnover accentuates

TABLE 7.5   AVERAGE PERCENT OF TOTAL
PURCHASES BY VALUE ORIGINATING WITHIN
FIFTEEN MILES OF RESPONDENT, AND
WITHIN SOUTHERN CALIFORNIA

	Establishment size (annual sales)			
	< $2 million		> $2 million	
	%	n	%	n
Within fifteen miles	25.3	36	18.4	30
Within Southern California	58.6	36	58.0	32

locational agglomeration by placing a premium on information and accessibility to alternative employment opportunities. The agglomeration economies of the region are yet further enhanced by the presence of large pools of habituated and socially differentiated workers in both upper and lower labor-market segments.

THE LOGIC OF INTERESTABLISHMENT LINKAGES

GENERAL PATTERNS OF PURCHASES AND SALES

One of the objectives of the questionnaire survey was to discover to what degree electronics establishments in Southern California are linked to the local economy, and to what degree they are linked to a geographically wider circle of input providers and customers. Respondents were therefore asked to indicate (a) what percentages of their total purchases come from within fifteen miles of their establishment, and what from within Southern California as a whole, and (b) what percentages of their total customers are located within the same two spatial ranges. Summaries of the results of this query are displayed in tables 7.5 and 7.6. Both tables have been constructed by first of all grouping respondents into one of two size categories and then averaging the results over each category, where the dividing line between categories is defined as the median value (i.e., $2 million) of the annual sales volume of all establishments in the sample. Also shown in both tables are the numbers of establishments providing information used in calculating the average percentages.

TABLE 7.6   AVERAGE PERCENT OF ALL
CUSTOMERS LOCATED WITHIN FIFTEEN MILES
OF RESPONDENT, AND WITHIN SOUTHERN
CALIFORNIA

	Establishment size (annual sales)			
	< $2 million		> $2 million	
	%	n	%	n
Within fifteen miles	21.2	37	8.6	32
Within Southern California	46.8	37	31.6	32

These two tables indicate that both small and large establishments are strongly linked in their upstream and downstream transactions to the local economy, though there are three important nuances to this judgment that need to be expressed. First, electronics establishments in Southern California do approximately one-third to two-thirds on average of their business with other firms in the same region; and they do significant amounts of business even with firms located within a narrowly defined circle of fifteen miles radius of their own locations. Second, as was observed in chapter 5, small establishments have more localized linkages than large, and in the case of sales linkages this discrepancy between the two groups is statistically significant at the 0.05 level by a test of the difference of means. Third, the pattern of purchases seems in general to be more spatially limited than the pattern of sales, though the differing measurements of these two variables make it necessary to append reservations to this remark. Oakey (1984) has noted parallel contrasts between the purchasing and sales patterns of high-technology firms in other regional contexts. Notwithstanding these differences between the upstream and downstream linkage structures of sample establishments, the correlation coefficients laid out in table 7.7 indicate that when an establishment has strong backward linkages to the local economy, it is likely also to have strong forward linkages. In addition, we find a simple correlation of 0.33 between (a) the percentage of any establishment's purchases that come from its top three suppliers and (b) the percentage of the same establishment's sales that go to its top three customers. For thirty-nine sample observations

TABLE 7.7   SIMPLE CORRELATIONS BETWEEN
PURCHASES AND SALES PATTERNS OF
SAMPLED ELECTRONICS ESTABLISHMENTS IN
SOUTHERN CALIFORNIA $(N = 61)$

	Percent purchases within fifteen miles	Percent purchases within Southern California
Percent customers within fifteen miles	0.49**	0.23*
Percent customers in Southern California	0.31**	0.19

* Significant at 0.05 level.
** Significant at 0.01 level.

this correlation is moderately significant at the 0.05 level. This observed relationship suggests that when an establishment's purchases are spread out over a large number of suppliers, its sales are likely to be similarly spread out; and when its purchases are concentrated on only a few suppliers, so too will its sales pattern be concentrated. Thus, when establishments are locked through their linkages into the local agglomeration, they are typically bound in both upstream and downstream directions.

One common and very important form of interestablishment linkage in the electronics industry of Southern California involves subcontracting activity in the form of the putting out and taking on of work. On average, sample establishments put out work to the value of 15.4 percent of total sales, and they take on work to the value of 20.2 percent of sales. In the questionnaire, respondents were asked to specify the individual locations of the top three subcontractors to whom they put out work. Figure 7.4 and table 7.8 summarize the responses that were received to this question. Figure 7.4 portrays the close locational symbiosis that exists between many electronics producers and their main subcontracting partners. Table 7.8 confirms this tendency by indicating that both small and large establishments in the sample overwhelmingly choose their major subcontracting partners from the local area. Large establishments have a somewhat lower propensity to use local subcontractors than small ones do, but there is no statistically significant difference between the two groups of establishments in this regard.

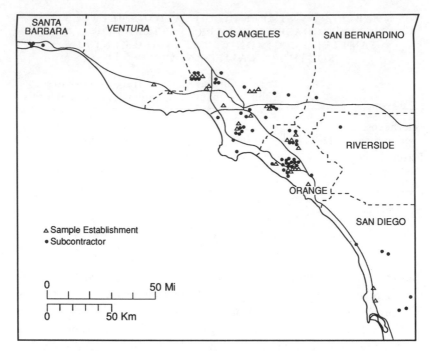

Figure 7.4. Location of sample electronics establishments and the major sub-contract firms that received work.

MODES OF TRANSACTING

In the questionnaire, an attempt was made to complement the data gathered on linkage structures with additional information on modes of transacting business. Specifically, respondents were requested to indicate the percentage of time allocated to different modes of transacting in the negotiations leading up to the sale of both a standard catalog item and a piece of subcontract work. The modes specified were telephone, face-to-face contact, mail, telex/fax, and other. Table 7.9 provides simple and weighted averages of responses to this question, where the weighted averages are computed in relation to the total sales volume of each establishment.

The data set out in table 7.9 reveal that telephone and face-to-face contact are by far the most common modes of transacting for both catalog item sales and subcontract sales. The telephone dominates for catalog item sales, but face-to-face contact becomes just as important, if not more so, when subcontract work is involved. As subcontracting

TABLE 7.8   PUTTING-OUT ACTIVITIES OF
SAMPLE ELECTRONICS ESTABLISHMENTS IN
SOUTHERN CALIFORNIA

		Size of establishment (annual sales)	
		< $2 million	*> $2 million*
a.	Number of respondents	18	15
b.	Total number of subcontractors mentioned by respondents	48	34
c.	Subcontractors in Southern California	46	29
d.	c as a percentage of b	95.8%	85.3%

TABLE 7.9   PERCENTAGE OF TIME ON
AVERAGE ALLOCATED TO DIFFERENT MODES
OF TRANSACTING IN THE NEGOTIATIONS
LEADING UP TO A SALE OF OUTPUT OR
SUBCONTRACT WORK

	Catalog item sale		Sale of subcontract work	
	Simple average (n = 53)	*Weighted average (n = 51)*	*Simple average (n = 50)*	*Weighted average (n = 47)*
Telephone	58.7	48.1	38.6	26.2
Face-to-face contact	19.0	26.7	37.6	52.4
Mail	86	9.4	8.4	11.1
Telex/fax	10.1	12.3	9.7	7.9
Other	2.5	3.5	1.6	3.1

usually entails considerable discussion between both parties about design specifications, materials, and ways of proceeding, it is not surpris-
ing that a particularly transactions-intensive mode of communication
is generally resorted to in this instance. It is worthy of note that the
weighted average allocation of time to face-to-face contact for the sale
of subcontract work is distinctly larger than the corresponding simple
average, which suggests that large electronics producers tend to have

more transactions-intensive subcontract relations than small. Mail, telex/fax, and other modes of communication are evidently of much less significance in terms of time allocation than the telephone and face-to-face contact.

LINKAGES AND LOCATION

The preceding discussion has demonstrated that both the upstream and downstream linkages of electronics producers in Southern California are highly localized, especially for smaller establishments, and that these linkages involve significant levels of transactions-intensive interaction between different producers. These characteristics of the local electronics complex are almost certainly interrelated with one another, in the sense that high spatially dependent transactions costs encourage locational agglomeration and discourage locational dispersal. Moreover, with deepening fragmentation of the local manufacturing system into increasingly specialized subsectors of production— thus leading to yet further transactional activity—the observed tendency of the entire system to agglomeration within a series of specialized industrial districts is reinforced. Within these districts, the clustering of small establishments is especially intense.

Despite the revealed biases in the sample data, these qualitative conclusions seem robust enough, especially if we take into account their consistency with the other bodies of evidence set forth throughout this book. Obviously, however, the sample data do not allow us to make stronger or more extended generalizations than these about the broad structure of electronics production activities in the region.

CONCLUSION

The electronics industry of Southern California has grown vigorously since World War II, and together with the aerospace industry, with which it is functionally and spatially allied, it constitutes one of the primary engines of the impressive expansion of the Southern Californian economy over the last few decades.

The peculiar pattern of development and growth of the industry in Southern California can in large part be understood in terms of the extremely high levels of federal defense spending that have been directed over a long period of time to the region, together with a series of employment and organizational attributes that have encouraged much specialization and agglomeration of the industry. These attributes involve on the one side, the emergence of large, multifaceted, and rapidly rotating local labor markets to which firms gain maximal access through mutual locational convergence, and on the other side, a proliferation of localized interfirm transactional relations binding the entire complex into a functionally integrated system. These transactional relations are very probably reinforced by the increasing tendency of many kinds of electronics firms, even small ones, to enter into joint ventures and strategic alliances with one another (cf. Gordon 1991).

Today, the electronics industry in Southern California is spatially organized in a series of dense agglomerations rooted in the west-central and northwestern sections of Los Angeles County as well as in the outer cities of the region. We must not lose sight of the fact that the electronics industries of Southern California are currently much buffeted by intensifying foreign competition, especially from Japan and the newly industrializing countries of East and Southeast Asia. They are also inserted into national and international systems of economic interaction, involving both the active relocation offshore of large standardized units of production (such as assembly plants), and the worldwide search for specialized inputs and markets. With increasing liberalization of U.S.–Mexican trade under the North American Free Trade Agreement, these problems are likely to be exacerbated by shifts of some kinds of low-wage electronics producers (in such subsectors as assembly subcontracting or printed circuit board production) to the Mexican side of the border. As in the cases of the aircraft industry and the missile and space industry, serious policy questions are raised by all such issues as these, and we shall return to them toward the end of this book.

PART IV

Local Labor Markets:
Two Contrasting Cases

CHAPTER 8

The Local Labor Market Dynamics of a Cohort of Engineers and Scientists

In this chapter and the next I describe two case studies of local labor markets within the high-technology industrial complex of Southern California. These case studies are representative of the two dominant labor-market fractions that characterize the complex, namely, on the one side, skilled professional workers, and on the other side, a group of unskilled and predominantly immigrant workers. The particular case examined in this chapter deals with engineering and scientific employees at three major Lockheed aircraft plants in the Los Angeles metropolitan area. In the subsequent chapter, we shall examine the local labor-market activity of low-wage workers employed in electronics assembly subcontract shops.

The three Lockheed plants that are the basis of the investigation here are located in the northern half of the area, at Burbank, Palmdale, and Rye Canyon (though note that the Burbank plant has subsequently closed down). In late 1988 they employed a total of 2,492 engineers and scientists. The local labor market constituted by these engineers and scientists is of much interest and significance in its own right, for it represents a major element of the high-technology industrial system of greater Los Angeles. At the same time, the case study that is developed in the pages that follow sheds much light on the ways in which the jobs-housing nexus operates in and around industrial agglomerations. While there is an enormous literature on particular aspects of this problem—e.g., on commuting behavior, residential mobility, job search, employment location, and so on—there is a paucity of analyses that attempt to fit the individual pieces together into a synthetic view of local labor markets as a whole (cf. Simpson 1987). There is especially little in the way of case-study material on local labor markets in relation to the operation of specialized industrial districts, and even less on the geography of skilled upper-tier workers in high-technology industries (though for a notable exception to this remark see Angel 1989).

ENGINEERS AND SCIENTISTS AT THE THREE LOCKHEED PLANTS: SOME SUMMARY DATA

DATA-COLLECTION PROCEDURES

The data-gathering phases of this research began in early 1989. At that time, a questionnaire was sent by mail to all 2,492 engineers and scientists then employed in the Lockheed plants at Burbank, Palmdale, and Rye Canyon. The addresses of these workers were provided by the Engineers and Scientists Guild, Lockheed Section. Each questionnaire was accompanied by a prepaid return envelope and a brief letter from the president of the Guild urging recipients to participate in the survey. Note that even though the Guild is the recognized collective bargaining unit at Lockheed for engineers and scientists, only some 25 percent of the individuals on the Guild's mailing list are actually paid-up members.

In total, 418 questionnaires were returned, representing a response rate of 16.8 percent. However, not all respondents answered all questions, which means that response rates differ from question to question (as indicated in the various statistical analyses that follow). The 418 responses received represent of course a self-selected sample, and there is a legitimate question about the sample's representativeness. In the absence of detailed information about the population from which the sample is drawn, it is difficult to adjudicate this issue with any finality, though in one important respect we *can* compare the sample with the population. The original address list of 2,492 engineers and scientists enables us to identify the residential location of each individual by zip code. In the greater Los Angeles area, there are 265 zip code areas with at least one such individual. The 418 engineers and scientists who responded to the questionnaire also indicated the zip code of their residence. From these two sets of information, we can construct counts of both the population and questionnaire respondents for each of the 265 zip codes. These two counts were then compared by means of matched

TABLE 8.1   ENGINEERS AND SCIENTISTS:
HIGHEST EDUCATIONAL LEVEL ATTAINED BY
QUESTIONNAIRE RESPONDENTS

	Number	Percent
High school	20	4.8
Two-year college	73	17.7
Four-year college	250	60.5
Master's degree	66	16.0
Doctoral degree	4	1.0
Total	413	

pairs, and it was found by a t-test that there is an extremely high probability (>0.99) that the sample is representative of the population. To this degree, then, the sample can be said to be unbiased. However, there obviously may be unsuspected biases elsewhere in the data, and as with all analyses based on sample data, a degree of interpretative caution is called for as we proceed.

A BRIEF STATISTICAL PROFILE

The questionnaire elicited information on a great variety of personal information (age, gender, education, marital status, children, income, etc.) together with data on job shifts and residential mobility over the period from 1980 to 1989.

On the basis of the information gathered, engineers and scientists at the three Lockheed plants under study here can at once be described as being to an overwhelming degree male (89.7 percent) and white (86.2 percent), with a further 6.3 percent of questionnaire respondents claiming an Asian ethnic background and 4.8 percent Hispanic. Only 1.7 percent of respondents were African-American. All are highly qualified, and most also possess a four-year college degree or better (table 8.1). Out of all questionnaire respondents, 69.8 percent are married, and 76.9 percent are owners rather than renters of their residential accommodation. The median age of these workers is forty-four, which is rather high, but they are also spread out over a wide range of different age groups with weak local maxima in the thirty to thirty-five and fifty to fifth-five ranges (table 8.2). The latter bulge in the age structure is a reflection of the large intake of engineers and scientists into

TABLE 8.2   ENGINEERS AND SCIENTISTS:
AGE DISTRIBUTION OF QUESTIONNAIRE
RESPONDENTS

Age in years	Number	Percent
20–25	12	2.9
25–30	62	14.9
30–35	75	18.0
35–40	35	8.4
40–45	35	8.4
45–50	30	7.2
50–55	50	12.0
55–60	48	11.5
60–65	38	9.1
65–70	28	6.7
70+	3	0.7
Total	416	

Lockheed during the boom years of the 1960s, and this observation is corroborated by the frequency distribution of respondents' job starts at the firm by year (table 8.3), which shows that there was a distinct upturn in the second half of the 1960s. Table 8.3 further tells us that there are many engineers and scientists at Lockheed who have been employed by the firm for considerable periods of time; and their lengthy tenure has no doubt been reinforced by their accumulation of seniority and firm-specific human capital, thus helping to shield them from layoff. Median annual salary is $45,500, but there is much individual variation around this figure (table 8.4).

From these data, we glean a first and unsurprising picture of the engineers and scientists at Lockheed as rather typical upper-tier technical and professional workers, with established and stable jobs.

THE SPATIAL ORGANIZATION OF THE LOCAL LABOR MARKET

THE BASIC GEOGRAPHY OF JOBS AND RESIDENCES

Figure 8.1 shows the residential locations of all questionnaire respondents together with the three Lockheed plants under study here. This

TABLE 8.3   ENGINEERS AND SCIENTISTS:
QUESTIONNAIRE RESPONDENTS' YEAR OF JOB
START AT LOCKHEED

	Number	Percent
1940–1944	3	0.7
1945–1949	1	0.3
1950–1954	19	4.7
1955–1959	36	8.8
1960–1964	23	5.6
1965–1969	47	11.5
1970–1974	16	3.9
1975–1979	47	11.5
1980–1984	88	21.6
1985–1989	128	31.4
Total	408	

TABLE 8.4   ENGINEERS AND SCIENTISTS:
ANNUAL SALARY OF QUESTIONAIRE
RESPONDENTS

Salary $'000	Number	Percent
20–25	1	0.2
25–30	8	1.9
30–35	36	8.7
35–40	62	15.0
40–45	80	19.4
45–50	65	15.7
50–55	72	17.4
55–60	36	8.7
60–65	42	10.2
65–70	9	2.2
70+	2	0.5
Total	413	

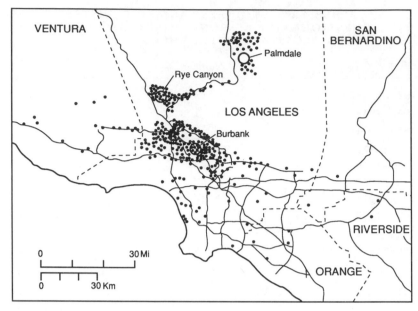

Figure 8.1. Locations of the three Lockheed plants and the residential locations of all engineers and scientists who responded to the questionnaire.
Residential locations are plotted by zip code and are approximate only.

complex of jobs and residences is focused upon the major plant at Burbank, with subsidiary foci at Palmdale and Rye Canyon. Observe that
workers' residences are for the most part confined to a remarkably restricted area relative to the entire metropolitan region. The local labor
market is not only circumscribed in its geographical extent, but it is
also organized so that the most dense development of workers' residences occurs in the immediate vicinity of major places of employment. This phenomenon is captured in figure 8.2, which shows the
residential density (D) of employees as an inverse function of commuting distance (d) from place of residence to place of employment,
where distance is codified in the figure in terms of discrete distance
bands centered on workplace. The two variables D and d relate to
each other through the negative exponential model first proposed
by Clark (1951), i.e., $D = 0.66\exp(-0.12d)$, where the parameters are
computed on the basis of aggregate data for all three plants. The value
of R^2 for this model is 0.97. The data on which figure 8.2 is based tell
us that over 50 percent of the residences of engineers and scientists are
located within fifteen miles of their place of work, and just under 75
percent are located within twenty miles.

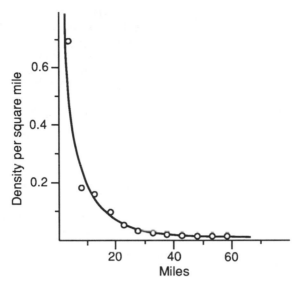

Figure 8.2.   Residential density per square mile of questionnaire respondents as a function of distance from place of employment. (Data for all three Lockheed plants are aggregated in this figure.)

BIRTHPLACE, EDUCATION, AND METHODS OF JOB SEARCH OF QUESTIONNAIRE RESPONDENTS

Let us now examine how the local labor market is constituted in terms of the origins, skill-acquisition, and job-finding capacities of its participants.

As table 8.5 indicates, only 27.3 percent of questionnaire respondents were actually born in Southern California. Table 8.5 also reveals, however, that 52.5 percent of all respondents received their highest level of education in the region. In table 8.6 are arrayed data indicating the colleges and universities from which questionnaire respondents who were educated in Southern California graduated. It was possible to identify thirty-five individual colleges and universities from the returns. Many of the more important of them are located in the northern half of the region, within or close to the engineers' and scientists' local labor market. The quality of the engineering and science programs offered by these institutions of higher education varies widely, but the top two or three (accounting for 26.2 percent to 38.9 percent of all locally educated engineers and scientists) are certainly of high repute. These institutions make a major contribution to the agglomeration economies available to the aerospace industry generally

TABLE 8.5   ENGINEERS AND SCIENTISTS:
BIRTHPLACE AND PLACE OF HIGHEST LEVEL
OF GRADUATION OF QUESTIONNAIRE
RESPONDENTS

	Birthplace		Place of graduation	
	Number	*Percent*	*Number*	*Percent*
Southern California	114	27.3	211	52.4
Rest of California	23	5.5	27	6.7
Rest of United States	249	59.7	155	38.5
Rest of world	31	7.4	10	2.5
Total	417		403	

TABLE 8.6   ENGINEERS AND SCIENTISTS:
SOUTHERN CALIFORNIAN COLLEGES AND
UNIVERSITIES ATTENDED BY QUESTIONNAIRE
RESPONDENTS

	Number of cases	Percent
University of California—Los Angeles	26	13.1
University of Southern California	26	13.1
California State University—Northridge	25	12.7
Los Angeles Valley College	12	6.1
California State Polytechnic University—San Luis Obispo	11	5.6
California State Polytechnic University—Pomona	11	5.6
California State Polytechnic University—San Diego	9	4.5
California State University—Los Angeles	9	4.5
Antelope Valley College	7	3.5
Glendale Community College	6	3.0
California Institute of Technology	5	2.5
Pepperdine University	5	2.5
University of LaVerne	5	2.5
Northrop University	4	2.0
University of California—Santa Barbara	4	2.0
University of California—San Diego	3	1.5
College of the Canyons	2	1.0

TABLE 8.6   (*cont.*)

	Number of cases	Percent
California State University—Fullerton	2	1.0
California State University—Long Beach	2	1.0
Harvey Mudd College	2	1.0
Los Angeles Community College	2	1.0
Los Angeles Trade Technical College	2	1.0
Loyola Marymount University	2	1.0
Pierce College	2	10
San Diego City College	2	1.0
West Coast University	2	1.0
California Lutheran College	1	0.5
California State University—Dominguez Hills	1	0.5
East Los Angeles College	1	0.5
Embry-Riddle Aeronautical University (March Air Force Base)	1	0.5
Immaculate Heart College	1	0.5
Long Beach Community College	1	0.5
Los Angeles Mission College	1	0.5
Pacific States University	1	0.5
Pomona College	1	0.5
Total	197	

in Southern California. It would, however, be a mistake to see them as being in some sense a prior causal factor in the growth of the industry in the region. Rather, we should view both the industry and its supportive institutions (not just educational programs but also such phenomena as subcontract services, R&D facilities, and the very labor market itself) as existing in relationship to one another in the form of an evolving structure of mutually interdependent activities.

Just as a large proportion of questionnaire respondents were educated in the local area, so too is it evident that many of them found their jobs at one of the three Lockheed plants on the basis of essentially local sources of information (see table 8.7). By far the greater number (35.6 percent) obtained information leading to their current job from friends or relatives—themselves presumably employees of Lock-

TABLE 8.7   METHOD BY WHICH INCUMBENT
LEARNED ABOUT JOB OPENING AT LOCKHEED

	Number of cases	Percent
Friends or relatives	142	35.6
Contacted by employer	63	15.8
Newspaper advertisement	51	12.8
Contacted employer	43	10.8
Other	100	25.1
Total	399	

heed. Others were either contacted by the employer (15.8 percent), or were recruited as a result of a newspaper advertisement (12.8 percent), or simply made direct inquiries at Lockheed (10.8 percent). A significant percentage of respondents (25.1 percent) marked the category "other" when responding to the question about job-search methods on the questionnaire, and on the basis of their written comments it is apparent that most of these respondents were recruited by the firm through college-placement services. None of these modes of information acquisition is necessarily purely local to Southern California, and in many cases we may be sure that they are not so; equally, it seems reasonable to presume that information about job opportunities is probably most densely developed in the local area with its strong infrastructure of personal contact networks. This remark is consistent with the findings of Hanson and Pratt (1990) and Granovetter (1974) on job-search behavior.

PATTERNS OF MOBILITY, 1980–1988

SOME OVERALL TENDENCIES

Questionnaire respondents were asked to provide detailed information on their past histories of job and residence mobility. They were asked to list by zip code whatever jobs they may have held prior to their current job at Lockheed, going as far back as January 1, 1980. They were also asked to indicate the zip code of their current residence and all previous residences back to the same date. Much useful information on inter- and intraregional mobility patterns was obtained in this man-

TABLE 8.8   ENGINEERS AND SCIENTISTS:
SHIFTS IN PLACE OF EMPLOYMENT AND
PLACE OF RESIDENCE, 1980–1988

| Number of shifts | Number of cases | |
	Employment shifts[a]	Residence shifts
0	283	246
1	66	74
2	44	57
3	16	24
4	6	13
5	3	3
6	0	1

[a] Employment shifts exclude first-time job entries.

ner, though the data collected must be treated prudently, for there were clearly many gaps and omissions in the responses received.

A total of 135 (32.2 percent) questionnaire respondents indicated that over the nine-year period from January 1, 1980, to December 31, 1988, they had changed their place of *employment* at least once; 172 respondents (41.1 percent) indicated that they had changed their place of *residence* at least once during the same period; and ninety-five (22.7 percent) indicated that they had changed *both* place of employment and place of residence at least once. The employment shifts noted, incidentally, do not include first-time entry-level hires, and they involve all job changes prior to and including the shift to Lockheed between January 1, 1980, and December 31, 1988. These mobility data can be broken down more finely so that they also show the number of different moves per worker over the nine-year period of observation. Moves per worker are recorded in table 8.8, which reveals a moderate degree of multiple shifting of jobs and residences. Table 8.8 also shows that there were in total 241 shifts of employment place and 333 shifts of residence, and on this basis, it would seem that residential mobility for this particular group of workers is on average of the order of 38 percent greater than employment mobility. Of the 241 recorded job moves for workers during the 1980–1988 period, only eighty-three

TABLE 8.9   PREVIOUS SECTOR OF
EMPLOYMENT BY STANDARD INDUSTRIAL
CATEGORY (SIC) FOR A SAMPLE OF
LOCKHEED ENGINEERS AND SCIENTISTS[a]

SIC	Description	Number of cases	Percent
372	Aircraft & parts*	37	30.8
366	Communications equipment*	11	9.1
376	Guided missiles, space vehicles, parts*	11	9.1
971	National security (armed forces)	11	9.1
822	Colleges & universities	9	7.5
357	Computer & office machines*	4	3.3
871	Engineering services*	4	3.3
873	R&D & testing services*	4	3.3
367	Electronic components*	3	2.5
951	Administration of environmental-quality programs	2	1.6
966	Space research and technology*	2	1.6
	Other	22	18.3
Total		120	

[a] Main high-technology sectors are marked with an asterisk.

(34.4 percent) were accompanied by some unemployment at the time of the change, and in over a third of these cases the unemployment was of one month or shorter duration.

Among questionnaire respondents, there were in total 216 new hires at Lockheed over the period from 1980 to 1988. Of these, 135 (62.5 percent) had held previous jobs, and eighty-one (37.5 percent) were entry-level hires. For most of the 135 engineers and scientists who had held previous jobs, it was possible to determine the SIC category of their previous place of employment. This information is arrayed in table 8.9, which shows that 65 percent of those providing usable information on previous place of employment had held jobs in various high-technology industrial sectors. Additionally, forty-two individuals (35 percent of this segment of the sample) were previously employed in a wide variety of other sectors, many of them far removed in functional terms from the aircraft industry, but all well represented in Southern California. As a corollary, it would seem that the sampled engineers and scientists have what we might call agglomeration-specific skills, permitting them to shift fairly readily between a wide range of sectors within one particular industrial locality. Here, the term *agglomeration-specific skills* designates skills that are especially useful in a given agglomeration but that may be deployed over a variety of different sectors within the agglomeration.

None of the above comments suggests that the engineers and scientists currently employed by Lockheed have been hypermobile during the past nine years; indeed, as table 8.8 reveals, 283 respondents (67.7 percent of the total) never moved their place of employment over the period from 1980 to 1988, and 246 (58.9 percent) never moved their residence. With this qualification in mind, the record does still indicate a fair degree of shifting around over this period of time, especially in the case of younger and less well-established workers, and the record moreover probably represents an underestimate of real mobility rates, for some questionnaire respondents evidently did not fully enumerate all job or residence shifts. Unfortunately, since data were collected only for current engineering and scientific employees of Lockheed, it is not possible to assess mobility patterns for workers who have moved elsewhere after a period of employment with the firm. Evidence assembled by Angel (1989) for the semiconductor industry in the United States indicates that the employment mobility of engineers is comparatively high in the small-firm sector, but much lower for employees of large firms with well-developed internal labor markets. If the same is true of the aircraft industry, we would expect employment mobility rates to fall markedly once workers have been taken on by Lockheed. Interviews with company representatives tend to confirm this speculation.

THE SPATIAL PATTERN OF JOB SHIFTS

As we have seen, 62.5 percent of Lockheed's new hires of engineers and scientists after 1980 had held previous jobs. Of these jobs, fully 74.1 percent were located in Southern California. Indeed, the spatial extent of workers' previous jobs is even more narrowly restricted than this, for it is largely limited to one particular locale within the Los Angeles metropolitan area. Figure 8.3 provides some first rough evidence in favor of this assertion by showing how the jobs held prior to workers' current employment at Lockheed (as well as the residences

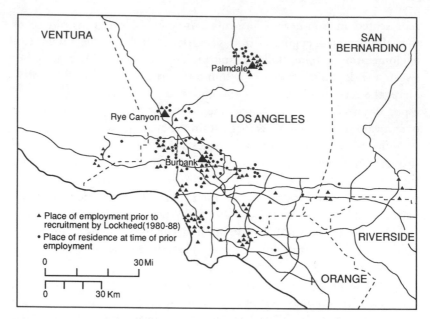

Figure 8.3. Locations of jobs held prior to current Lockheed job, and residences occupied at time of prior job, for the period 1980–1988. A handful of prior jobs and associated residences lie in the rest of Southern California beyond the confines of the map. Locations shown are plotted by zip code and are approximate only.

they occupied at that time) have a distinct locational bias towards the three Lockheed facilities.

A further piece of evidence is laid out in table 8.10, which shows, for eighty-five questionnaire respondents, the distance between the job that they held prior to their recruitment by Lockheed and the plant at which they are now employed. Table 8.10 records only intraregional shifts. The table shows that more than 50 percent of the eighty-five respondents' prior places of employment are located within twenty miles of their job at Lockheed. Moreover, the density per square mile of these prior employment places declines in a clear negative exponential fashion with distance from the Lockheed place of employment. The subsidiary peaks in the density surface corresponding to the fifteen to twenty and the twenty-five to thirty mile distance bands evidently pick up the flow of engineers and scientists from the large aircraft manufacturing facilities located in the El Segundo-Hawthorne-Inglewood area (above all Northrop and Rockwell North American) and in Long Beach (McDonnell Douglas).

TABLE 8.10   DISTANCE BETWEEN PRIOR JOB
AND CURRENT LOCKHEED JOB (FOR
INTRAREGIONAL JOB SHIFTS ONLY)

Distance band	Number of cases	Density per square mile
0–5	5	0.064
5–10	4	0.017
10–15	14	0.036
15–20	21	0.038
20–25	6	0.008
25–30	10	0.012
30–35	5	0.005
35–40	3	0.002
40–45	8	0.006
45–50	0	0.000
50–55	1	0.000
55–60	2	0.000
60+	6	0.000
Total	85	

THE SPATIAL PATTERN OF RESIDENCE SHIFTS

The high degree of localization of labor-market activity among these
workers is also reflected in residential behavior. Here, we look specifically at intraregional residential mobility patterns for those engineers
and scientists who shifted jobs between 1980 and 1988. These individuals are categorized into two subgroups, one consisting of those
who shifted their place of residence, the other consisting of those who
did not. At the outset, however, we are faced with a difficult definitional problem. This problem arises because we have no explicit
means on the basis of the questionnaire data of distinguishing residence shifts that are directly related to job shifts (either as cause or
effect) from residence shifts that have no relation whatever to a shift of
job. For want of more precise criteria, the problem is resolved as follows. First, where an individual has moved residence a number of
times, the move that is closest in time to the job shift is taken to be the
relevant job-related move, no matter whether it precedes or succeeds
the job shift. Second, where an individual who has been taken on at
Lockheed has moved residence only once over the nine-year time

frame under investigation here, this move is defined as job related, however distant in time it may be from the actual job shift. These definitions mean that the time lag between the two moves may be considerable. That said, the sample data portrayed in figure 8.4 reveal that in practice more than 25 percent of all residence shifts occurred within a five-month period before or after the shift to Lockheed, and close to 50 percent occurred within a ten-month period. Again, it must be noted that the directions of causality in this relation are unspecified, and presumably they operate in different directions in different cases. Figure 8.4 also reveals a small (but in statistical terms, nonsignificant) tendency for the residence shift to come after the job shift in time. The data set out in the figure are both right and left censored, for the questionnaire returns record no residence moves prior to January 1, 1980, or subsequent to December 31, 1988. Thus, there must be some bias in the figure, especially for cases where the shift to Lockheed was either early or late in the nine-year period.

Now consider table 8.11, which displays distances between respondents' residential locations at the time of their previous job and their current Lockheed employment location. The data presented in the table are disaggregated into residential movers and nonmovers. It is at once apparent that the majority of those who shifted to Lockheed from another job (whether they are residence changers or not) also resided at the time of the previous job well within the Lockheed local labor-market area. A similar relationship between home-place and job-shifts is reported for employed persons in Worcester, Massachusetts, by Hanson and Pratt (1988). Despite the rather low number of cases, an attempt was made to test statistically for differences between the frequency distributions of movers and nonmovers given in table 8.11. The hypothesis here is that those engineers and scientists whose residence during their prior job was relatively distant from Lockheed would have a greater propensity to change residential locations than those who lived closer to Lockheed. This hypothesis (though different in the manner of its formulation) is consistent with the proposition of Clark and Burt (1980) to the effect that workers evince a tendency to move closer to their place of work as the distance between homeplace and workplace increases. However, even though the average distance to Lockheed for residence movers (25.6 miles) is greater than the distance for nonmovers (20.8 miles), there is no significant difference between the two distributions on the basis of a one-tailed Kolmogorov-Smirnov test. These results help to reinforce the notion

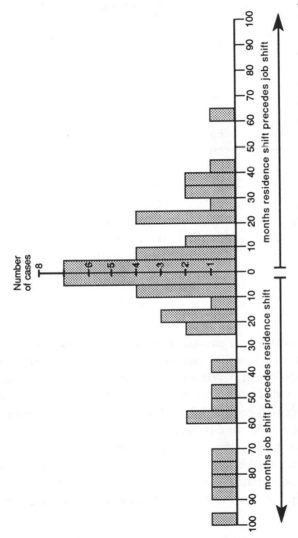

Figure 8.4. Time lag between job shift and residence shift for engineers and scientists who moved from a previous job to Lockheed in the period 1980–1988, and who changed their place of residence at least once in the same period.

TABLE 8.11   DISTANCE BETWEEN
RESIDENTIAL LOCATION AT TIME OF
PREVIOUS JOB AND CURRENT LOCKHEED
EMPLOYMENT LOCATION, DISAGGREGATED
BY RESIDENTIAL MOVERS AND NONMOVERS

Distance band	Movers		Nonmovers		All workers	
	Number	Percent	Number	Percent	Number	Percent
0–5	4	9.3	2	9.5	6	9.4
5–10	6	14.0	3	14.3	9	14.0
10–15	5	11.6	4	19.0	9	14.0
15–20	7	16.3	4	19.0	11	17.2
20–25	4	9.3	1	4.8	5	7.8
25–30	3	7.0	1	4.8	4	6.3
30–35	1	2.3	3	14.3	4	6.3
35–40	4	9.3	0	0.0	4	6.3
40–45	4	9.3	1	4.8	5	7.8
45–50	0	0.0	1	4.8	1	1.6
50–55	2	4.7	1	4.8	3	4.7
55+	3	7.0	0	0.0	3	4.7
Total	43		21		64	

that sampled workers are strongly rooted in one particular local labor market, and even when they change both jobs and residences, significant numbers of them nevertheless tend to remain in the same area. This phenomenon is evident again in the observation that the average distance between *all* recorded intraregional job moves between 1980 and 1988 is 26.5 miles, and between *all* residence moves over the same period is 23.1 miles, signifying an extremely localized pattern of mobility relative to the total urbanized area of Southern California. The same restricted pattern of mobility has been observed by Mattingly (1991) for production workers at Rockwell North American in El Segundo.

A LOGIT MODEL OF RESIDENTIAL MOBILITY

A further attempt was made to probe the rather unexpected findings about the geographically restricted range of the engineers' and scientists' local labor market as reported above, using a binomial logit model of workers' decisions to move or not to move residence in association with their being taken on by Lockheed.

The data for the model refer to the sixty-four sampled workers alluded to in table 8.11. The idea here is to examine the effects of changes in commuting distance on the decision to move residence, while holding constant the effects of a variety of other socioeconomic variables, such as age, income, family status, ethnicity, gender, spouse's workplace, and so on (cf. Clark [1982], Quigley and Weinberg [1977]). However, out of all the socioeconomic variables examined in addition to distance, only age was found to have any significant effect. The terms of the final model are defined as follows: p_i is the probability that the ith sampled worker will shift residence some time before or after shifting jobs to Lockheed (see above for clarification of this relationship); a_i is the age of the ith worker, and d_i is the distance between (a) the worker's place of residence while occupied in the previous job and (b) the current place of employment with Lockheed. The computed binomial logit model is

$$p_i = 1/[1 + \exp(-2.6121 + 0.0528a_i - 0.0127d_i)],$$

which has an associated ρ^2 of 0.07 which is just significant at the 0.05 level by a chi-squared test with 2 degrees of freedom. The parameter attached to the variable a_i is also significant at the 0.05 level, but the parameter attached to d_i is nonsignificant. Both parameters have the expected sign. Thus, age has an inverse relationship to the propensity to move residence, and commuting distance has a positive relationship. However, the effects of the distance variable are nonsignificant as noted, presumably because so many job-shifters already resided at reasonably accessible locations to their new job.

The evident inference from this analysis is that workers tend to search for jobs within a given restricted range of their current residence. Even when attempts are made to correct the analysis for the fact that earlier shifters (of jobs or residences) have had a greater opportunity to adjust (residences or jobs, respectively) than later shifters, the significance of d_i remains null. Moreover, if we examine commuting distances for those workers who also shifted residence we find (contrary to the conclusions of Clark and Burt [1980]) that they are actually greater—by 6.9 miles on average—after the move than before. This finding, no doubt, is in part an indication of the geographical peculiarities of this local labor market with its extensive westward sweep into the suburban reaches of the San Fernando Valley, where relatively easier access to suitable housing is to be found than in the denser eastern end of the Valley.

SOME WIDER IMPLICATIONS: LOCAL LABOR MARKETS IN THE LARGE TECHNOPOLIS

In all of the above, a detailed geographical and statistical sketch of the local labor market for engineers and scientists employed by Lockheed at Burbank, Palmdale, and Rye Canyon has been laid out. This local labor market is embedded within a wider complex of activities comprising the whole of the specialized high-technology industrial district that has developed in the San Fernando Valley since World War II. In terms of the main residential pattern of sampled engineers and scientists, the local labor market coincides with a territorial expanse centered on the main Lockheed facility at Burbank and largely contained within a circle of fifteen- or twenty-mile radius from the same facility. In a certain sense, then, the local labor market is like an island rising out of the surrounding urban area.

Even though many of the workers in this local labor market enjoyed stable and long-standing jobs at Lockheed, there is also a certain degree of fluidity in its mode of operation. This fluidity consists above all in a steady passage of workers, prior to their employment with Lockheed, through a variety of industrial sectors and job locations. A particularly revealing finding is that so much of this mobility occurs within quite narrow geographical limits. To be sure, there is much in-migration from outside the region, especially of younger workers from other parts of the country, and some long-distance intraregional moves also occur. The weight of the evidence laid out above, however, points to a labor market dominated by localized job shifts and equally localized adjustments of residential locations. Some exchange of qualified workers between different aircraft and aircraft-parts-manufacturing districts in the Los Angeles metropolitan area is detectable, but again the actual magnitude of this activity falls far below what would in principle be observable under conditions of a free flow of workers between different local labor markets in the metropolitan area.

These general remarks encourage the conjecture that significant agglomeration economies may be generated in local labor markets of the type under investigation here. Four main points are now tentatively offered in regard to this notion. First, the local labor market delineated in figure 8.1 is evidently a repository of significant agglomeration-specific skills that can be tapped by a wide variety of employers. Second, the concentration of many high-technology industrial employers in the area means that workers have potential employment alternatives nearby as and when they may be needed. Third, the high density of both jobs and workers in the local area almost certainly reduces job search and recruitment costs by facilitating the retrieval of local labor market information at low marginal cost. Fourth, the large market for skilled aircraft and other high-technology workers in Southern California as a whole is in part based upon (and in turn has stimulated the emergence of) a rich infrastructure of local educational institutions, many of which have programs geared explicitly to the training of qualified technical labor. Lockheed itself has clearly taken advantage of the latter sorts of agglomeration economies by recruiting the majority of its engineers and scientists from firms and educational institutions in the local area. Whether or not there is a countervailing flow of qualified labor from Lockheed back to other employers remains an open question at this stage, though as already pointed out it is probably fairly limited, especially to the small-firm sector. Smaller firms within the area, however, do gain strong compensating advantages from their locations through their direct and indirect sales and subcontracting linkages to large local producers.

At the same time, there are almost certainly definite upper limits to the agglomeration economies sustainable within the local labor market. One noteworthy feature of the spatial organization of the aircraft industry in Southern California is that the very largest assembly plants tend to be spread out over different and widely separated industrial districts. This locational strategy reduces overcrowding by large employers in given local labor market areas and thus helps to diminish competition for labor and the upward pressure on wage levels that such competition would tend to beget. This line of reasoning, perhaps, may in part explain why it is that aircraft and aircraft-parts-manufacturing activities are not located all together in the urban area but rather in a series of discrete industrial districts scattered over the length and breadth of Southern California. By the same token, when one of the leading employers within any given local labor market closes down (as has now occurred at Lockheed Burbank) a period of painful economic decline and restructuring is apt to ensue in the surrounding local labor market.

Despite their great relevance to the study of regional economic systems, detailed case studies of the geography of local labor markets like the one presented here are something of a rarity in the literature, with a handful of recent exceptions. There is accordingly an urgent need for the accumulation of more investigative research, and in particular— given the markedly idiosyncratic nature of different local labor markets in different historical, geographical, and occupational contexts— of much more empirical material. The need is all the more pressing because local labor markets undoubtedly represent one of the most enigmatic and complicated levels of structured human behavior within industrial localities. In the next chapter we shall press forward with this agenda by looking at a low-wage immigrant local labor market and at the effects of ethnicity and gender on the intrafirm division of labor.

CHAPTER 9

Electronics Assembly Workers in Southern California

The electronics assembly industry is a typical example of an unstable, low-skill sector, and it is all the more intriguing as an object of research because it constitutes an element of the lower stratum of sweatshops and secondary labor-market activity within the high-technology industrial complex of Southern California. It subsists by supplying an array of electronics and aerospace producers with subcontract assembly services involving such tasks as the attachment of various electronic components to printed circuit boards, as well as other activities such as wire-wrapping, cable harnessing, chassis assembly, testing, and so on. Most establishments in the industry are restricted in size, and virtually all of them are engaged in highly competitive forms of small batch production. The labor force of these establishments consists primarily of female and ethnic workers, a large proportion of whom are recent Asian and Hispanic immigrants (Fernandez-Kelly 1987; Green 1983; Keller 1983; Sassen-Koob 1982; Snow 1983). If local press reports are to be believed, a significant number of the immigrant workers in the industry in the Los Angeles area are undocumented.

The focus of the present investigation is on the social and spatial organization of the labor market for these workers in Southern California. In this manner, I hope to add to the understanding of the geographical dynamics of secondary labor markets, a topic that remains something of a puzzle in many important respects despite the large literature that exists on the topic. A further objective of the study is to capture a broad sense of the role of low-wage workers in the kinds of

179

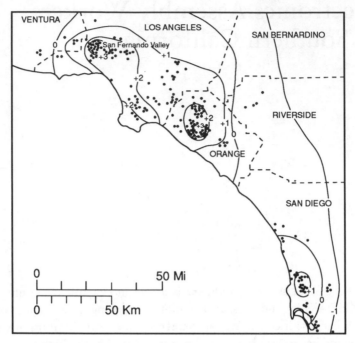

Figure 9.1. Electronics assembly subcontractors in Southern California. Isolines define levels of accessibility to other electronics manufacturing establishments in the region.

high-technology industrial complexes that have mushroomed in Southern California and other parts of the United States over the last two or three decades.

THE ELECTRONICS ASSEMBLY INDUSTRY IN SOUTHERN CALIFORNIA

In 1989 there was a total of 262 electronics assembly establishments in the seven counties of Southern California. Figure 9.1 maps out the spatial distribution of these establishments in relation to a set of isolines defining levels of accessibility to all other electronics producers in Southern California.[1] As one would expect, assembly establishments clearly gravitate toward the most accessible locations in the region. Average employment per assembly establishment is estimated at 34.2,

---

1. The measure of accessibility applied here is described in chapter 3.

and median employment at 15 (cf. Scott 1991). The majority of these establishments are markedly labor intensive. A few large establishments in the area make use of sophisticated robotized technologies, but none of these enters into the sample of establishments considered below.

In a typical electronics assembly establishment, work flows through a series of eleven sequential stages. These are, in order: (a) checking and sorting incoming parts, (b) assembling printed circuit boards and components, (c) soldering components into place on the boards, (d) cleaning the soldered assembly, (e) touching up, (f) clipping away surplus wire, (g) inspection, (h) reworking, (i) testing, (j) packing finished assemblies for shipment back to the customer, and (k) other activities consisting mainly of managerial, supervisorial, technical, and secretarial tasks. In most (but not all) of these tasks, little or no formal skill is required. There is, however, in the industry a persistent pattern of differentiated allocation of workers to jobs, taking the form, in part, of a division of labor along gender and ethnic lines. Labor markets are quite unstable in the industry, with turnover rates typically exceeding 30 percent a year (Scott 1991).

A SAMPLE SURVEY

One of the great problems in carrying out research on local labor markets is targeting subjects for sampling by labor-force fraction and/or place of work. This is sufficiently difficult where workers are concentrated in large workplaces and are represented by formal labor organizations, but it is an even more daunting problem where (as in the present case) establishments are small and scattered, workers are totally unorganized and often unable to speak English, and much of the industry is constantly brushing against illegalities of one sort or another.

As this research moved into the survey phase, various experiments were undertaken with different ways of sampling electronics assembly workers, from contacting community groups to sending questionnaires to employers through the mail with the request that they distribute them to their workers. None of these methods produced significant results. In the late spring and early summer of 1991, therefore, another line of attack was tried, which involved sending undergraduate students to visit assembly establishments in order to hand-deliver worker questionnaires to the person in charge and to explain the purposes of the survey. Each visit was preceded by a brief introductory letter. The

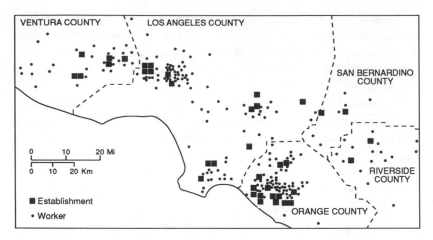

Figure 9.2. Locations of sampled electronics assembly establishments, and the residences of questionnaire respondents.

person taking delivery of the questionnaires was asked to give a copy to every worker in the establishment, and to collect the completed questionnaires again within a week. The entire set of completed questionnaires was then picked up in person by the student who delivered them. This method turned out to be reasonably successful.

Because of the costs incurred by this method of survey, only electronics establishments in Los Angeles County and the four adjacent counties (i.e., Orange, Riverside, San Bernardino, and Ventura) were surveyed. Addresses for establishments included in the survey were taken from industrial directories and the yellow pages of the several telephone directories that cover the region. A total of 314 establishment addresses was recorded, and all of these establishments were visited in early 1991 in an attempt to deliver questionnaires. However, only 203 establishments out of this total were found in the end to be *bona fide* electronics assembly units. Of these 203 establishments, 38 (18.7 percent) agreed to participate in the survey, and eventually these yielded up a total of 236 completed (or partially completed) worker questionnaires, i.e., on average, 6.2 questionnaires per establishment. The geographical locations of these thirty-eight establishments are shown in figure 9.2 together with the locations of the residences of sampled workers. It is worth remarking at this stage how workers' residences tend to cluster around individual workplaces.

Even though the distribution of sampled establishments seems, on visual inspection, to correlate with the distribution of all establishments, a statistical comparison of the two (by means of a chi-squared test of the incidence of establishments by county) indicates that they are significantly different at the 0.01 significance level. There are also probably other kinds of bias in the sample. Questionnaires were made available in both English and Spanish, but not, it needs to be stressed, in any Asian language. This was because of the cost and difficulty of translating the questionnaire into the requisite languages (i.e., Cambodian, Chinese, Korean, and Vietnamese, among others). Moreover, many workers in the industry are probably unable to read or write effectively, while numbers of others are undocumented immigrants—both factors representing strong impediments to filling out a questionnaire. For all of these reasons, we should in no sense take the sample to be unbiased. Despite this caveat, given the extraordinary difficulty of surveying these workers, and given the interest and significance of such little information as we can obtain on them, it seems worthwhile to press forward with the analysis in the anticipation of gaining at least a few guarded insights into the processes shaping this peculiar local labor market system.

A SOCIAL PROFILE OF SAMPLED WORKERS

To begin, what are the main gender and ethnic characteristics of the surveyed labor force? A total of 135 females and 101 males returned questionnaires, thus giving a female/male ratio of 1.34. Of the workers who provided information on their racial and ethnic identity, 45 (19.1 percent) were Asians, 137 (58.1 percent) were Hispanics, while just two African-Americans were found in the entire sample (see table 9.1).

Table 9.2 shows the country of birth for assembly workers. Outside of the United States, workers come from nineteen different countries. Major foreign countries of origin are Mexico, El Salvador, Vietnam, Korea, and China. In total, 54.6 percent of all respondents indicated that they were not U.S. citizens. Of those workers who were born in the United States, 56.1 percent were born in California, and the vast majority of these were born in Southern California. It would have been extremely useful to have had information on documented and undocumented status of immigrant workers, but in the interests of

TABLE 9.1   ELECTRONICS ASSEMBLY
WORKERS: GENDER AND ETHNIC
COMPOSITION OF QUESTIONNAIRE
RESPONDENTS

	Female		Male		Total	
	Number	*Percent*	*Number*	*Percent*	*Number*	*Percent*
Asian	21	15.6	24	24.0	45	19.1
Hispanic	78	57.8	59	58.4	137	58.1
African-American	2	1.5	0	0.0	2	0.9
Non-Hispanic white	28	20.7	16	15.8	44	18.6
Not identifiable	6	4.4	2	2.0	8	3.4
Total	135	100.0	101	100.0	236	100.0

securing a reasonable response rate it was decided not to probe this issue in the questionnaire (cf. Cornelius 1982). Both Bonacich (1989–90) and Cornelius (1989–90) have recently argued that illegal immigration into Southern California continues apace, and that the 1986 Immigration Reform and Control Act has done little to staunch the flow.

The median age of respondents was found to be 30.5 years. Female workers had a median age of thirty-two and male workers a median age of twenty-seven, with the difference being explicable perhaps in terms of the greater upward mobility of males through the labor market so that they are able more easily to move on to more attractive jobs in other sectors. Most workers (i.e., 74.7 percent) had received only a pre-high school or high school education, with the remaining 25.3 percent having completed two years or more of college. Differences in levels of educational attainment represent the single most significant means of distinguishing statistically between Asians and Hispanics in this sample of workers. Discriminant analysis shows that Asians consistently and significantly score higher on level of education than Hispanics, a finding that is also echoed by Uto (1990) in a study of industrial workers in Orange County. With data for 130 Hispanics and 39 Asians, the canonical correlation for this discriminant analysis is given as 0.31, which has a highly significant F-value of 32.2.

TABLE 9.2   ELECTRONICS ASSEMBLY
WORKERS: COUNTRY OF BIRTH OF
QUESTIONNAIRE RESPONDENTS

	Number	Percent
Mexico	99	42.3
United States	56	23.9
El Salvador	16	6.8
Vietnam	14	6.0
South Korea	10	4.3
China	7	3.0
Guatemala	6	2.6
Cambodia	4	1.7
India	3	1.3
Chile	3	1.3
Nicaragua	3	1.3
Costa Rica	2	0.9
Cuba	2	0.9
Laos	2	0.9
Germany	2	0.9
Argentina	1	0.4
Columbia	1	0.4
Dominican Republic	1	0.4
Egypt	1	0.4
Philippines	1	0.4
Total	234	

THE EMPLOYMENT RELATION

The preceding description rather clearly identifies questionnaire respondents as being for the most part secondary labor-market participants. In short, they are predominantly female, Asian and Hispanic,
mainly immigrants, on average fairly young, and with an educational
level that only occasionally goes beyond the high-school level (Boston
1990; Gordon et al. 1982; Morrison 1990; Wilkinson 1981). The
ways in which these workers are actually deployed through the electronics assembly labor market confirm and add several important new
shades of meaning to this characterization.

TABLE 9.3   ELECTRONICS ASSEMBLY
WORKERS' LENGTH OF TENURE IN CURRENT
JOB

Quartile	Months (median value)
First	4
Second	15
Third	32
Fourth	67

n = 229

CONDITIONS OF EMPLOYMENT, RECRUITMENT, AND JOB MOBILITY

Electronics assembly workers in Southern California face unstable and precarious labor-market conditions. There is no union representation of these workers whatsoever, and virtually no job security beyond the personalized assurances that workers can individually negotiate with their employers. Sampled workers were found to have spent a median time of twenty months with their current employer. Table 9.3 shows months of current job tenure by quartile fractions of the labor force. The median length of job tenure for the bottom quartile is only four months, and the median for the top quartile is sixty-seven months (though we must remember that the data measure as-yet-uncompleted spells of job tenure). Thus, there evidently is much turnover in the industry, but there is also a group of workers who have relatively steady jobs, and the questionnaire data suggest that these workers tend to be more educated and better paid than the workforce as a whole.

Almost all of the workers surveyed (i.e., more than 99 percent) considered their jobs to be nontemporary, and even more were full-time employees. To this degree, then, the secondary workers in electronics assembly establishments in Southern California are *not* subject to some of the more important forms of employment flexibility (i.e., temporary and part-time work) as described in the literature (e.g., Atkinson [1985]; Christopherson and Noyelle [1992]; Storper and Scott [1990]). Workers were almost entirely paid by the hour rather than on a piece-rate basis, which is probably because there is enough variability in the work to make implementation of piece-rate schedules impracticable. Just fewer than half of the workers had had some previous

TABLE 9.4   HOURLY WAGE RATES OF
SAMPLED ELECTRONICS ASSEMBLY WORKERS

Quartile	$ (median value)
First	4.75
Second	5.75
Third	6.50
Fourth	8.50

n = 209

experience in electronics assembly before their current job, and almost 20 percent had engaged at one time or another in electronics assembly at home (Dangler 1989; Fernandez-Kelly and Garcia 1989).

The median hourly wage for sampled workers was $6, which is $1.75 above the statutory minimum wage. However, some variation in wage rates was observable (see table 9.4), with wages ranging from the legal minimum itself to as much as $17 an hour. The fact that only one worker claimed to earn an hourly wage below the legal minimum suggests that the law on this matter is being largely respected by employers, though of course it may also be the case that only those employers who do respect the law were amenable to having their workers surveyed.

An attempt was made by means of multiple regression to isolate those personal characteristics of workers that have an effect on the wages they are paid. For the ith worker, the hourly wage rate (W_i) can be expressed as

$$W_i = 6.1571 \exp(0.0025L_i + 0.0734E_i - 0.1724H_i)$$
$$\qquad\quad (0.0004) \quad (0.0314) \quad (0.0325)$$

where L_i is length of tenure at the current place of employment, E_i is a binary variable indicating whether or not the worker has had electronics assembly experience in a previous job, and H_i is a binary variable indicating whether or not the worker is Hispanic. This equation was computed over a total of 185 observations. The value of R^2 is a modest but very significant 0.27, and all the regression coefficients are highly significant as indicated by the standard errors shown in parentheses. Thus accumulated experience (both in the current job and in previous jobs) tends to enhance wage rates, while being Hispanic

TABLE 9.5   ELECTRONICS ASSEMBLY
WORKERS: PRIMARY SOURCES OF JOB-
RECRUITMENT INFORMATION

	Percent
Friends or relatives	55.0
Newspaper advertisements	10.4
Made direct inquiries with prospective employer by phone or in person	8.8
Employment agency	7.6
School placement office	7.6
Contacted by employer	6.4
Other	4.4

n = 215

tends to depress them. The variable H_i has a simple correlation of
−0.41 with level of education (measured on a tripartite scale), and to
some degree its dampening effect on wages can be seen as residing in
the relatively low level of formal education of the Hispanic respondents. Obviously, however, educational level accounts for only part of
this effect, and much is presumably an outcome of the social and political marginality of recent Hispanic immigrants (Cornelius 1989–90;
DeFreitas 1988; Ong and Morales 1988). This theme will be taken up
again below. Contrary to prior expectations, gender was found to
have no significant effect on W_i, either directly or indirectly (e.g., via
the variable H_i).

In conformity with previous findings on the job search strategies of
secondary labor market participants, most of the workers surveyed
here found their jobs by word of mouth (Anderson 1974; Granovetter
1974; Hanson and Pratt 1991). Table 9.5 shows that well over half of
all jobs were obtained through social networks involving friends or
relatives. More formalized channels of recruitment such as newspaper
advertisements or employment agencies were also used but to a much
lesser extent.

Table 9.6 lays out data on the types of job held by questionnaire respondents immediately prior to their current job. We may note that of
all respondents who had held a previous job, almost half were in the
electronics industry itself. This point echoes what was said earlier to

TABLE 9.6   ELECTRONICS ASSEMBLY
WORKERS: PREVIOUS JOBS HELD BY
QUESTIONNAIRE RESPONDENTS

	Percent of cases
Electronics assembly	49.5
Sales clerk/cashier	7.5
Packing	3.8
Cleaning	3.8
Machine operator	3.2
Agriculture/gardening	2.7
Restaurant work	2.2
Clothing industry	1.6
Plastics industry	1.6
Food industry	1.6
Miscellaneous	20.4

n = 186

the effect that about half of all workers had had some electronics assembly experience before they came to their present job. Conversely, in just over half of all cases, the previous job was frequently far removed from anything even approaching electronics assembly. Thus, sales work and cleaning jobs figure prominently in table 9.6, as do jobs in industries like agriculture, clothing, plastics, and food. For the great majority of workers (i.e., 60.6 percent), the period of unemployment between their previous job and the current job was three months or less.

If we look at where the previous jobs of respondents were located, we find that they are remarkably closely correlated with the locations of the current job. Thus 36.2 percent of all previous jobs are located within just five miles of the present workplace, and as many as 62.6 percent are located within ten miles. This information suggests at once that workers tend to carry out job-search activities within a fairly narrowly circumscribed local labor-market area. For the engineers and scientists examined in the previous chapter, the equivalent values for the same respective distance bands are 5.9 percent and 10.6 percent.

TABLE 9.7   ELECTRONICS ASSEMBLY
WORKERS: TASK ASSIGNMENTS BY GENDER
AND ETHNICITY; DATA ARE DEFINED IN
TERMS OF THE AGGREGATE ALLOCATION OF
WORK HOURS PER WEEK BY EACH GROUP TO
INDIVIDUAL TASKS

	Females	Asians	Hispanics	Non-Hispanic whites	All workers
Checking & sorting	306.8	114.8	285.2	106.8	544.8
Assembly	1187.2	482.8	1183.6	294.4	2046.0
Soldering	767.2	210.4	815.6	147.2	1255.6
Cleaning	253.2	122.4	440.0	50.0	627.6
Touching up	482.0	114.4	469.6	69.2	706.0
Clipping	297.6	66.8	367.2	44.4	510.8
Inspection	322.8	288.4	338.0	128.8	781.2
Reworking	171.6	30.0	241.2	54.8	344.8
Testing	186.8	128.4	273.2	79.6	487.2
Final packing	309.6	139.6	300.4	149.2	608.4
Other	315.2	102.0	126.0	251.6	503.6
Number of observations	115	45	121	34	210

THE TASK ASSIGNMENT PROCESS

How, we may ask, are workers assigned to different tasks in the electronics assembly industry? In particular, what role do gender and ethnicity play in this process?

Table 9.7 indicates the aggregate number of hours per week spent in each major task by different groups of workers. The table immediately pinpoints the high concentration of female workers in assembly tasks as such, though given possible undersampling of female workers in the questionnaire survey, the actual concentration is probably higher. The figures given in table 9.7 are a reflection of the absolute numbers of workers in each gender and ethnic group; a more interesting perspective on the same data is given in table 9.8, which informs us about the percentage allocation of time per task for each group. A review of table 9.8 reveals three broad tendencies in job assignments. First, there is a mix of females, Asians, and Hispanics in

TABLE 9.8   ELECTRONICS ASSEMBLY
WORKERS: TASK ASSIGNMENTS BY GENDER
AND ETHNICITY; DATA ARE DEFINED IN
TERMS OF THE PERCENTAGE ALLOCATION OF
WORK HOURS BY EACH GROUP TO
INDIVIDUAL TASKS

	Females	Asians	Hispanics	Non-Hispanic whites	All workers
Checking & sorting	6.7	6.4	5.9	**7.8**	6.5
Assembly	25.8	**26.8**	24.5	21.4	24.3
Soldering	16.7	11.7	**16.9**	10.7	14.9
Cleaning	5.5	6.8	**9.1**	3.6	7.5
Touching up	**10.5**	6.4	9.7	5.0	8.4
Clipping	6.5	3.7	**7.6**	3.2	6.1
Inspection	7.0	**16.0**	7.0	9.4	9.3
Reworking	3.7	1.6	**5.0**	4.0	4.1
Testing	4.1	**7.1**	5.6	5.8	5.8
Final packing	6.7	7.6	6.2	**10.8**	7.2
Other	6.9	5.7	2.6	**18.3**	6.0
Number of observations	115	45	121	34	210

Maximum value in each row is in bold.

a series of tasks involving assembly, soldering, cleaning, touch-up, clipping, and reworking. These tasks constitute the basic, largely unskilled central core of assembly work. Second, in proportional terms, Asians dominate inspection and testing, both of which tasks call for a degree of skill and technical experience. Third, non-Hispanic whites (many of whom are also owner-entrepreneurs) are most in evidence in tasks that involve responsibility for ensuring the successful initiation, termination, and supervision of the assembly process, i.e., checking and sorting, final packing, and "other" tasks as defined earlier. What meaning, if any, can be attached to these empirical observations?

In order to probe this question more fully, an attempt was made to investigate the specific content and attributes of each particular task. The thirty-eight establishments that had participated in the worker questionnaire survey were sent (by mail) a further questionnaire to be

TABLE 9.9   FACTOR ANALYSIS OF
DESCRIPTORS OF TASK REQUIREMENTS AND
CHARACTERISTICS

Descriptor	Factor 1	Factor 2
Dexterity	−0.31	0.86
Patience	0.37	0.70
Strength	0.02	−0.26
Experience	0.45	0.57
Technical knowledge	0.71	0.35
Education	0.93	0.04
Speak English	0.93	−0.11
Write English	0.89	−0.13
Concentration	0.43	0.68
Reliability	0.68	0.69
Initiative	0.64	0.43
Imagination	0.14	0.45
Responsibility	0.68	0.70
Honesty	0.84	0.49
Cooperativeness	0.46	0.83
Need for supervision	0.02	0.91
Tediousness	−0.01	0.80
Dirtiness	−0.23	0.03
Danger	−0.34	0.14
Toxicity	−0.22	0.16
Variance explained	6.14	6.02

filled out by the owner or manager and which asked respondents to score the eleven tasks laid out in tables 9.7 and 9.8 on a simple binary scale according to a series of criteria. These criteria covered a wide assortment of task requirements and characteristics such as dexterity, patience, strength, etc. (see table 9.9), and they intentionally made no direct reference to the ethnic or racial attributes of the workers who perform these tasks. Of the thirty-eight questionnaires sent out, a total of twenty-two were eventually returned in fully completed form. Once all the responses to them were tabulated, it became clear that there was considerable confusion over the "other" task category, and in telephone follow-ups it was evident that some respondents had understood it as signifying administrative/clerical tasks, while others had understood it as meaning residual manual tasks like janitorial or maintenance work. Accordingly, this task was eliminated from the subsequent analyses.

The answers to these twenty-two questionnaires were then averaged and subjected to factor analysis. Two meaningful factors were extracted by rotation, and their loadings are laid out in table 9.9. Factor 1 has high positive loadings on such task descriptors as education, ability to speak English, ability to write English, honesty, and technical knowledge; and it has negative loadings on dangerousness, dexterity, and dirtiness. The factor may thus be interpreted in terms of an opposition between key technical and quality-control tasks on the one hand, and manual work on the other. Factor 2 loads positively on the need for supervision, dexterity, cooperativeness, tediousness, patience, responsibility, reliability, and concentration, and negatively on physical strength, and (very weakly) on ability to read and write English. This second factor may be viewed as representing an ordering of manual tasks from those involving detailed and narrowly defined maneuvers to more open-ended forms of physical work. Note that the simple correlation of factor 1 with average wage rates in each of our ten assembly tasks (i.e., omitting "other") is 0.82, while wage rates have no significant correlation with factor 2. A graph of the factor scores of the ten tasks on factors 1 and 2 is shown in figure 9.3. Here, two main clusters of tasks make their definite appearance. One is constituted out of the unskilled central core of assembly work—except cleaning—alluded to above; this cluster may be labeled "repetitious manual jobs." The other involves checking and sorting, inspection, testing, and final packing, and we may designate this cluster "responsible key jobs."

Let us now consider how the gender and ethnic division of labor relates to the two factors identified in the previous paragraph. Table 9.10 lays out the results of three regression analyses. In each case, the dependent variable is the ratio of one group's average time allocation per task to another group's average time allocation. The groups defining the ratios are (a) females/males, (b) Asians/Hispanics, and (c) non-Hispanic whites/all other workers. By taking ratios in this way, the dependent variable is made completely independent of the absolute amounts of time invested in each task. The independent variables are the scores of each task on factor 1 and factor 2. The regressions defined in table 9.10 are extremely problematical because they have such

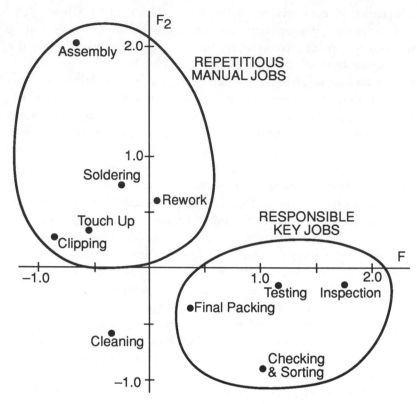

Figure 9.3.   Scores of ten major electronics assembly tasks on factors 1 and 2.

TABLE 9.10   REGRESSION RESULTS FOR ANALYSES OF THE EFFECTS OF FACTOR SCORES ON TASK ASSIGNMENTS BY GENDER AND ETHNICITY

	Regression coefficients		Constant	R^2
	Factor 1	*Factor 2*		
Females/males	−0.00014	0.00008	0.91	0.37
Asians/Hispanics	0.00058**	0.00018	0.85	0.66
Non-Hispanic whites/all others	0.00024*	0.00003	0.84	0.40

*Significant at the 0.05 level.
**Significant at the 0.01 level.

limited degrees of freedom, and levels of overall significance are not high. However, the pattern of relationships that emerges bears some affinity to what we have already learned about this particular labor market. Tasks that score high on factor 1 tend to be disproportionately assigned to Asians in preference to Hispanics; and they are also disproportionately assigned to non-Hispanic whites. The ratio of females to males is negatively but nonsignificantly correlated with factor 1. Factor 2 does not appear to induce any significant bias in task allocation by gender or ethnicity, though again, the extreme tentativeness of this proposition must be emphasized.

On the basis of the information that is summarized in tables 9.7, 9.8, 9.9 and 9.10, and figure 9.3, a roughly threefold hierarchy of jobs and workers in the electronics assembly industry in Southern California is discernible. The top of the hierarchy seems to be marked by two substrata. One of these corresponds to a class of managerial and quality-control jobs dominated by white males; the other is principally occupied by a cadre of male Asians performing tasks like inspection and testing, and who have a relatively advanced general education together with a superior level of special training in electronics assembly (51.2 percent of Asians but only 27.3 percent of Hispanics indicated that they had received such training). At the second and numerically most important level, there is a large absolute representation of Hispanic females, followed by Hispanic males, and with a disproportionately high representation of Asian females. This second level entails largely routine unskilled work that may be characterized in terms of the descriptors laid out in table 9.9 as involving considerable "tediousness," and calling for much "patience" and "cooperativeness" on the part of workers (Beneira 1987; Morrison 1990). At the very bottom of the hierarchy it is possible to identify a small group of Hispanic males engaged in cleaning electronics assemblies, and constituting the most marginal and lowest-paid workers in the industry. Cleaning tasks typically evoke descriptors like "danger," "dirtiness," "strength," and "toxicity," suggesting that the work is both physically disagreeable and strenuous.

The evidence marshaled here suggests that gender and ethnicity do play a role in the assignment of workers to different tasks. The question is, are these variables merely proxies for other critical variables, such as education, experience, or skill, or do they have some independent effect? Unfortunately, the data on which the present research is based make it infeasible to evaluate this particular issue with any degree of finality. Analysts such as Boston (1990), Hanson and Pratt (1990) and Tienda and Guhleman (1985), among many others, have suggested that secondary labor-market participation in general can only partially be explained by an absence of "human capital," and that workers are also pigeonholed by their gender and ethnic characteristics into particular kinds of labor-market niches. We have noted above that Hispanic ethnicity as such has a depressive effect on wage rates. And the information before us certainly makes it amply clear that employers do preferentially assign to low-wage unskilled tasks the very kinds of workers who are in social and political terms the least capable of putting up any resistance to their conditions of pay and employment, i.e., women and immigrants. No doubt this same structure of preferences also helps to account for the conspicuous absence of both non-Hispanic whites and African-Americans from routine electronics assembly work.

RESIDENTIAL PATTERNS AND COMMUTING BEHAVIOR

Local labor markets are made up not just of workplace phenomena, but also of the homeplaces of workers and the commuting behavior that ties workplaces and homeplaces together into a functioning activity system (Hanson and Pratt 1988; Schreuder 1989, 1990; Topel 1986).

The residential location of workers is especially important because residence helps to anchor individuals to particular local labor-market areas. In fact, electronics assembly workers are rather more bound to their residences than they are to their jobs. The length of tenure at current residence for the median worker is twenty-seven months, as compared with twenty months for job tenure. For the upper quartile of workers, the median length of residential tenure is more than 60 percent greater than the median length of job tenure (compare tables 9.3 and 9.11). Moreover, a total of 43 percent of all surveyed workers live in the same municipal area today that they lived in 1986. We need to contrast the latter piece of information, however, with the further observation that 23.9 percent of all questionnaire respondents were living in another country in the same year.

Figure 9.4 shows the residences of surveyed Asian and Hispanic workers relative to the broad geographical distribution of the Asian and Hispanic populations of the entire five-county area. The figure dis-

TABLE 9.11   ELECTRONICS ASSEMBLY
WORKERS' LENGTH OF TENURE AT CURRENT
PLACE OF RESIDENCE

Quartile	Months (median value)
First	5
Second	18
Third	36
Fourth	104

n = 226

plays two sets of isolines defining levels of accessibility to Asians and Hispanics as computed from census data for 1990. Here (in conformity with the accessibility measure described in chapter 3) accessibility for any given point, i, is defined as $\ln(\sum P_j/D_{ij}^2)$, where P_j is the population (Asian or Hispanic, as the case may be) of the jth census tract in the five-county area, and D_{ij} is the distance from i to j. Two main issues now need to be dealt with in relation to this accessibility index. First, it would seem reasonable to ask if the relative accessibility of sampled workplaces to Asians and Hispanics as a whole has any influence on the ethnic differentiation of task assignments as discussed earlier. Extensive statistical testing, however, revealed no relationship whatever between accessibility and ethnicity in task assignments. Second, a comparative scrutiny of figures 9.2 and 9.4 suggests that while workplaces tend to have good accessibility to Asians and Hispanics in general, there are also parts of the five-county area with very high levels of accessibility, and yet with comparatively few electronics assembly establishments. As shown in figure 9.1, assembly establishments *are* strongly clustered around locations that have absolutely maximum accessibility to the main purchasers of assembly services in the greater Los Angeles region. A possible deduction from these observations is that assembly establishments are somewhat more sensitive in their locational behavior to interindustrial linkage structures than they are to the geographical distribution of potential workers. However, much more rigorous statistical analysis (including some attempt to hold constant the locational effects of land prices) is necessary before this proposition can be advanced with confidence.

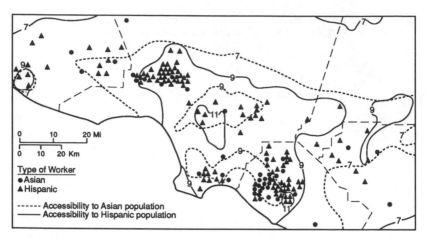

Figure 9.4. Workers' residences by major ethnic group; selected accessibility isolines are shown.

The tendency for surveyed workers to live near to their place of work, as indicated by figures 9.2 and 9.4, is confirmed by the information given in table 9.12. This information consists of frequency distributions of home-to-work commuting times for workers. The table shows that well over half of all workers live within a twenty-minute commute of their work, and that there is surprisingly little difference in commuting times by gender or ethnic group (even between non-Hispanic whites and other groups). In chapter 8, it was shown that about 50 percent of engineers and scientists in the aircraft industry in the Los Angeles area live within a fifteen-mile radius of their work. If we optimistically estimate current average commuting speed at peak periods in Los Angeles at twenty miles an hour (Commuter Transportation Services, 1990) this fifteen-mile radius corresponds to a commuting time of forty-five minutes. Thus, if electronics assembly workers differ little among themselves in the matter of their journey-to-work behavior, they certainly seem in this regard to differ greatly from the cohort of engineers and scientists examined in the previous chapter (cf. Hanson and Pratt 1990).

CONCLUSION

The electronics assembly workers in the greater Los Angeles region constitute a type of labor market whose geographical dynamics are in

TABLE 9.12   DISTRIBUTION OF REPORTED
COMMUTING TIMES FOR SAMPLED
ELECTRONICS ASSEMBLY WORKERS;
PERCENTAGE INCIDENCE PER TIME ZONE

Minutes	Females	Asians	Hispanics	Non-Hispanic Whites	All workers
0–5	8.5	8.2	8.8	8.8	8.7
5–10	17.7	14.3	15.3	11.8	18.3
10–15	16.2	18.4	13.1	17.6	14.9
15–20	24.6	22.4	21.2	23.5	21.6
20–25	6.9	8.2	7.3	11.8	8.3
25–30	12.3	14.3	21.2	11.8	16.6
30–35	0.8	0.0	1.5	0.0	0.8
35–40	3.1	4.1	2.2	5.9	2.9
40+	10.0	10.2	9.5	5.9	7.9
Number of cases	130	49	137	34	231

general little understood, i.e., a secondary labor market dominated by low-wage female and ethnic workers. Such labor markets are particularly difficult to investigate precisely because of the problems that are encountered in any effort to glean meaningful information on the individuals that make them up. My method of attack has consisted in rather blunt efforts to implement a questionnaire survey, and then to lay out an ordered series of descriptions of the labor market based on the data gathered. It needs to be stressed once more that the data on which this study is based are probably quite defective in several important respects.

That said, the composite view of the labor market for electronics assembly workers that finally emerges here has a certain coherence and plausibility. These workers for the most part face rather unstable employment conditions; they are also caught up in a somewhat blurred but discernible gender and ethnic division of labor; and while many of them come from far afield to work in Southern California, once they are established in the region, they seem to move between jobs within a relatively small local labor-market area. Further, while they may shift their residences only a little less frequently than they shift jobs, they also tend to remain within a particular community. These conclusions are consistent with the claim recently advanced by Cornelius (1989–90) that in the specific case of Mexican immigrants there has been a shift from shuttle migration to long-term settlement. Recall that a similar pattern of limited geographical mobility within a given local labor-market area was also observed to prevail in the case of the aircraft industry engineers and scientists examined in chapter 8. Presumably this relative residential immobility of workers represents a potent agglomeration economy for producers.

There remains, of course, considerable scope for further description and analysis of the labor-market processes alluded to above. In particular, further and more searching attempts to explore the question of the relations between gender and ethnicity on the one side and the intrafirm division of labor on the other are much to be encouraged. A longer temporal view of the job and housing mobility patterns of different ethnic groups would also add much to our comprehension of the changing shape and form of these local labor markets. The present case study has accomplished two major purposes. It has shown how secondary labor markets are in practice subject to considerable internal differentiation combined with elements of both precariousness and permanence; and it has thrown some light on the shadowy underside of high-technology industrial development in Southern California. As such, it represents a further contribution to industrial geography conceived of as the study of place-specific ensembles of production technologies, organizational structures, and labor markets.

PART V

Industrial Organization, Innovation, and Location

Subcontracting Relations and Locational Agglomeration in the Printed Circuits Industry

One of the distinguishing characteristics of industrial agglomerations is the large amount of subcontracting activity that usually goes on within them. In the present chapter I investigate this theme in much detail by means of a case study of the subcontracting behavior and propensities of printed circuit-board producers in Southern California. The printed circuits industry is a small but critical element of Southern California's high-technology industrial complex, and its organizational structure reveals much about the logic of industrial subcontracting in general.

In the light of the theoretical ideas presented in chapter 2, three primary analytical expectations may be set out in advance of the discussion that follows. In the first place, printed circuits producers facing conditions that intensify internal economies of scope may be expected to adopt vertically integrated organizational structures, just as those facing conditions that engender *dis*economies of scope may be expected to opt for vertical disintegration. The substantive conditions underlying these contrasting tendencies will be identified at a later stage. Second, printed circuits producers that fail to achieve an adequate level of scale may be expected to evince some degree of vertical disintegration since there may be particular manufacturing operations (especially if they involve expensive machinery and equipment) that they will not be able to carry out efficiently. Third, where subcontracting relations are strongly developed we may also expect to ob-

serve some mutual locational attraction (leading to agglomeration) between printed circuits plants and their associated subcontractors. This
follows from the properties of agglomeration as a strategy for reducing spatially dependent external transactions costs. Conversely, where
locational agglomeration occurs, subcontracting is likely to be all the
more highly developed because of concomitant economies in external
transacting.

THE PRINTED CIRCUITS INDUSTRY

The printed circuits industry is an essential link in the social division
of labor in modern electronics production. The industry takes inputs
of copper-clad epoxy laminates and various chemicals and transforms
these into boards with electrical circuitry etched onto them. Three
main classes of boards are produced, each class being defined in terms
of a number of circuit layers, i.e., (a) single-sided, (b) double-sided,
and (c) multilayer. Production of the boards is a customized batch
process *par excellence*. It is initiated only when a purchaser places an
order for a set of boards conforming to given design specifications.
Once the boards are finished and delivered to the customer they are
then mounted with a variety of electronic components such as capaci-
tators, resistors, memory chips, microprocessors, and so on.

   The manufacturing process itself varies according to the type of
board being produced. I shall first of all describe the process for simple
single-sided and double-sided boards, and then indicate how it is mod-
ified for the more complex case of multilayer boards. At the outset, the
copper-clad laminate material is cut into individual panels of the
requisite size and shape, and a designated pattern of holes is drilled
into them. The number of holes may vary from a mere handful to
many thousands. A circuit image is photographically imprinted on
every board and the resulting pattern is then solder-plated. This operation allows exposed areas of copper to be chemically etched away,
thus physically creating the circuitry of the board. If the boards have
edge-connector fingers, these are commonly plated with gold. In addition, in the case of double-sided boards, the inner surfaces of the
board holes are copper-plated to ensure connectivity between the two
circuit layers. The boards are then covered with solder mask, which
protects their circuits from any subsequent soldering work; however, a

small area (or pad) around each hole is usually left uncovered, and this is coated with solder (in a process known as solder-leveling) so that when the boards are finally assembled, components can be easily soldered into place. The production process ends with the inspection and testing of the boards and their shipment to the customer.

Multilayer board production is somewhat more complicated than this, for it involves the incorporation of an additional number of steps into the manufacturing process. In this instance, several individual boards are first of all etched, and then they are laminated together between two outer layers of copper-clad epoxy material. The composite laminated board is then drilled, and this operation must be performed with special care to ensure the correct positioning of the holes through the board. After drilling it is often necessary to subject the board to a plasma-etch process in which excess or smeared resin is removed from the insides of the holes. The circuitry of the outer layers of the board is then created by normal etching. As in the case of double-sided boards, the inner surfaces of all board holes are plated with copper.

In practice, the process of manufacturing printed circuit boards involves many more details than those indicated here. This brief description, however, is adequate for present purposes. With the exception of drilling, which is usually executed by skilled operators, the diverse labor tasks performed in the printed circuits industry are largely unskilled. In the case of Southern Californian producers, unskilled labor is provided for the most part by Asian or Hispanic immigrants. Some firms internalize all sets of production tasks (from the purchase of basic inputs to the final shipment of the boards) within a vertically integrated organizational structure, whereas other firms subcontract out various combinations of activities. Eight particular production tasks (representing the functions most often subcontracted out in the printed circuits industry of Southern California) are isolated for particular scrutiny in what follows. They are (a) copper-plating, (b) drilling, (c) gold-plating, (d) laminating, (e) plasma etch, (f) solder-leveling, (g) solder-masking, and (h) testing. All of them have been alluded to in the above description of the manufacturing process, and further details on each are provided in Appendix D. Most printed circuits producers are themselves vertically disintegrated from their downstream customers; some, however, are integrated as captive plants into general electronics firms. In this study, only independent printed circuits producers are investigated.

DATA-COLLECTION PROCEDURES AND A
PRELIMINARY OVERVIEW OF THE INDUSTRY IN
SOUTHERN CALIFORNIA

THE DATA BASE

The research was initiated by constructing a list of the addresses of all firms thought to be printed circuits manufacturers in the seven counties of Southern California. In total, an initial listing of 372 firms was extracted in this way. In early January 1988 a questionnaire and cover letter were mailed to all of these firms. Out of the initial mailing forty replies were received, twenty-two of which were from printed circuits producers, and eighteen of which turned out to be from other kinds of manufacturers (some of them offering subcontract services to the printed circuits industry). In addition, thirty-nine questionnaires were returned unopened by the post office, signifying that the designated recipients had either gone out of business or (less likely) had moved elsewhere. This left 293 firms in the original address list unaccounted for. Thus, six weeks after the initial mailing, these 293 firms were sent a duplicate questionnaire and a reminder letter. On this occasion, forty-two replies were received, fourteen of them from printed circuits producers, and twenty-eight from other kinds of firms; ten post office returns were also received. A total of 241 firms thus now remained unaccounted for. These firms were rechecked in industrial directories, and if necessary by telephone, and the result of these operations was to reduce their number to 169 genuine printed circuits producers. The total population of independent printed circuits producers in Southern California at the time of the research, then, consisted of these 169 firms plus the thirty-six questionnaire respondents, i.e., a total of 205 firms. The thirty-six questionnaire respondents hence also represent a response rate of 17.6 percent out of the total set of printed circuits producers. It is possible that the information gathered by the questionnaire is biased due to the self-selection of respondents. However, there was found to be a statistically significant correspondence across counties between the distribution of respondents and the population.

The questionnaire elicited information on a diversity of firm characteristics thought to be relevant to an understanding of subcontracting behavior, e.g., number of workers employed, total revenue, manufacturing turnaround time, percentage of work performed to military specifications, type of output, and so on. A series of questions was also directed explicitly to subcontracting activity as such. In particular, firms were asked to report (a) the annual dollar value of all work that they had put out over the previous year, (b) the proportion of all production tasks of the eight varieties mentioned earlier that they put out, and (c) the names and addresses of their principal subcontract partners for each kind of activity. In practice, respondents tended to provide the name and address of only their most significant subcontract partner. With this limited information, combined with additional scrutiny of directory sources, a list of the addresses of forty-five subcontractors—categorized by type—in the Southern California region was compiled. The list is thought to include all subcontractors serving the printed circuits industry.

SOME ELEMENTARY GEOGRAPHICAL PATTERNS AND RELATIONSHIPS

In an earlier investigation of the printed circuits industry described in Scott (1983), it was found that there were 150 independent printed circuits producers in the Greater Los Angeles region (i.e., Los Angeles County plus the four adjacent counties). The average number of workers employed at each of these 150 plants was forty-five. Of the 205 producers found to exist in the seven-county area of Southern California in 1988, 159 are located in the Greater Los Angeles region. Average plant size for the thirty-six respondents to the questionnaire is 108.5, though this figure is skewed by the presence of one unusually large firm in the sample. If we exclude this firm, average plant size in the sample falls to 65.9. Firms surveyed are all, with one exception, single-establishment enterprises.

The locations of all 205 printed circuits producers found in Southern California in 1988 are shown in figure 10.1. The revealed pattern displays strong signs of spatial agglomeration, and, indeed, as found earlier (Scott 1983), printed circuits producers tend to converge locationally around points that are maximally accessible to their main customers, comprising for the most part a variety of electronics and aerospace producers. The densest concentration of printed circuits producers coincides with the great agglomeration of high-technology firms in the northern half of Orange County. For the rest, there are distinctive clusters of producers in the San Fernando Valley to the northwest of Los Angeles, and in San Diego County, and to a minor

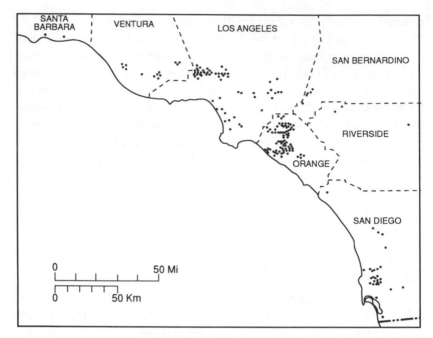

Figure 10.1. The printed circuits industry in Southern California. One dot equals one manufacturing establishment.

degree elsewhere (fig. 10.1). There is also a thin scattering of printed circuits plants over the central portions of the study area.

Consider now the forty-five subcontractors serving these printed circuits producers. Figure 10.2 depicts the locations of these subcontractors superimposed upon a map of isolines, each of which traces out a locus of points with equal accessibility to the total set of 205 printed circuits producers. The figure demonstrates at once the marked proclivity of subcontractors to seek out locations that offer high levels of accessibility to printed circuit-board producers in general. Note especially the major concentration of subcontractors in Orange County, where the printed circuits industry itself is most insistently developed. It is also apparent that subcontractors generally locate just to one side of peak values in the graphed accessibility surface—presumably as a response to differential land-rent mechanisms. The spatial pattern of subcontractors is evidently even more clustered than that of printed circuits producers themselves.

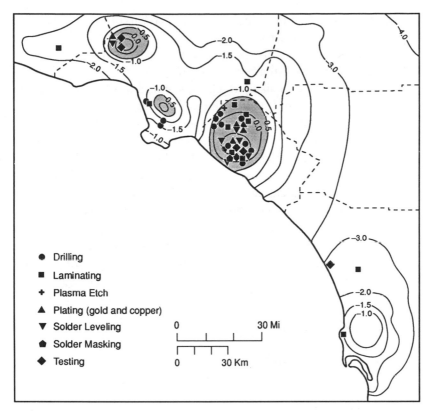

Figure 10.2. Subcontractors serving the printed circuits industry in Southern California. The isolines shown are defined in terms of the logarithm of a gravity-potential measure of accessibility to all printed circuits producers in the region. Areas where this gravity-potential measure exceeds −0.5 are shaded.

THE FUNCTIONAL AND SPATIAL BASES OF SUBCONTRACTING IN THE PRINTED CIRCUITS INDUSTRY: A LOGIT ANALYSIS

Out of the thirty-six printed circuits producers who responded to the questionnaire, thirty-three provided usable information on the total dollar value of work that they had subcontracted out over the previous year. For these thirty-three producers, the average expenditure on sub-contracting services came to $1.96 *per circuit board*, or 3.8 percent of the average sales value of $51.77 per board. These data, however, vary widely from producer to producer, and, in fact, subcontracting expenditures range from a high of 24.9 percent of sales value per board to a low close to zero.

What factors, we may ask, account for these observed phenomena? Above, it was suggested that economies of scale and scope and external transactions costs are likely to play a significant role in shaping the subcontracting function. I now examine this suggestion by means of a statistical analysis of the dollar value of work subcontracted out by each plant expressed as a proportion of total revenues. Let us designate this proportion by the symbol S_i for the ith printed circuits producer. We may now attempt to scrutinize the behavior of S_i in relation to three main independent variables, namely, (a) E_i, total employment at the ith plant, (b) M_i, the proportion of the plant's physical output that conforms to military specifications, and (c) G_i^*, which is a gravity-potential measure (analogous to accessibility as defined in chapters 3 and 9), representing the overall accessibility of the ith plant to the forty-five subcontractors shown in figure 10.2. A logit regression analysis is now defined. The logit model is appropriate here since S_i is a true proportion with its lower bound defined by zero and its upper bound by unity. The computed model is

$$S_i = 1/[1 + 2.326\,esp\,(0.704lnE_i + 0.375M_i - 0.480lnG_i^*)], \quad (10.1)$$
$$(0.343) \qquad (0.118) \qquad (0.223)$$

$$R^2 = 0.41; \ F = 6.78; \ d.f. = 3,29,$$

where the figures appended immediately below each regression coefficent are standard error terms. The standard errors indicate that all regression coefficients are significant at the 0.05 level or better. For purposes of comparison, we may note that in the previously published study of the printed circuits industry cited above (Scott 1983), a logit model of the behavior of S_i was also computed. In the earlier study the model was identified as

$$S_i = 1/[1 + 2.184(exp\,0.885lnE_i)], \qquad (10.2)$$
$$(0.212)$$

$$R^2 = 0.57; \ F = 20.96; \ d.f. = 1,16.$$

Even though the two sample sets underlying equations (10.1) and (10.2) are quite distinct from one another, there is no statistically significant difference between the regression coefficients attached to E_i in the two cases. Thus, the impact of E_i on S_i has, it seems, changed little over recent years, and with an enlarged number of degrees of freedom, the model for the later year is now able to accommodate the effects of two additional independent variables. Some comment on the meaning of the variables E_i, M_i, and G_i^* in equation (10.1) is in order at this stage.

First, the variable E_i may be taken in practice as a fairly direct measure of the hypothesized scale effect in subcontracting behavior. The parameter attached to this variable suggests that as plant size increases, subcontracting (vertical disintegration) decreases, and vice versa. That said, the possibility that E_i is also in part dependent on S_i cannot be entirely discounted here. Observe that the variable E_i is transformed to logarithms in equation (10.1) because its impact on S_i is presumed to be constant after some specifiable threshold is passed.

Second, the variable M_i functions as a broad proxy for scope effects. Military specifications in manufacturing consist of a series of product quality and documentation standards that must be met before a firm can sell (directly or indirectly) to the U.S. Department of Defense. In order to satisfy these standards, strict managerial control and supervision must be maintained at all stages in the production process. This does not absolutely prevent the subcontracting out of work, though it is a significant discouragement to do so, and it is reinforced by the fact that any subcontractors used must themselves be certified as meeting the standards defined by military specifications. Accordingly, those printed circuits producers who work to military specifications tend to internalize this work to a significant degree. A total of twenty-two plants in the overall sample was found to do at least some of their work to military specifications, and of these, nine plants do at least 50 percent of all their work to military specifications.

Third, the independent variable G_i^* tells us that printed circuits producers with high levels of accessibility to subcontractors will tend to put out more work than producers with low levels. As in the case of E_i, the variable G_i^* is expressed in logarithmic form to reflect its relatively constant effect beyond some critical threshold value. Where subcontractors are readily accessible, external transactions costs will be limited, and producers will accordingly be encouraged to put out relatively large quantities of work; but where subcontractors are not so accessible, producers will face comparatively high external transactions costs, and thus will have an inducement to economize on these by internalizing work. This reasoning is consistent with the findings of Del Monte and Martinelli (1987) who have shown for a sample of electronics producers in Italy that firms located in dense manufacturing regions tend to be more vertically disintegrated than firms located in less-developed regions. At the same time, at least some of the evident spatial symbiosis between printed circuits manufacturers and their dependent subcontractors in Southern California is presumably actively brought about by the locational behavior of firms as a strategy for reducing spatially dependent transactions costs and thereby creating external economies for themselves. No doubt both sets of firms are motivated to achieve this sort of symbiosis, though the dependency of each upon the other is certainly not symmetrical. Printed circuits producers are at least in part locationally tied to plants in the electronics and aerospace sectors generally, whereas subcontractors are virtually exclusively linked to printed circuits producers. These observations are indirectly borne out by the comparatively greater spatial agglomeration of subcontractors (see figs. 10.1 and 10.2).

In spite of the overall statistical significance of the computed logit equation for the 1988 sample data, the value of R^2 is only a modest 0.41, and even though our analytical results are encouraging so far, they remain somewhat limited. Let us therefore now press forward into a more detailed scrutiny of subcontracting activities in the printed circuits industry of Southern California.

THE DIMENSIONS OF SUBCONTRACTING IN THE PRINTED CIRCUITS INDUSTRY

FACTOR ANALYSIS OF SUBCONTRACTING ACTIVITIES

Recall that sample data were obtained on the percentage amount of each of eight different production activities that printed circuits producers subcontract out. All thirty-six producers in the sample provided complete data on this issue, and these data were subjected to factor analysis in an effort to reveal some of their internal dimensions.

The loadings resulting from the factor analysis are laid out in table 10.1. Two factors only were extracted after varimax rotation. An initial rough interpretation of the two factors is proposed, after which an attempt is made to justify in detail the interpretation advanced. First, then, factor 1 appears to represent an ordering of subcontracting activities running approximately from those that are associated with small printed circuits producers (high factor loadings) to those that are associated with large producers (low factor loadings). Second, factor 2

TABLE 10.1   ROTATED FACTOR LOADINGS
FOR SUBCONTRACTING ACTIVITIES[a]

	Factor 1	Factor 2
Copper-plating	0.19	0.83
Drilling	0.13	0.80
Gold-plating	0.60	0.49
Laminating	0.78	−0.07
Plasma etch	0.36	−0.48
Solder-leveling	0.58	0.08
Solder-masking	−0.53	−0.09
Testing	0.80	0.09
Variance explained	2.38	1.80

[a] See appendix D for descriptions of the subcontracting activities mentioned in this table.

seems to identify an ordering whose polar extremities are represented on the one hand by the subcontracting activities of single-sided and double-sided board producers (high factor loadings) and on the other hand by the subcontracting activities of multilayer board producers (low factor loadings). Identification of the meaning of the two factors is clarified by inspecting table 10.2, which shows simple coefficients of correlation between the factor scores for individual plants and selected measures of plant activity. The information displayed in table 10.2 indicates that factor 1 correlates positively with an imaginary continuum defined at its positive end by small plants, fast manufacturing turnaround times, and high rates of subcontracting; and at its negative end by large plants, slow turnaround times, and relatively restricted rates of subcontracting. Factor 2 correlates positively with a continuum whose positive end is equated to small plants with a high proportion of their output composed of single-sided and double-sided boards (i.e., a low proportion of multilayer boards) and high rates of subcontracting, and whose negative end is represented by large multilayer producers who do little putting out of work.

Factor 1, then, would seem largely to reflect the hypothesized scale effect in subcontracting behavior (with the turnaround time variable making its appearance not so much because it is correlated with subcontracting activity as it is with plant size). Thus, plants with high

TABLE 10.2   SIMPLE CORRELATIONS OF
FACTOR SCORES WITH SELECTED MEASURES
OF PRINTED CIRCUITS ESTABLISHMENT
ACTIVITY

	Factor 1	Factor 2
Employment (lnE_i)	−0.33*	−0.41*
Percent output conforming to military specifications (M_i)	−0.15	−0.29
Gravity-potential measure of accessibility to subcontractors ($lnG_i{}^*$)	−0.31	−0.06
Percent output (by value) made up of multilayer boards	−0.14	−0.42**
Manufacturing turnaround time	−0.32*	−0.01
Value of all work put out as a % of sales (S_i)	0.52**	0.38*

* Significant at the 0.05 level.
** Significant at the 0.01 level.

scores on factor 1 are small and vertically disintegrated, and tend especially to put out work that incurs high capital-equipment costs; plants with low scores are large and vertically integrated, and they tend only to subcontract out occasional overflow work (cf. Holmes 1986) or work that calls for highly specialized equipment, such as dry-film solder masking—see below. By contrast, factor 2 can be interpreted as representing the differential play of internal economies and diseconomies of scope as embodied in a multilayer-nonmultilayer dimension. Multilayer board production (much of it performed to military specifications) is, of course, much more complex than single-sided or double-sided board production. It calls for more intensive managerial supervision and more carefully coordinated work at every stage of the manufacturing process. This means that particular production activities that generate internal diseconomies of scope in single-sided or double-sided board production facilities will often be associated with positive internal economies of scope in multilayer facilities. The net result is that as the proportion of multilayer boards in any establishment's final output increases—and after discounting for the effects of capital cost—vertical integration will tend to increase. It should be pointed out at once that this interpretation of factor 2 remains as yet somewhat speculative, but it will be reinforced as the analysis pro-

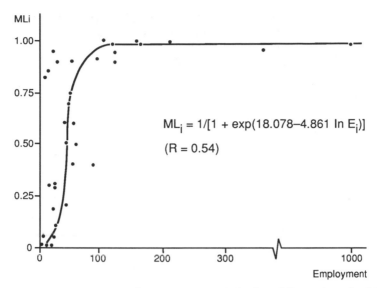

Figure 10.3. Proportion of output composed of multilayer boards (ML_i) graphed against employment (E_i) for sample printed circuits producers.

ceeds. At the same time, factor 2 is strongly correlated (as indicated above) with employment, which introduces a scale factor into its dimensionality. As suggested by figure 10.3, producers whose output is composed primarily of multilayer boards are on average large, whereas producers whose output is composed primarily of single-sided and double-sided boards are on average small. This circumstance means that any factor that loads highly on multilayer producers is by definition, and as a statistical artifact, likely also to load highly (and in the same direction) on employment.

Both factor 1 and factor 2 correlate negatively with the proportion of output that is manufactured to military specifications (table 10.2), a result that is consistent with the role of the variable M_i in the logit analysis above. In neither instance is the correlation statistically significant, though in the case of factor 2 it lies just short of the 0.05 level. Why the latter correlation is not more significant remains something of a puzzle. Both factors also correlate negatively, but anomalously, with overall levels of accessibility to subcontractors. This finding seems to suggest that the influence of accessibility on subcontracting—as ascertained above—becomes detectable only after internal scale and scope effects have been accounted for; and indeed, the suggestion is borne out by the circumstance that the simple correlation of

TABLE 10.3   SIMPLE CORRELATIONS OF
ROTATED FACTOR LOADINGS WITH
ESTIMATED CAPITAL COST AND
INSTALLATION ORDER OF SUBCONTRACTING
FUNCTIONS

	Factor 1	Factor 2
Estimated capital cost	0.34	0.56
Estimated order of installation	−0.11	−0.71*

* Significant at the 0.05 level.

S_i on G_i* (i.e., before the effects of E_i and M_i have been neutralized as in equation 10.1) is both negative and nonsignificant.

FURTHER EMPIRICAL EVIDENCE OF SCALE AND SCOPE EFFECTS

We can begin to make additional sense out of these results in the light of a second short questionnaire that was sent to all thirty-six producers who responded to the original survey. The short questionnaire asked producers for estimates of (a) the capital costs of installing each of the eight functions mentioned in table 10.1, and (b) the relative order (first being designated by 1 and last by 8) in which each function would be installed as plant expansion occurs. A total of twenty replies to the questionnaire (not all of them fully usable) was received. After averaging the responses for each type of subcontracting activity, simple correlation coefficients were computed between the two sets of responses on the one hand, and the factor loadings shown in table 10.1 on the other hand. These correlation coefficients are presented in table 10.3. They are based only on eight observations and their levels of statistical significance are not high, though the direction of correlation is as expected. The estimated capital cost of each subcontracting function correlates positively with the loadings for factor 1; and the estimated order of installation correlates negatively with the loadings for factor 2. Manufacturers thus seem to recognize that where economies of scale and scope are readily available, a particular function will to that extent be all the sooner internalized in the order of installation. At the same time, estimated capital cost is also positively correlated with factor 2, for this factor, as noted, contains a definite scale element.

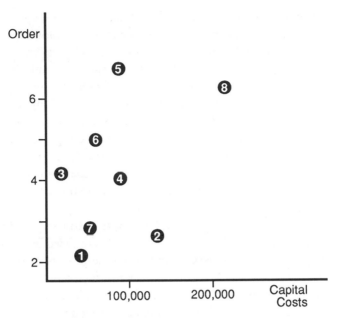

Figure 10.4.   Average estimated capital costs versus average estimated order of installation for eight subcontracting functions. Key to numbers used in figure: 1, copper plating; 2, drilling; 3, gold plating; 4, laminating; 5, plasma etch; 6, solder-leveling; 7, solder-masking; 8, testing.

The relationship between estimated capital cost and order of installation of specific subcontracting activities is portrayed in figure 10.4. The two variables seem to be positively related to each other, though the actual correlation coefficient is a nonsignificant 0.44. The particular scattering of data points in figure 10.4 helps us to understand something of the precise loading of each of the eight subcontracting functions on the two factors shown in table 10.1. Copper-plating, gold-plating, laminating, solder-leveling, and testing appear to be relatively unproblematic. They all score positively and (with the exception of copper-plating) highly on factor 1. They are also arranged fairly regularly and predictably across the axes of figure 10.4, signifying that they are internalized into the printed circuits production process in an order that corresponds roughly to their capital cost. Drilling, plasma etch, and solder-masking call for more detailed attention (see also appendix D). As we shall see, some additional commentary is also in order for the cases of copper- and gold-plating.

First, then, out of all the different production processes involved in the printed circuits industry, drilling is certainly the most demanding in terms of its need for managerial control and care in execution (Clark 1988). This is reflected in the industry rule of thumb that errors in locating holes on printed circuit boards should not in general exceed one five-hundredth of an inch. Because of this, drilling tends to be internalized at an early stage in the development of any plant even though the capital costs of drilling equipment are high ($132,000 on average). As suggested by its heavy loading on factor 2, drilling is subcontracted out to a significant degree only by small single-sided and double-sided board producers, i.e., by the most marginal producers in the industry.

Second, plasma etch is a process that is restricted to multilayer producers. For this reason alone, it tends to be internalized at a relatively late stage in the development of any plant, despite its fairly modest capital cost; and because only multilayer producers make use of this process (hence are the only kinds of printed circuits producers to subcontract the process out) it has a strong negative loading on factor 2.

Third, solder-masking can in practice be performed in two different ways, one (a liquid film process) that is general purpose, cheap to install, and easy to operate, and another (a dry film process) that is expensive to install and is usually applied only to boards with extremely dense and fine circuitry etched on them so that high-precision work is necessary. Ordinary solder-masking is virtually universally internalized by printed circuits producers. By contrast, the dry film process (which is also subject to erratic demands) is frequently subcontracted out, and it is accordingly this process (rather than the liquid film process) that registers in the factor-analytic results reported in table 10.1. Moreover, since it is a process that is for the most part restricted to large and sophisticated producers, it scores negatively on both factors, but especially on factor 1. The apparently unexceptional position of solder-masking in figure 10.4 is accounted for by the fact that the short questionnaire did not distinguish between the two different types of solder-masking, and the averaging out of responses has eliminated much of the variability in the answers given.

Lastly, we should note that copper-plating, and to a lesser extent gold-plating, have high positive loadings on factor 2, suggesting that these operations yield positive internal economies of scope at a relatively low threshold of scale. Metal-plating in general is subject to rigorous environmental and planning regulations governing toxic waste disposal in Southern California, and even though the direct capital costs of metal-plating facilities are not high, the indirect costs in terms of waste-treatment facilities can sometimes be prohibitive for small and relatively unsophisticated producers. Such producers will often find it most economical to subcontract these functions out to specialist metal-plating firms with the requisite disposal capacity. However, somewhat larger and more sophisticated printed circuits producers can more easily deal with the toxic-waste problem, and once they install a system to manage one kind of waste, it is usually cost-effective to have the system handle several different kinds, and from this there flows a series of positive internal economies of scope.

INDUSTRIAL ORGANIZATION AND LOCATION

Thus, in complex but comprehensible ways, economies and diseconomies of scale and scope engender varying patterns of subcontracting behavior in the printed circuits industry. Subcontracting, in turn, involves a proliferation of external (and highly variable) interlinkages between printed circuits producers and their dependent subcontractors. The net result is the definite locational implosion of the entire production system, as indicated by figures 10.1 and 10.2. This implosion is particularly marked in the case of subcontractors for whom ready access to large numbers of printed circuits producers is a crucial condition of their continued survival.

CONCLUSION

One of the great difficulties faced by previous research on the interrelations between forms of industrial organization and location has been to demonstrate in empirical terms how these two levels of economic reality interact with each other by way of the effects of scale, scope, and transactions costs. In this chapter, a substantive resolution of this problem has been at least in part achieved. First, I have shown that economies and diseconomies of scale (and not just scope effects, as implied in the Williamsonian view) play a significant role in processes of vertical integration and disintegration. Second, I have been able to identify, indirectly but nonetheless firmly, economies and diseconomies of scope in the printed circuits industry, and their effects on subcontracting activity. Third, I have adduced evidence to show that the external transactions costs associated with vertical disintegration have definite impacts on patterns of industrial location, and tend in particular to encourage spatial agglomeration and polarization. These findings are specific to the printed circuits industry, but they are also entirely consistent with the theoretical ideas laid out in chapter 2, and they are indicative of many of the intricately detailed inner workings of Southern California's high-technology industrial complex as a whole.

CHAPTER 11

Innovation, New Firm Formation, and Location in Southern California's Medical Device Industry

The medical device industry represents a relatively recent development within the high-technology industrial ensemble of Southern California. Medical device manufacturers of course serve very different markets from those served by the main aerospace-electronics industry of the region, though they have drawn much support from the high-technology industrial milieu that the latter industry has engendered. Employment and output in the medical device industry have grown at an extremely rapid pace over the last couple of decades, and the industry is now also of considerable interest and importance as a focus of technological innovation.

The central objective of this chapter is to reveal some of the complex relationships between technological innovation, the formation of new firms, and locational structure. To begin with, a statistical overview of the medical device industry in the United States as a whole and in Southern California is provided. A few conceptual preliminaries about processes of innovation, new firm formation, and location are outlined. On the basis of data collected by questionnaire survey methods, some of the mainsprings of innovation and new firm formation in the medical device industry of Southern California are examined, paying particular attention to spinoff activities. In the penultimate section of the chapter, a close analysis of the industry's dynamic core in Orange County is presented, and with the aid of discriminant

This chapter was co-authored by Jan-Maarten de Vet.

221

analysis, evidence is adduced in favor of the view that geographical agglomeration is positively associated with innovation and new firm formation.

THE MEDICAL DEVICE INDUSTRY IN THE UNITED STATES

SOME DEFINITIONS

In the nomenclature of the Standard Industrial Classification of 1972 (as in the earlier 1967 classification) the medical device industry as a whole can be defined as comprising five four-digit SIC categories, i.e., SIC 3693, SIC 3841, SIC 3842, SIC 3843, and SIC 3851, as indicated in table 11.1. In the revised classification of 1987, the old SIC 3693 was divided into two new categories labeled SIC 3844 and SIC 3845 (table 11.1), while all other categories remained unchanged. Much of the statistical information discussed here covers the period before and including 1987, and hence it will be organized along the lines of the 1972 classification; however, when a switch is made in the second half of the chapter to an analysis of up-to-date questionnaire data, many of the results are reported in terms of the 1987 classification.

One of the first things we need to know about the various four-digit sectors that make up the medical device industry is their degree of technology intensiveness. Unfortunately, comprehensive data that might facilitate a resolution of this issue (e.g., scientific and technical workers employed, or R&D expenditures) are not available at the four-digit level. Hence, an attempt has been made simply to divide sectors into a "high-technology" group and a "low-technology" group on the basis of a scrutiny of industrial profiles published by the Office of Technology Assessment (1984) and the U.S. Department of Commerce (1989). The high-technology group is defined—in terms of the 1972 Standard Industrial Classification—as comprising SIC 3693 and SIC 3841 (or SIC 3841, SIC 3844, and SIC 3845 in terms of the 1987 classification); this group of sectors is engaged in the production of outputs such as high-quality medical apparatus, surgical instruments, electromedical equipment, and so on. The low-technology group is defined as comprising SIC 3842, SIC 3843, and SIC 3851; these sectors produce outputs like bandages, wheelchairs, dentures, and eyeglasses. This categorization of sectors by level of technology is supported by the survey data for Southern Californian producers (see below) in which 15 percent of all employees in sampled establishments in SIC

TABLE 11.1   THE MEDICAL DEVICE
INDUSTRY: 1972 AND 1987 STANDARD
INDUSTRIAL CLASSIFICATIONS COMPARED

1972		1987	
SIC code	Description	SIC code	Description
3693	Radiographic X-ray, Fluoro-scopic Therapeutic X-ray, and other Apparatus and Tubes; Electromedical and Electrotherapeutic Apparatus		
384	SURGICAL, MEDICAL, AND DENTAL INSTRUMENTS AND SUPPLIES	384	SURGICAL, MEDICAL, AND DENTAL INSTRUMENTS AND SUPPLIES
3841	Surgical and Medical Instruments and Apparatus	3841	Surgical and Medical Instruments and Apparatus
3842	Orthopedic, Prosthetic, and Surgical Appliances and Supplies	3842	Orthopedic, Prosthetic, and Surgical Appliances and Supplies
3843	Dental Equipment and Supplies	3843	Dental Equipment and Supplies
		3844	X-Ray Apparatus and Tubes and Related Irradiation Equipment
		3845	Electromedical and Electrotherapeutic Apparatus
385	OPHTHALMIC GOODS	385	OPHTHALMIC GOODS
3851	Ophthalmic goods	3851	Ophthalmic goods

SOURCE: Office of Management and Budget: *Standard Industrial Classification Manual*, 1972 and 1987.

3841, 10 percent in SIC 3844, and 22 percent in SIC 3845 were found to be R&D workers, whereas only 7 percent of employees in SIC 3842, 1 percent in SIC 3843, and 3 percent in SIC 3851 were R&D workers.

GENERAL PATTERNS OF GROWTH AND LOCATION

In the United States as a whole, the medical device industry has grown with great rapidity over the last couple of decades. Between 1967 and

TABLE 11.2   THE MEDICAL DEVICE
INDUSTRY IN THE UNITED STATES (SICs
3693, 3841, 3842, 3843, 3851):
ESTABLISHMENTS AND EMPLOYMENT,
1967–1987

Year	Establishments	Employment
1967	1,832	90,865
1972	2,125	124,285
1977	2,908	169,010
1982	3,144	215,398
1987	3,850	224,524

SOURCE: U.S. Department of Commerce, Bureau of the Census: *County Business Patterns.*

1987, the number of establishments grew 110.2 percent from 1,832 to 3,850, and employment grew 147.1 percent from 90,865 to 224,524 (table 11.2). Growth rates for the individual four-digit sectors differ greatly, however. As indicated by figure 11.1, SIC 3841 and SIC 3842 have grown most rapidly, with the other sectors lagging fairly far behind.

At the same time, much of this growth has been confined to only a handful of geographic areas. It has been shown in the literature that the instruments industry in general has a tendency to locational agglomeration (Gibson 1970; Oakey 1983; Malecki 1985). Thus, Oakey (1983) found that 52 percent of employment in the British instruments industry is located in southeast England. Gibson (1970) has noted that the instruments industry in the United States is concentrated in the Northeast and in California. More recently, Hekman (1980) has shown that production of medical instruments is concentrated in Boston, the New York area, and California. Data from *County Business Patterns* support these contentions (table 11.3). The medical device industry in the United States is focused on five states, i.e., California, Florida, Illinois, Massachusetts, and New York, which in 1987 collectively accounted for 41.6 percent of the country's establishments and 41.8 percent of its total employment. Of these five states, California is by far the most important with 17.6 percent of the country's establishments and 17.0 percent of its employment.

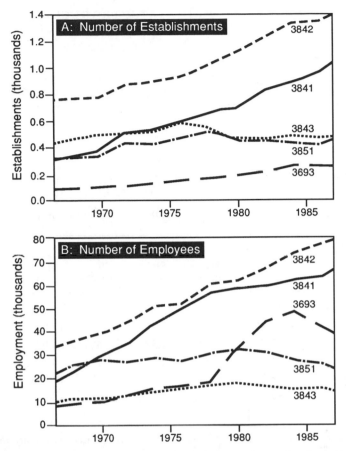

Figure 11.1. Trends in the U.S. medical device industry by four-digit SIC category, 1967–1987.

THE MEDICAL DEVICE INDUSTRY IN SOUTHERN CALIFORNIA

A STATISTICAL AND CARTOGRAPHIC DESCRIPTION

Within California, it is the southern part that contains the majority of medical device producers. This seven-county megalopolis stretching from Santa Barbara in the north to San Diego in the south contains 66.9 percent of California's medical device establishments and 81.2 percent of its total employment. Three counties (Los Angeles, Orange, and San Diego) alone account for 57.1 percent of establishments and 68.5 percent of employment in the region (table 11.4). The growth of

TABLE 11.3   MAIN STATES PRODUCING
MEDICAL DEVICES AS PERCENT OF NATIONAL
TOTAL, 1987

Establishments

State	SIC 3693	SIC 3841	SIC 3842	SIC 3843	SIC 3851	Total
California	16.9%	20.6%	14.5%	22.3%	15.4%	17.6%
Florida	6.6%	4.6%	5.8%	3.6%	6.7%	5.3%
Illinois	8.7%	5.1%	4.3%	7.3%	6.1%	5.4%
Massachusetts	7.9%	6.8%	3.4%	2.2%	5.1%	4.8%
New York	6.6%	8.1%	8.0%	9.5%	10.8%	8.5%
U.S. total:	242	1,113	1,481	507	507	3,850

*Employment**

State	SIC 3693	SIC 3841	SIC 3842	SIC 3843	SIC 3851	Total
California	16.4%	21.1%	13.5%	27.8%	11.9%	17.0%
Florida	9.8%	2.9%	2.2%	1.3%	11.9%	4.8%
Illinois	2.5%	3.8%	3.5%	6.6%	4.9%	3.8%
Massachusetts	11.2%	11.4%	3.1%	1.2%	10.6%	7.7%
New York	6.8%	9.0%	5.7%	10.7%	17.7%	8.6%
U.S. total:	38,919	65,795	79,176	14,296	26,338	224,524

SOURCE: U.S. Department of Commerce, Bureau of the Census: *County Business Patterns*, 1986.
* Employment figures partly derived from class means.

the industry in these three counties has been extremely rapid over the 1967–1987 period. The major four-digit medical device industry in the region is SIC 3841, which accounts for 32.1 percent of the region's device establishments and 33.9 percent of employment.

The locations of actual establishments in the medical device industry in Southern California are depicted in figures 11.2 and 11.3. Figure 11.2 represents the high-technology segment of the industry (214 establishments belonging to SICs 3841, 3844, and 3845), and figure 11.3 the low-technology segment (142 establishments belonging to SICs 3842, 3843, and 3851). Both figures display a scattering of establishments across the region, but the high-technology segment of the

TABLE 11.4   THE MEDICAL DEVICE
INDUSTRY IN SOUTHERN CALIFORNIA:
ESTABLISHMENTS AND EMPLOYMENT, 1987

County	Establishments		Employment*	
	Number	Percent	Number	Percent
Los Angeles	204	30.2%	10,763	28.3%
Orange	111	16.4%	8,148	21.4%
Riverside	11	1.6%	643	1.7%
San Bernardino	12	1.8%	274	0.7%
San Diego	71	10.5%	7,166	18.8%
Santa Barbara	19	2.8%	1,431	3.8%
Ventura	24	3.6%	2,509	6.6%
Southern California	452	66.9%	30,934	81.2%
California	676	100.0%	38,099	100.0%

SOURCE: U.S. Department of Commerce, Bureau of the Census: *County Business Patterns*, 1986.
    * Employment figures are derived partly from class means.

industry also has a propensity to agglomerate in the Irvine area of Orange County. The contrast in locational patterns between the high- and low-technology segments of the industry is brought out by entropy measures, which (expressed as percentages of maximum possible entropy) are 66.3 percent for figure 11.2 and 71 percent for figure 11.3. These measures indicate that both patterns are characterized by considerable dispersion, but that the high-technology segment is somewhat more clustered than the low. As is shown at a later stage, the Orange County cluster represents an especially interesting and significant nexus of (high-technology) establishments, and some comment on the historical development of the industry in the county is thus in order at this stage.

HISTORICAL DEVELOPMENT OF THE MEDICAL DEVICE INDUSTRY IN ORANGE COUNTY

At the end of the 1950s, Arnold O. Beckman founded Beckman Instruments in Fullerton, Orange County. This was one of the first major

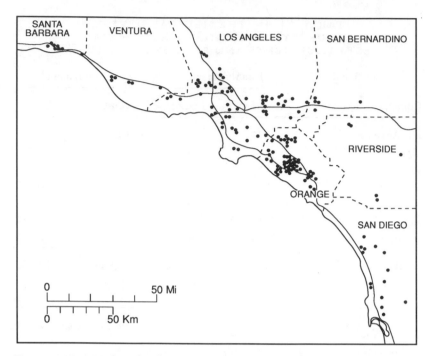

Figure 11.2. High-technology segment of the medical device industry in Southern California. (Data from *California Manufacturers Register*, 1989, and *Directory Systems*, 1987.)

manufacturing firms to enter the county and it was certainly the first to do so in the field of medical devices. However, despite its long-established presence in Orange County (today it employs 1,000 workers in Brea), it has actually had little impact on local industrial development. Lowell Edwards, the cofounder of Edwards Laboratories, is usually credited as representing the initial spark that set off the growth of the Orange County medical device industry (Applegate 1984; Doyle and Friedenreich 1988; Grant 1988; Robischon 1988). Edwards was a retired aircraft fuel-pump designer from Oregon who together with Albert Star, a cardiovascular surgeon, opened Edwards Laboratories in 1961 in a Santa Ana machine shop, conveniently placed between Edwards's second home in Palm Springs and the Long Beach shop of a friend (Grant 1988). Edwards correctly judged that Southern California provided more and better business opportunities than Oregon. The new company achieved a breakthrough in the development of a mechanical heart valve, and was able to attract

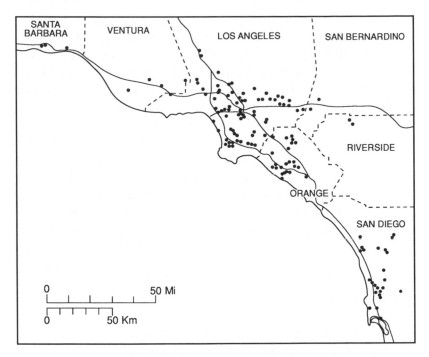

Figure 11.3. Low-technology segment of the medical device industry in Southern California. (Data from *California Manufacturers Register*, 1989, and *Directory Systems*, 1987.)

first-rate biomedical-device engineers from all over the United States. During the 1960s and 1970s, Edwards Laboratories was a source of numerous spinoffs in cardiovascular and related fields.

At the outset, the chief engineer of Edwards Laboratories, Don Shiley, developed a new type of artificial heart valve, and he started his own company in 1963 to manufacture the product. By the late 1980s, Shiley Laboratories had become a 1,800-employee company located in Irvine (Grant 1988). In 1964, Jim Bentley also resigned from Edwards Laboratories and founded Bentley Laboratories, producing a new type of blood oxygenator; the company is now (with 800 employees) the largest oxygenator producer in the country. Several other Edwards engineers followed behind. One of these was William Hancock, who developed the porcine heart valve and started Hancock Laboratories in 1967. The latter firm's bioprosthetic heart valve is now a standard alternative for the mechanical heart valve (Grant 1988).

This first phase of spin-offs was followed by a number of developments that reinforced the localized growth of the industry in Orange County. In 1968, American Hospital Supply moved some of its operations to adjacent San Diego County. That same year Orange County Airport opened its passenger terminal. The University of California at Irvine was founded in 1967, and its Medical School started in 1970—though it was only later that the Medical School began seriously to establish relations with device firms in its immediate vicinity (Scott 1988a). The aerospace-electronics industry, which was already well represented in Orange County, contracted in the early to mid-1970s due to a decrease in defense spending. This motivated many of the key personnel in aerospace-electronics to search for opportunities in other sectors. The medical device industry was one such sector, particularly as many techniques (e.g., durability testing and clean-room processing) commonly used in aerospace-electronics production were also being used in medical device production. In addition, in the early 1970s, a second wave of spin-offs took place, thus bolstering the growth of the Orange County complex. William Harvey Research Corporation, Vorhauer Laboratories, Retroperfusion Systems, and Gish Biomedical are some of the spin-offs, which came directly or indirectly from Edwards at that time. Moreover, the spin-off process has continued to proliferate in the county down to the present moment.

Figure 11.4 is an attempt to trace out the main genealogy of spin-offs in the Orange County medical device industry over the last couple of decades. Both the older spin-offs from Edwards Laboratories, like Shiley and Bentley, as well as some of the newer (indirect) ones, such as Xenotech and Hemascience, are shown. The figure is schematic and incomplete, but it is a good illustration of the vigor of the spin-off process in the industry in Orange County. Today, the county is a leading center for cardiovascular products and related specialty devices in the fields of respiratory care and pulmonary medicine.

PRODUCT INNOVATION, NEW FIRM FORMATION, AND LOCATION: BACKGROUND AND HYPOTHESIS FORMULATION

PRODUCT INNOVATION AND THE REGULATORY ENVIRONMENT

Innovation in industrial systems may take one of two major forms: process or product innovation. In practice these are often difficult to

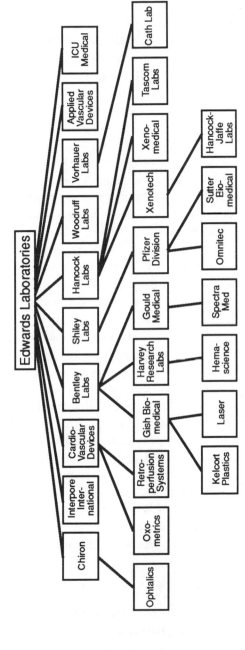

Figure 11.4. Selected spin-offs in Orange County's medical device industry.

distinguish from each other, and what for one sector may look like a process innovation may for another sector be perfectly tradable as a product innovation. In any case, in this analysis the focus is restricted to product innovation, which is particularly important in the current phase of development of the medical device industry, and is also—a pragmatic issue—crudely but relatively easily measurable by questionnaire methods. This form of technological change, moreover, often gives rise to spinoff phenomena and new firm formation.

Product innovations may be engendered either within the individual firm (Myers and Marquis 1969; Rothwell and Zegfeld 1981) or at the interface between a firm and any sort of interlocutor, such as a customer or an input supplier (Russo 1985; Von Hippel 1976). In several recent studies it has been suggested that doctors and surgeons (i.e., the major users of medical devices) are significant sources of innovative ideas for medical device manufacturers (Roberts and Hauptman 1986; Von Hippel and Finkelstein 1979). These ideas may be transferred from medical practitioners to manufacturers either by personal contacts (e.g., sales personnel), by means of scientific publication, or through information garnered at medical conferences and congresses.

The actual production and sale of innovative devices are tightly controlled by the Food and Drug Administration (FDA), especially since the passage of the Medical Device Amendments to the Food, Drug and Cosmetics Act in 1976 (Romeo 1988). The FDA classifies products into three main categories, depending on the medical risks they incur. These categories range from Class I (low risk) to Class III (high risk), with clinical trials being mandated for Class III products (Office of Technology Assessment, 1984). The FDA regulations certainly impose added costs on producers, but they also eventually ease market entry, for FDA approval helps to smooth out the process of coverage and payment decisions on the part of major medical insurers such as Medicare, Medicaid, Blue Cross/Blue Shield, and other private insurers. Indeed, the growth of health-care insurance over the last few decades has been a major factor in the expansion of the industry and in the widening diversity of products that it brings to market.

NEW FIRM FORMATION

Several analysts have claimed that product innovation forms one of the mainstays of new entrepreneurial activity, especially in industries where patenting of designs is feasible, thus protecting investments. Gordon, Dilts and Kimball (1990), for example, have indicated that

66.6 percent of small and medium-sized enterprises in Silicon Valley were started for the purpose of commercializing new products. Oakey, Rothwell and Cooper (1988) and Myers and Marquis (1969) have argued that radical forms of product innovation are likely to be found in new and small firms while older and larger firms are more prone to be engaged in incremental improvement of existing products (Dosi 1988). This claim is reinforced by the studies of Roberts (1988) and Roberts and Hauptman (1986), who show that in the medical device industry radical product innovations are preeminently the preserve of the small firm. There is evidence, then, that when radical product innovations occur they often tend to induce much spin-off and the formation of new small firms. Such spin-off may represent either horizontal or vertical disintegration of functions, though in the medical device industry horizontal disintegration appears to be the more usual case.

Key personnel (i.e., experienced and knowledgeable workers in charge of crucial firm operations) are central to the spinoff process. Certainly these are among the individuals most strategically placed both to perceive new commercial opportunities and to take advantage of them. Cooper (1985) shows in a study of growth-oriented firms that their founders had often started businesses before, and that they rarely acted alone but (in 70 percent of all cases) created a new firm with one or more partners. In the medical device industry, founding teams usually consist of a technical specialist who is able to develop the engineering and manufacturing side of the operation, and a management specialist who is more skilled in general business activities (Roberts and Hauptman 1986). Venture capital also plays a major role, especially in the high-technology segment of the medical device industry. Indeed, in 1988, the medical/health-care industry received 13 percent of all venture-capital disbursements in the United States, second only to the computer industry (Venture Economics 1989). The early Schumpeter (1934) seemed to have the medical-device industry in mind when he characterized innovative entrepreneurs in general as individuals who set up a new firm to exploit an invention, borrow most of the necessary capital, and then once the firm is established, move on to new horizons.

AGGLOMERATION

One major point needs to be added to these preliminaries. If active spin-off of new firms is occurring, and if founding entrepreneurs are at least to some degree residentially immobile, a simple agglomeration may start to form spontaneously. However, industrial agglomerations are usually more than just inert masses of producers contingently clustered in one place. What basically engenders industrial agglomerations and holds them together over long periods of time is, as we have seen, a set of structured and organic relationships in which local labor markets and linkage networks play a crucial role. Agglomeration will be further accentuated where firms are constantly innovating, and therefore (a) have unpredictable demands for skilled labor, and hence to that degree must have access to a revolving pool of such labor, and (b) frequently change process and product configurations, necessitating that they be close to a wide constellation of allied firms and specialized suppliers. In turn, and building on the insights developed by Russo (1985), innovation is likely to be enhanced by agglomeration because it is especially in dense localized networks of producers that the flow of information is maximized and new technological and commercial opportunities most visible.

A QUESTIONNAIRE SURVEY OF SOUTHERN CALIFORNIAN MEDICAL DEVICE PRODUCERS

The 356 medical device establishments shown cartographically in figures 11.2 and 11.3 were all surveyed by mail questionnaire over 1989.

The final questionnaire (which is described more fully in de Vet [1990]) was four pages long and requested information on a series of four main topics: (a) general characteristics of the establishment, (b) product innovation and R&D activities, (c) new firm formation and spin-offs, and (d) production processes and linkages. All establishments in the designated population were sent a first questionnaire and cover letter in July 1989. The response to this mailing yielded only twenty-three filled-out questionnaires. A second questionnaire plus a reminder letter were therefore sent out in August 1989 to all establishments that had not responded. In response to this mailing, twenty-nine usable questionnaires were returned, thus giving a total of fifty-two. At the same time, forty-one questionnaires (from both mailings) were returned by the post office without any forwarding address. Thus, if we take it that the effective sampled population was $356 - 41 = 311$, our returned fifty-two questionnaires represent a response rate of 16.7 percent, which is reasonably satisfactory for this kind of survey.

What biases if any affect our (self-selected) sample? In the absence of detailed data on the population of establishments, it is difficult to assess this issue with finality. However, we *do* have information on the locations and SIC codes of the establishments that form the population, and this information can be used as a rough standard against which to judge the sample. As shown by table 11.5, the distribution of sample establishments by county differs widely from that of the population. Los Angeles County is underrepresented (34.6 percent of the sample, compared to 45.2 percent of the population), and Orange County is overrepresented (36.5 percent of the sample versus 30.6 percent of the population). By contrast, the distribution of sample establishments by high- or low-technology sector is quite similiar to that of the population (57.8 percent of establishments from the sample and 59.6 percent from the population belong to the high-technology sector). A chi-squared test of the overall distribution of establishments in the population and the sample cross-classified as in table 11.5 reveals that the two data sets are significantly different from each other at the 99 percent confidence level (chi-squared = 46.7, with three degrees of freedom). This test does not of course tell us anything direct about possible biases in other sample measures, such as indicators of innovation or new firm formation, but it does suggest that we need always to be extremely careful in our interpretations of the sample results.

AN EMPIRICAL DESCRIPTION OF PRODUCT INNOVATION AND NEW FIRM FORMATION IN SOUTHERN CALIFORNIA'S MEDICAL DEVICE MANUFACTURING COMPLEX

THE SOURCES OF INNOVATIVE IDEAS

As indicated earlier, one of the major findings in the literature on the medical device industry is that product innovation is derived mainly from ideas that originate in medical practice. The sample data set out in table 11.6 suggest that this proposition does *not* hold for the case of Southern Californian producers. In total, 61.5 percent of sample establishments reported that the person who created the main idea underlying their most important product is or was one of their own employees. In fact, for establishments in this sample, the external environment is of secondary importance as a source of product ideas, and only 7.7 percent of establishments indicated that their main product idea originated in a university or academic hospital. However, as table 11.6 indicates, high-technology establishments were more than twice as likely to obtain their main product ideas from universities or academic hospitals than low.

TABLE 11.5 POPULATION AND SAMPLE ESTABLISHMENTS CROSS-CLASSIFIED BY COUNTY AND TECHNOLOGICAL LEVEL

County	Population			Sample		
	High technology	Low technology	Total	High technology	Low technology	Total
Los Angeles	22.8%	22.5%	45.2%	9.6%	25.0%	34.6%
Orange	23.9%	6.7%	30.6%	30.8%	5.8%	36.5%
San Diego	5.9%	7.6%	13.5%	7.8%	5.8%	13.5%
Other	7.0%	3.7%	10.7%	9.6%	5.7%	15.4%
Total establishments	212	144	356	30	22	52
Percent	(59.6%)	(40.4%)	(100%)	(57.8%)	(42.2%)	(100%)

TABLE 11.6 ORIGINS OF INNOVATIVE IDEAS FOR THE ESTABLISHMENT'S MOST
IMPORTANT PRODUCT

Origin of idea	High-technology establishments	Low-technology establishments	All establishments	
			Percent	Number
Individual within this company	66.6%	54.6%	61.5%	32
Individual in other company	16.7%	9.1%	13.5%	7
University/academic hospital	10.0%	4.5%	7.7%	4
Other	6.7%	4.5%	5.8%	3
Not applicable	0.0%	27.3%	11.5%	6
Number of establishments	30	22	52	

Value of chi-squared = 5.11
degrees of freedom = 4
significance = 0.279

The finding that innovation in the medical device industry is for the greater part internally generated may of course be in part tilted by exaggerated self-evaluation on the part of questionnaire respondents. In fact, other information elicited by the questionnaire provides a partial corrective to this finding. Thus, about 20 percent of respondents (all of them high-technology producers) indicated that they had initiated formalized contacts with one or more academic institutions. Moreover, formalized contacts with universities and academic hospitals are significantly more common for establishments with more than twenty-five employees (48 percent of them have such contacts) than for establishments with fewer than twenty-five employees (7.4 percent).

Several establishments were found to have formal contacts with more than one university, and one establishment indicated that it had contacts with ten universities. Table 11.7 lists the universities and affiliated medical centers involved in the reported contacts. Thirty percent of these contacts refer to institutions that are located in Southern California, an additional 15 percent concern universities in Northern California. Contacts with the University of California at Irvine are unexpectedly low. Although a substantial number of innovative establishments are extremely close to this university, only one establishment in the entire sample indicated that it had a formal contact with it. That said, the University of California at Irvine has recently set up a Medical Research Education Society to stimulate transfers of innovative technologies to the industry, and more active local relations are now evidently being created.

R&D, PATENTING, AND INNOVATION

R&D functions are of considerable importance in the medical device industry of Southern California, and all the more so as product innovation is apparently largely internally engendered. Table 11.8 describes the employment structure of R&D departments in the fifty-two sample establishments. The industry deals with developmental questions that are primarily engineering in nature, in contrast with other parts of the health-care industry that face more fundamental scientific questions, requiring life scientists (biotechnology) or chemists (pharmaceuticals) to resolve them. Table 11.8 amply corroborates the dominance of engineers in the medical device industry: their number is more than ten times larger than the numbers of life scientists and other scientists. R&D engineers form 5.9 percent of the total labor force of

TABLE 11.7   UNIVERSITIES/ACADEMIC
HOSPITALS INVOLVED IN FORMAL CONTACTS
WITH MEDICAL DEVICE ESTABLISHMENTS IN
SOUTHERN CALIFORNIA

	Reported contacts	
University/academic hospital	*Number*	*Percent*
California		
* University of California—Los Angeles	3	15%
* University of Southern California	2	10%
* University of California—San Francisco	2	10%
* Stanford Medical Center	1	5%
* University of California—Irvine	1	5%
Rest of United States		
* University of Utah Medical Center	2	10%
* Columbia University Medical Center	1	5%
* Duke University	1	5%
* Johns Hopkins University	1	5%
* Massachusetts General Hospital	1	5%
* New York University	1	5%
* University of Colorado Medical Center	1	5%
* University of Virginia	1	5%
* Yale	1	5%
Outside United States		
* University of Hamburg (Germany)	1	5%
Total	20	100%

sample establishments and the percentage is even higher (9.3 percent) for those establishments classified as high-technology. The presence of medical doctors in R&D activities in the medical device industry is negligible, which is consistent with results from other research in other regions (Roberts and Hauptman 1986).

The percentage of engineers in the labor force is one rough proxy for innovative thrust, and patenting activity is another. As the Office of Technology Assessment (1984) has indicated, commercially viable product ideas in the industry are typically registered with the Patents Office. These two measures are strongly related to each other in sam-

TABLE 11.8   EMPLOYMENT STRUCTURE OF
RESEARCH AND DEVELOPMENT DEPARTMENTS
IN SAMPLE ESTABLISHMENTS

R&D field	Total number of R&D employees	As a weighted % of total employment	Percent of establishments with this activity
Engineers	266	5.87%	61.5%
Life scientists	21	0.46%	17.3%
Medical doctors	1	0.02%	3.8%
Other scientists	19	0.42%	17.3%

pled establishments. Thus, 73.0 percent of establishments that manufacture patented products have more than 3 percent of their labor force employed as R&D engineers. Only 7 percent of establishments without patented products have a similar percentage of their workers employed as R&D engineers. A difference-of-proportions test indicates that these two values are significantly different from each other at the 99 percent confidence level.

Patent protection also correlates strongly with several other indices of innovation. Altogether, some 50 percent of sampled establishments introduced medical devices that were new to U.S. and world markets, and of these, almost all were engaged in the production of patented products. The same is true of the 44 percent of sampled establishments that introduced medical products that replaced fundamentally different technologies or practices. Manufacturers of patented products are significantly more likely to carry Class III products than other establishments. Moreover, while patenting activity is not necessarily in principle restricted to high-technology establishments, 93.3 percent of such establishments manufacture patented products, whereas only 40.9 percent of low-technology establishments do so (table 11.9). These two values are different from each other at more than the 99 percent confidence level by a difference-of-proportions test.

Thus, patenting activity seems to hold up well as a useful though certainly imperfect yardstick of broad innovative effort, and it is now brought into play as a general proxy variable to assay the effects of interestablishment interactions (strategic alliances and subcontracting) upon rates of innovation.

TABLE 11.9   SIC CATEGORIES IN RELATION
TO PRODUCTION OF PATENTED PRODUCTS

SIC code	Patented products?		Number of establishments
	Yes	No	
	(% of establishments)		
3841*	92.0	8.0	25
3842	41.2	58.8	17
3843	33.3	66.7	3
3844*	100.0	0.0	1
3845*	100.0	0.0	4
3851	50.0	50.0	2
High-technology establishments	93.3	6.7	30
Low-technology establishments	40.9	59.1	22
Number of establishments	37	15	52

* High-technology sectors

INTERESTABLISHMENT INTERACTIONS AND INNOVATION

Many medical device manufacturers interact with their external milieu through formalized strategic alliances directed to activities such as R&D, technology transfer, exchanges of manufacturing capacity, marketing, and so on. A surprisingly high 41.2 percent of all sampled establishments reported that they have such alliances with other companies, and more specifically, 29.4 percent have alliances in the field of R&D. For establishments that are engaged in the manufacture of patented products, 48.6 percent have one or more alliances with other companies; for establishments that do not manufacture patented products, only 21.4 percent have such alliances (see table 11.10). When we look only at R&D alliances, the contrast between the two groups of establishments is even more pronounced (and significantly different according to a chi-squared test). Manufacturers of patented products are five times more likely to be engaged in R&D alliances than all other establishments. Establishment size was found not to have any impact on these relationships.

TABLE 11.10   STRATEGIC ALLIANCES IN
RELATION TO PRODUCTION OF PATENTED
PRODUCTS

Manufacture patented products?	Alliances?		Number of establishments
	Yes	No	
Yes	48.6%	51.4%	37
No	21.4%	78.6%	14
Number of establishments	30	21	51

Value of chi-squared = 2.08; degrees of freedom = 1; significance = 0.0780

Manufacture patented products?	R&D alliances?		Number of establishments
	Yes	No	
Yes	37.8%	62.2%	37
No	7.1%	92.9%	14
Number of establishments	15	36	51

Chi-square = 4.61; degrees of freedom = 1; significance = 0.0318

Subcontracting is another sort of external relation that seems to correlate with innovative activity. As suggested earlier, innovative establishments require much flexibility to be able to experiment to the maximum degree with process and product configurations, and subcontracting can greatly facilitate such activity. Table 11.11 shows the relationship between the use of subcontractors and the manufacture of patented products for sample establishments. Almost three out of four establishments (73.5 percent) make use of subcontractors. However, manufacturers of patented products are twice as likely to subcontract out as other establishments. We may note in passing that most of this subcontracting involves tasks such as plastic molding (by injection and extrusion), machining, and electronic work such as printed circuit-board assembly. The locations of subcontractors mentioned in the questionnaires could be traced in thirty-seven out of sixty-four cases. Most device manufacturers use local subcontractors, and 54 percent of all subcontractors are located in the same county as the establishment

TABLE 11.11   USE OF SUBCONTRACTORS IN
RELATION TO PRODUCTION OF PATENTED
PRODUCTS

Manufacture patented products?	Use subcontractors?		Number of establishments
	Yes	*No*	
Yes	85.7%	14.3%	35
No	42.9%	57.1%	14
Number of establishments	36	13	49

Value of chi-squared = 9.42; degrees of freedom = 1; significance = 0.0021

that mentioned them. A further 24 percent are located in the rest of California, almost always in an adjacent county within the Southern Californian metropolitan area.

EMPIRICAL EVIDENCE ON NEW FIRM FORMATION

New firm formation has proceeded vigorously in the medical device industry of Southern California over the last few decades, especially in the high-technology segment. The median year of founding of sample establishments was 1972. Half of the low-technology establishments were founded before 1970, whereas 73.3 percent of the high-technology establishments were created after that date, and 33.3 percent were created after 1980.

Spin-off is one of the main forms in which new firm formation occurs. The survey data indicate that spin-off occurs with greatest frequency from establishments with patented products. In total, 31.4 percent of establishments with patented products had had other firms spun off from them, whereas *no* spin-offs were observed from establishments that do not make patented products. In line with the data presented earlier on previous employment of firm founders, parent establishments reported that nearly all their spin-offs started operations in the medical device industry. Furthermore, while the new spin-offs usually began immediately to develop and/or manufacture their own product lines, these were often closely related to the products of the parent firm, so that spin-off chiefly represents a process of horizontal disintegration in *optima forma*.

TABLE 11.12   FORMER EMPLOYMENT OF
ESTABLISHMENT FOUNDER(S)

Former employment	High-technology establishments	Low-technology establishments	All establishments	
			Percent	Number
Medical device industry	59%	67%	62%	26
Other industries	22%	13%	19%	8
Medical practice/ hospital	8%	20%	12%	5
University	11%	0%	7%	3
Number of establishments	23	19	42	

The majority (62 percent) of the founders of medical device establishments in Southern California were originally employed in the industry itself (table 11.12). Here, data on founders include multiple
founders where this is the case. Previous employment in a medical or
university environment is of relatively minor importance: only 19 percent of founders have such employment experience. However, when
we look at the educational attainments of founders, we find that
academic or medical credentials are extremely important, at least for
high-technology establishments (table 11.13). By far the greater majority of founders of high-technology establishments have an educational
background in biology, medicine, engineering, or physics. Some 32.7
percent of all founders had set up one or more businesses prior to their
present venture, though this is on the low side compared to the
findings of Cooper (1985).

AN INTERIM SUMMARY

The preliminary theoretical sketch of innovation and new firm formation laid out earlier seems so far to be reasonably well reflected in the
empirical record of medical device manufacturing in Southern California. Major product ideas come less from the external environment
than is expected, but still there is much evidence of influences permeat-
ing through from hospitals and universities to the industry. In conformity to expectations, product innovation is most intense in the

TABLE 11.13 EDUCATIONAL LEVEL OF
ESTABLISHMENT FOUNDER(S) BY HIGHEST
OBTAINED DEGREE

	High-technology establishments	Low-technology establishments	Total cases*	
			Percent	Number
High school	0.0%	33.3%	14.5%	8
High school plus	12.9%	20.8%	16.5%	9
Bachelor's degree	38.7%	20.8%	30.9%	17
Master's degree	9.7%	20.8%	14.5%	8
MD/DDS	16.1%	4.3%	10.9%	6
Doctor's degree (Ph.D.)	22.6%	0.0%	12.7%	7
Number of establishments	31	24	55	

* More than one answer per establishment is possible.

high-technology segment of the industry. Strategic alliances and sub-contracting activity are more common in the high-technology segment than in the low, and these relationships seem to stimulate innovatory capacity, the first by widening the range of possibilities that any individual establishment can effectively scan, the second by enhancing the flexibility of production. Lastly, spin-offs are numerous in the more innovative portions of the industry, as anticipated.

We have already seen in a small way that innovative and high-technology device manufacturers tend to cluster together in geographical space. This relationship is now scrutinized more closely by means of a statistical analysis of the main contrasts between (a) the dominant core group of high-technology establishments in Orange County and (b) the set of more heterogeneous establishments dispersed throughout the rest of Southern California.

A DISCRIMINANT ANALYSIS OF THE MEDICAL DEVICE INDUSTRY IN SOUTHERN CALIFORNIA

The maps presented earlier of the medical device industry in Southern California (figs. 11.2 and 11.3) strongly suggest that the industry can be geographically divided into two distinctive groups: a cluster in a confined area within the core of Orange County and another group scattered across the rest of the region. The Orange County core group is defined as all establishments located in zip code areas 92680 (Tustin), 92705 (Santa Ana), 92714, and 92718 (the latter two in Irvine). An attempt was now made to distinguish between the two groups on the basis of linear discriminant analysis.

A total of forty sample establishments was subjected to analysis, the remaining twelve being eliminated because of missing-data problems. The Orange County core group consists of ten establishments and the group representing the rest of Southern California consists of thirty. The discrepancy in size between the two groups should be kept in mind when interpreting the statistical results presented below, though it does not invalidate the main assumptions of the technique. A set of twenty-eight variables derived from the questionnaire survey turned out to be potentially appropriate for the discriminant analysis, from both theoretical and practical points of view. Some of these variables were transformed in various ways to eliminate simple scale effects (see de Vet [1990] for details). A combination of three variables was finally found to be most useful and effective in the analysis. The variables are: (a) the number of engineers in R&D activities as a percentage of total employment, (b) the number of spun-off employees per 100 employees divided by the number of years the establishment has been in business (thus giving a rate per annum), and (b) a binary variable indicating whether or not venture-capital funding was used in the foundation of the establishment.

The computed standardized canonical discriminant function coefficients show that these variables discriminate significantly between establishments in the Orange County core and in the remainder of Southern California (table 11.14). Orange County core establishments employ more R&D engineers, spin-off companies at a higher rate, and are more likely to be supported by venture capital than establishments elsewhere in the region. Summary statistics show that the overall discriminant function is significant at the 0.004 level with a Wilks's Lambda of 0.678 and a canonical correlation coefficient of 0.567 (table 11.15). In all, 84 percent of the establishments are correctly classified by the analysis.

Each of the three discriminating variables is now discussed in turn. The first variable (R&D engineers) is in part an index of innovative activity, as suggested earlier. In the Orange County core group of

TABLE 11.14   STANDARDIZED CANONICAL
DISCRIMINANT-FUNCTION COEFFICIENTS
FOR THE ORANGE COUNTY CORE VERSUS THE
REMAINDER OF SOUTHERN CALIFORNIA

Discriminant variable	Standardized canonical discriminant-function coefficient	Statistical significance
Number of engineers in R&D activities as a % of total employment	0.770	0.04
Number of spun-off employees per 100 employees per annum	0.706	0.01
Use of venture-capital funding at time of founding of the establishment (binary)	0.553	0.05

TABLE 11.15   SUMMARY STATISTICS FOR
THE LINEAR-DISCRIMINANT ANALYSIS

	Orange County core	Remainder of Southern California	Total
* Number of establishments analyzed	10	40	50
* Percentage of establishments correctly classified	80%	85%	84%
* Wilks's Lambda	—	—	0.678
* Canonical correlation coefficient	—	—	0.567
* Significance level	—	—	0.004

establishments such engineers make up 12.3 percent of the workforce, and in establishments in the remainder of Southern California they make up 5.5 percent. The second variable (employees spun off) performs at a highly significant level in the discriminant analysis, and the results indicate that the new firm formation rate in the Orange County core is higher than in the remainder of Southern California. The third variable (venture capital) is somewhat less significant than the others but is still quite indicative. Among Orange County core establishments, 30 percent had received venture capital funding at the time of their foundation, but only 6 percent of the establishments in the remainder of Southern California had been given such support. However, it must also be acknowledged that venture-capital financing is a relatively recent phenomenon and that the Orange County core establishments—most of them started after 1980—had a finance opportunity that was not widely available at an earlier time when many other establishments in the remainder of Southern California were founded. If one keeps in mind the need for interpretative caution, we may tentatively infer from these results that Orange County core establishments are more innovative, more actively engaged in spin-off, and perhaps more likely to call upon venture capitalists in the early stages of their formation.

The value of the discriminant analysis can now be extended by looking at the remaining twenty-five variables that were excluded from the first round of analysis, but that nevertheless contain valuable information. Table 11.16 presents coefficients of correlation for these individual variables and the computed discriminant function. A high correlation coefficient (close to $+1$) means that the associated variable is strongly related to the Orange County core group, while a low coefficient (close to -1) indicates the opposite. Five variables, in addition to those that actually define the discriminant function, have significant correlations. They are: (a) proportion of total personnel in R&D; (b) proportion of personnel in production (negative coefficient); (c) R&D life scientists as a percentage of total employment; (d) year of foundation (recent foundings being associated with the Orange County core); and (e) formalized contacts with universities. Other variables that are not significantly related to the discriminant function but that still collectively reinforce the emerging interpretation are subcontracting activity, patenting activity, the role of the founder in creating the firm's main product idea, and alliances, all of them with a positive correlation. Thus, on all these counts, Orange County core establishments are relatively innovative, R&D intensive, limited in their blue-collar activities, linked to academic institutions, and (to a lesser extent) prone to subcontracting and alliance formation. These findings point to a conception of key high-technology agglomerations as centers of innovation, new firm formation, and transactions-intensive production.

TABLE 11.16 CORRELATION COEFFICIENTS FOR INDIVIDUAL VARIABLES AND THE DISCRIMINANT FUNCTION

Proportion of total personnel in R&D	0.727**
R&D engineers as % of total employment	0.529**
Founded with venture capital (binary)	0.479**
Proportion of personnel in production	−0.467**
Number of spin-offs per 100 employees per year	0.450**
R&D life scientists as % of total employment	0.399**
Year of foundation	0.378*
Formalized contacts with universities (binary)	0.337*
Number of subcontractors per 100 employees	0.273
Product represents new technology (binary)	0.270
Establishment acquired/taken over (binary)	0.270
Manufacture of patented products (binary)	0.265
Proportion of output sold abroad	0.243
Founder as originator of main product idea (binary)	0.213
Alliances with other firms (binary)	0.197
Scope of new medical devices (binary)	0.183
Proportion of purchases made within 15 miles	−0.129
Companies previously founded (binary)	0.128
Other establishments owned by firm (binary)	0.108
Proportion of females in production personnel	0.089
Proportion of Hispanics in production personnel	−0.073
Proportion of output sold within 15 miles	−0.070
FDA-approval class III (binary)	0.035
Proportion of purchases abroad	0.023
Proportion of Asians in production personnel	−0.019
Other R&D scientists as % of total employment	−0.005
R&D medical doctors as % of total employment	−0.004
Total number of employees	0.003

Variables set in italics are elements of the discriminant function.
  * significant at the 0.05 level
** significant at the 0.01 level

CONCLUSION

Despite stagnation in some branches of U.S. manufacturing over the last few decades, a number of flexible production sectors have tended to grow at a rapid pace. Both the high-technology and low-technology segments of the medical device industry represent a remarkable but often unnoticed example of this trend, most especially in Southern California.

A crucial question is whether or not the growth of the industry is likely to continue in the near future. The 1970s and 1980s were a very favorable time for the industry, especially given the great expansion of the U.S. health-care system during this period. More restrictive medical reimbursement practices in the future may have a dampening effect on further expansion, and already the cost-containment policies of major insurers are cutting into the industry's growth. At the same time, the core agglomeration of high-technology producers in Orange County is facing many difficulties. In recent years production costs and urbanization diseconomies (in the form of shortages of cheap labor, extremely high land prices, traffic congestion, and pollution) have been rising sharply in Orange County. It is difficult to predict whether these increasing costs will offset the positive agglomeration economies that have shaped earlier rounds of growth. Several medical device firms have already relocated their more routinized production facilities outside of Orange County (a parallel phenomenon to the shift of semiconductor assembly work out of Silicon Valley).

If this trend continues, it could have an adverse effect on the regional economy of Southern California. This is doubly untoward given the dependence of other industrial sectors in the region on federal defense spending, which is now rapidly declining. It is doubtful, of course, that any future possible growth in the medical device industry would offset employment declines induced by reductions in Department of Defense spending. Nevertheless, the industry (along with biotechnology) represents one of the few high-technology sectors in the region that is almost entirely independent of such spending, and its role in helping to reorient Southern California's economy could therefore become significant, providing the dynamic of innovation and new firm formation continues in the future as it has in the past.

PART VI

Finale

CHAPTER 12

Questions of Policy and Strategic Choice

Collective Action and Regional Development in the New Global Economy

THE TURNING POINT

Southern California is now at a critical turning point in its evolutionary pathway, just as it was in the early decades of the twentieth century and again after World War II. Its industrial fabric today is jeopardized on a variety of fronts, and its future is extremely problematical. This judgment applies with special force to Southern California's complement of high-technology industries, but it also applies to many of the low-technology sectors that also proliferate throughout the region.

Between 1987 and 1990, according to data published by the Employment Development Department of the State of California (1991), employment in high-technology industries in Los Angeles County declined from 302,800 workers to 259,600 workers, giving a total loss of 43,200 workers or 14.3 percent. In Los Angeles, Orange, and San Diego counties combined, the aggregate loss was 56,500 workers or 12.3 percent.[1] Assuming a direct and indirect multiplier effect somewhere in the range of 1.5 to 2.5, this decline of 56,500 jobs could translate into an *additional* drop of anything from 84,750 jobs to 141,250 (Economic Roundtable 1992). Some of these losses are of course due to recessionary conditions.

---

1. Data from the Employment Development Department do not allow us to pinpoint employment in high-technology sectors for the other counties of Southern California, i.e., Riverside, San Bernardino, Santa Barbara, and Ventura.

However, beyond the current cyclical downswing there are long-term structural problems of a major sort that the region faces. Two of these have been stressed at length in all the previous discussion. One involves declining Department of Defense expenditures, and this decline will almost certainly continue for several years to come. Moreover, the downtrend brings with it a withering of the visible hand of the federal defense establishment, which has certainly been one of the most aggressive and successful agents of broad industrial policy in the United States over the entire postwar epoch. The other structural problem resides in the rising tide of foreign competition in aerospace and electronics products from Europe, Japan, and many of the newly industrializing countries. The combined effects of these pressures are already apparent in an incipient restructuring of the old pattern of organized interaction between the systems houses of the region and surrounding cohorts of flexible subcontractors and service providers. In the face of the uncertainties and difficulties of the current conjuncture, the systems houses are downsizing with great alacrity and are now beginning to compete aggressively for short-run gains (as opposed to efforts to create more stable long-run relations with suppliers, customers, and workers). Defense firms face the additional problem of trying to wean themselves from a technological and managerial culture that has been geared above all to cost-plus pricing, and they must now deal more resolutely with the hard realities of commercial (and internationalized) markets.

A further downward spiral has been observable in many segments of the Southern Californian economy over the last few decades. At various points in the industrial system, a relentlessly cutthroat and virtually unregulated competitive environment has led to the development of an immense and expanding sweatshop system in many of the industries serving core high-technology producers, e.g., in electronics assembly, printed circuits production, plastics molding, metal fabrication, machining, and so on. The same trend is apparent in many of the low-technology, labor-intensive industries of the region such as furniture, clothing, and jewelry. Within this system, low skills, low wages, and price gouging are the watchwords, and in many cases outputs compete to an ever-increasing degree not with the world's highest-quality producers, but with the lowest. We may add to this litany of problems the crisis of local government in Southern California, where a disjointed and irrational mosaic of seven counties and close to 200 municipalities attempt to manage an urban region whose dense internal interdependencies extend far beyond the bounds of any single local administrative unit. It is true that some effort has been made to deal with the most egregious problems of collective regional order by the formation of special-purpose agencies (like the Metropolitan Water District of Southern California or the South Coast Air Quality Management District). These, however, are at best stopgap measures that cannot substitute for a coherent and coordinated administrative apparatus with a clear and focused overview of the region's problems as a whole. It would seem, in short, that some form of regional government is long overdue, and any such rationalization would be beneficial for industrial growth because it would facilitate overall harmonization of urban development projects across the whole region.

In the absence of a concerted attack on these difficulties and dilemmas, Southern California's high-technology industrial economy—despite a number of bright spots like the medical device industry or the emerging biotechnology industry—could conceivably go from bad to worse. One possible scenario of future trends might envisage massive closure of defense-industry plants combined with the ascendancy of a hyperflexible production complex characterized by a widening circle of sweatshops, deteriorating work conditions, erosion of the region's skill base, and continued falling wage rates for the majority of industrial workers. Indeed, elements of this Dickensian vision are already firmly in place, with widespread press reports of a resurgence of child labor to complete the picture. Cases are legion of formerly thriving industrial agglomerations that have started to unwind because they could no longer find ways of dealing with mounting internal and external threats. The Birmingham gun industry in the 1850s is one such case, as are the Ulster linen industry in the 1960s and the Detroit car industry in the 1970s and 1980s. There is no reason why Southern California should be absolved in principle from this possible fate. But can there be ways in practice of achieving its antithesis? To begin the task of addressing this question, one needs to stand back to a significant degree from the particular case of high-technology industry in Southern California, and to examine the problem of regional policy and strategic choice in general. Most especially, we must consider the new problems of regional development that have been brought to the fore as flexible production organization and economic globalization have simultaneously left their indelible marks on contemporary capitalism.

REGIONAL POLICIES IN NORTH AMERICA AND
WESTERN EUROPE: A BRIEF HISTORICAL CONSPECTUS

In the immediate postwar decades—as we saw briefly in chapter 2—patterns of regional development in North America and Western Europe took on a highly distinctive form. On the one hand, there was a set of dynamic industrial-urban regions whose economies were concentrated on large-scale fordist mass production; on the other hand, there was a peripheral and subservient set of agricultural regions and older industrial regions (such as Appalachia or the Central Valley of Scotland) whose economic bases were stagnant or declining. This was an era in which regional development theorists such as Hirschman (1958) and Myrdal (1957) argued that the core regions tended to sweep up skills, talents, and resources from peripheral regions, with countervailing (but far from compensating) flows of low-wage, de-skilled branch plants from the core to the periphery.

In the period of fordist mass production, regional problems were for the most part conceived of in terms of these apparently stubborn disparities between core and peripheral regions, and regional policy in much of North America and Western Europe was thus focused on attempts at geographical redistribution and equalization (Camagni et al. 1990). Various governmental bodies (such as the EDA in the U.S., DREE in Canada, the DEA in Britain, DATAR in France, and the Cassa per il Mezzogiorno in Italy) were directed to deal with this problem, and a wide range of administrative and statutory measures was deployed. These attempted in one way or another to reduce regional development disparities, especially by seeking to stimulate growth in lagging regions by means of infrastructure investments, capital subsidies, and worker retraining programs. In some cases (e.g., Fos-sur-Mer in France, and parts of the Third World) efforts were made to create important new industrial growth centers, though with very limited success. Indeed, while regional policy in general in the fordist era undoubtedly achieved some marginal improvement in the economic well-being of peripheral areas, on the whole it did remarkably little to turn the tide of growth away from core industrial regions.

That said, by the early 1970s, many of the major manufacturing sectors in core areas were clearly in difficulties, and planners in a number of countries now began to withdraw from geographically redistributive measures. Instead, increasing attention was paid to industrial rationalization (as in the case of the Industrial Reorganization Corporation in Britain), and to the fostering of "national champions" (such as Renault in France) which were to be the vanguard of a new economic offensive. The death knell of redistributive regional policy was sounded by the aggressively neoconservative governments that came to power in several of the major capitalist countries in the late 1970s and early 1980s, unleashing waves of privatization and deregulatory activity (Alonso 1989; Martin 1989; Wren 1990). As central authorities sought to reduce their commitments to redistribution, localities were to an increasing degree left to fend for themselves, and many of them responded by now seeking to lure investment capital by whatever means were at their disposal, often in an assertively entrepreneurial way (Goodman 1979; Harvey 1989; Wiewel et al. 1984). The 1980s was a period in which many localities saw their salvation in high-technology industry, and the problem of "growing the next Silicon Valley" was firmly ensconced on the policy agenda (Clarke 1990; Miller and Cote 1987; Peltz and Weiss 1984; Rees and Lewington 1990; Schmandt and Wilson 1987). Efforts were made in several quarters to provide a theoretical comprehension of the problem by means of a rediscovered "location factors" approach to economic geography in which it was suggested that certain critical catalysts—military bases, a research university, a science park, venture-capital resources, recreational facilities and amenities, access to international airports, and all the rest—would spark off local high-technology industrial growth (Markusen et al. 1986; OTA 1984; Premus 1982). Numerous state and local governments actually tried to pursue policies based on this approach, and if these sometimes succeeded in persuading firms to locate new facilities in their jurisdictions, they for the most part failed to accomplish their wider goals of sustained economic development. A major factor underlying this failure is that it is extraordinarily difficult to identify dynamic new sectors of production *before* they have started to grow, and yet once growth has begun and agglomerative forces have set in, the chances of creating a new agglomeration elsewhere are much diminished, for the first-mover advantages and localized external economies that accrue to the original case help to crowd out late imitators (cf. Arthur 1988, 1990; David 1985; Scott and Storper 1992). The entrepreneurial regional policy efforts of the 1980s were fairly consistently a case of *much too little far too late*. Moreover, the pursuit of a finite quantum of industrial growth by many different public agencies is in the end a zero-sum game whose costs tend to be far in excess of the benefits.

This entrepreneurial phase is by no means over even yet in North America and Western Europe, though its meager results and the growing awareness that its main beneficiaries are company stockholders rather than local interests is currently encouraging much reconsideration. As flexible production organization begins to supplant mass production as the leading edge of capitalist development, a clearer sense of the difficulties of radical local economic transformation seems to be in the air, and more realistic attempts to build incrementally on what already exists are now a major focus of attention. This situation is underscored by the widening internationalization of production and markets, and the imperative of maintaining the competitiveness not so much of lagging regions as of leading regions. In this, the needs of growing flexible production agglomerations have become paramount. Thus, innumerable trial efforts in institution-building and social regulation directed to heightened innovativeness and the search for superior product quality in such agglomerations are now on foot in many different countries, e.g., the United States (cf. Ahlbrandt 1990; Osborne 1988), France (Benko 1991; de Bernardy and Boisgontier 1990; OECD 1985), Germany (cf. Sabel et al. 1987; Sternberg 1989, 1990), Italy (cf. Bianchi 1992; Martinelli 1989), Japan (cf. Dore 1986, 1987; Friedmann 1988), and other parts of the world. An extensive but scattered corpus of theoretical speculation about the appropriate forms and functions of collective action in flexible-production agglomerations has also started to unfold. Some stock-taking seems to be in order.

FLEXIBLE-PRODUCTION AGGLOMERATIONS IN NORTH AMERICA AND WESTERN EUROPE

While many older industrial regions in North America and Western Europe remain economically active, there is a widening domain of industrial regions that were largely marginal to fordist industrialization processes, and that have now come to the fore as major growth centers. The latter regions are to be found especially (but not exclusively) in the Sunbelt, as in the cases of Southern California, Silicon Valley, Phoenix, Austin, and so on, and in selected parts of Western Europe, such as the Third Italy, much of southern Germany, and the Scientific City of the Paris Basin. We might also include in our catalog selected regions in an assortment of newly industrializing countries, such as Hong Kong, Singapore, Taiwan, and Brazil. The economic bases of these regions consist primarily of flexibly organized production sectors, and above all, of a wide selection of both high-technology and artisanal industries. Frequently, such complexes give evidence of potent entrepreneurial and innovative energies stemming from the very intensity of interaction between local producers. They also tend to be associated with quite heterogeneous local labor markets comprising many different kinds of skills and human attributes.

As suggested by much of the discussion in this book, the flexible-production agglomerations that come into being in this manner are often, in their internal workings, extremely competitive and uncertain places. They usually contain many producers in several different subsectors, linked together in transactional systems that may be subject to rapid and continual change; and their local labor markets are invariably quite fluid as a result of limited security of job tenure and the ups and downs of production. Friedman and Friedman (1980) have suggested that these sorts of market conditions are a sine qua non of efficiency and growth, and they have proposed that Hong Kong—where flexible production organization is particularly well developed—be taken as a prime exemplar of what a rational economic order ought to be. As I shall argue at length below, however, flexible-production agglomerations that approximate to this normative laissez-faire vision are liable to suboptimal outcomes, both because of their susceptibility to severe internal market failure and because there are demonstrably superior benefits to be obtained by judicious mixes of competition and cooperation. Thus, such agglomerations are also likely to face deepening predicaments as their outputs come face-to-face on national and international markets with similar outputs from agglomerations whose problems of system coordination are being addressed. Indeed, some of the leading flexible-production agglomerations today are permeated with institutions of collective order, or what Bianchi (1992) has called "intangible assets." Furthermore, as Castells et al. (1991) have forcefully indicated, even Hong Kong has enjoyed the success it has largely because it has been subject to enormous collective control on two critical fronts: in the first place, all land is publicly owned, thus stabilizing the Colony's finances and facilitating planning of the land-development process; in the second place, high-quality public housing is supplied in massive amounts out of the governmental revenues from land, and this subsidizes wages and helps to underpin Hong Kong's remarkable political quiescence. In any case, competition can never be "pure" as though it were nothing more than an anonymous confrontation between faceless buyers and sellers haggling, short-term, over a counter. Rather, competition itself is commonly and variously structured by institutional and cultural frameworks that tie buyers and sellers together in customary ties of familiarity, reciprocity, and legal obligation. This, in turn, encourages forms of cooperation that often enhance the comparative economic advantages of particular industrial localities.

The problem of institutional order in flexible-production agglomerations is threefold: it involves questions of scale, scope, and strategic choice. Let us deal with each in turn. First, in the matter of scale, individual firms are often too small to provide internally for themselves certain critical services (e.g., marketing, accounting, R&D). Nevertheless, as a group they may well constitute a critical mass that when mobilized could secure an appropriate supply of such services. Second, the scope of each agglomeration (i.e., its internal sectoral variety) is characteristically very wide, and significant synergies flow from the manifold interactions engendered by this state of affairs. Various forms of social coordination may be critical here in order to secure optimal flows of information and to ensure minimal fiduciary standards in transacting behavior. Third, because each agglomeration is also made up of masses of interdependent establishments and workers, structures of governance will be essential in order to steer the system over time, all the more so as trajectories of development tend to become locked in once they are established, and hence care must be exercised to ensure that developmental choices that may be promising in the short run but deleterious in the long run are avoided. Of course, some of the problems alluded to here may be resolvable by means of interstitial entrepreneurial activity (as in the cases of private R&D laboratories, credit bureaus, employment agencies, and so on). Sometimes, however, market failures impede the emergence of this kind of spontaneous entrepreneurial activity so that other kinds of responses are called for, while in other cases even better results can be obtained by alternative nonmarket rules of order, especially where these build upon existing social and cultural conditions.

COLLECTIVE ACTION AND STRATEGIC CHOICE IN FLEXIBLE-PRODUCTION AGGLOMERATIONS

A brief revisitation of the theory of transactions costs helps to reinforce the argument advanced in the previous section. Neoclassical equilibrium theory considers all economic behavior as the competitive action of independent and irreducible firms and households, with transactions between them governed by markets and price signals. Transactions cost theory takes its point of departure in the idea that in addition to the market, there are hierarchically organized economic agents with intraorganizational transactions being carried out by non-market forms of negotiation and command. Firms, in this view, are constituted as vertically integrated units of governance, with a relatively stable configuration of their aliquot parts. As already suggested, transactions-cost theory also makes it clear that in addition to purely market and purely hierarchical forms of economic activity, there are viable intermediate institutional arrangements that combine varying degrees of centralized and decentralized decision making. Japanese *keiretsu*, multidivisional corporations, joint ventures, and strategic alliances belong to this intermediate category; so too do such organizations as trade associations, private-industry councils, fair-practice committees, and so on. It is possible, then (and is in fact invariably the case) that overall economic efficiency will be achieved by way of a mixture of market structures, hierarchical organizations, and hybrid formations, though what precise mixture is most desirable in any given case still remains an open question. Note, in passing, that this argument does not even (yet) take into account the desideratum of collective intervention to secure noneconomic, social goals.

In part, the emergence of nonmarket or quasimarket forms of economic coordination depends on the fact that the assumptions under which perfect competition and hence theoretically optimal resource allocation can occur (i.e., full information, freedom of entry and exit, convertibility of sunk investments, absence of externalities, and so on) are never fully realized in practice. In part, it also hinges on the circumstance that under certain conditions, the very existence of competitive markets undercuts or subverts the possibility of efficient outcomes. For example, the imperfect appropriability of knowledge often discourages firms from investing in research that would otherwise be beneficial to them, just as the potential mobility of labor may make firms reluctant to divert resources into worker training. Similarly, because of the possibility of fraud in some kinds of contractual arrangements, firms may choose to internalize activities that might under other circumstances be more efficiently externalized. Without some structure of governance transcending market relations, problems like these will undermine overall productivity. Such a structure, if it is well designed, will capture latent positive externalities and will diminish or eliminate negative externalities, and what is more, the design can, in principle at least, be fine-tuned to the needs of particular agglomerations. Likewise, given the nature of much innovative activity where continual marginal improvements in product and process configurations occur as firms interact with one another in the course of business, institutional arrangements that allow them to share more of their knowledge and expertise without fear of competitive danger will be apt to yield significant improvements in economic performance (cf. Dertouzos et al. 1989; Florida and Kenny 1990; Sabel 1990). From these remarks it seems likely that flexible production agglomerations— as potentially productive as they may be—do not have high chances of survival in the new global economy if their economies are tilted too far in the direction of purely competitive markets. In the absence of appropriate kinds of collective order, they are prone to self-destruction or inertia, as was evidently the case in the 1970s and 1980s with the north London furniture industry (Best 1989), or the textile and clothing industries of the French Choletais (Courlet and Pecqueur 1992; Renard 1989). But what, we might ask, constitutes appropriate kinds of collective order? Without in any sense attempting to address this question exhaustively, let us attempt to advance the discussion by considering five main types.

1. R&D and the transformation of research results into commercializable products is an endemic problem, both for high- and low-technology sectors. One important means of attacking the problem is by the public provision of agglomeration-specific innovation centers, and this approach is in fact now being widely adopted in many parts of North America and Western Europe (Benko 1991). Examples are the highly successful CONNECT program at the University of California, San Diego, which intermediates between university researchers and the local biotechnology industry, or Pennsylvania's Ben Franklin Partnership, formed in 1982, which successfully stimulated 208 new startups in its first thirty months of operation (Allen and Levine 1986). An example of a similar kind of activity serving low-technology industry is the Emilia-Romagna Textiles Information Center (CITER), a limited-liability consortium that supplies its subscribers with information on textile machinery and equipment, fashion trends, and market opportunities.

2. The creation and upgrading of labor skills are also major concerns in flexible-production agglomerations, as is the encouragement

of relevant forms of worker socialization. The latter activity is particularly important insofar as modern flexible-production activities frequently seek to incorporate the worker as an actively creative agent into the labor process. These objectives may be attained through apprenticeship programs, vocational training schemes, local universities, and so on, and institutions such as these play an important role in industrial localities today. This is also a domain of collective action in which labor unions can and do play an important part.

3. Many firms in modern flexible-production agglomerations are unable efficiently to internalize such basic services as accounting, design, payroll preparation, marketing information, and the like. However, precisely because they are geographically agglomerated, it is often feasible to provide these services on a collective basis. Business associations and municipalities in the craft-industrial districts of the Third Italy have excelled in making such services available to local firms. In particular, the marketing and export associations that operate throughout the Third Italy have been extremely successful in projecting local products onto world markets, despite the fact that the actual producers themselves are generally quite small in size.

4. As shown above, cooperative interactions between firms in industrial agglomerations can be a significant stimulus to innovation and continual technological upgrading. Japanese firms have carried this sort of cooperation particularly far. Just-in-time processing networks linking Japanese producers and their subcontractors ensure not only a dramatic acceleration in the rotation of circulating capital, but also a means of sharing technological information and market risk in a high-trust environment. Joint ventures, strategic alliances, trade associations, and the like also help to provide environments within which these sorts of interfirm synergies can develop (Humphrey et al. 1989; Storper and Harrison 1991). An outstanding example of this phenomenon is the socioindustrial networks of Baden-Würtemberg, described by Sabel et al. (1987) where trade associations, banks, labor unions, research institutes, vocational schools, and other groups have succeeded by their joint efforts and interaction in maintaining high levels of industrial performance. Sabel (1990) has also characterized Pennsylvania's Manufacturing Innovation Networks Program, established in 1989, as a conscious effort to create active synergies through public sponsorship of interfirm information networks.

5. Industrial agglomerations, by their nature, are typically located within units of local government, which play a crucial role in manag-

ing the systemic market failures and externalities endemic to dense concentrations of land use. This role involves both traditional functions of local government, such as infrastructure provision and land-use planning, but may also extend into more novel forms of activity such as the laying out and operation of science parks, the underwriting of venture-capital activities, the organization of worker-training programs, the formation of private-public development corporations, and so on. Again, the municipalities of the Third Italy have been in the vanguard of this sort of intervention, as in the case of the carefully planned industrial estates developed by the municipality of Modena, or the telematic network (SPRINT) linking together firms within the woolen textile-manufacturing district of Prato, and financed in part by local government. And of course the Japanese technopolis program represents a major experiment in the conscious public creation of industrial growth centers, though with what ultimate degree of success remains to be seen (Masser 1990; Tatsuno 1986). These are all domains of activity in which a putative regional government in Southern California could play a major role.

In all of the above arguments, I have emphasized the idea that flexible-production agglomerations in modern capitalism cannot persist in the long run by seeking to evolve in the direction of some idealized vision of laissez-faire competition. On the contrary, there is much evidence, both in theory and practice, to suggest that it is precisely those agglomerations that manage to build for themselves a complementary fabric of institutional and cultural infrastructures that are most viable and dynamic. Concomitantly, decaying agglomerations might in principle be revivable by local economic-development policies based on the principles adduced above, though again there can be no guarantees of success, as the experience of the Greater London Enterprise Board during the 1980s illustrates (Best 1989; Eisenschitz and North 1986). There does not seem to be any strict formula for prescribing the shape and form of these infrastructures, beyond the broad recommendation that each agglomeration must find its own best compromise—consistent with local social conditions—between competition and cooperation. In some instances these infrastructures will be provided by governmental agencies, in others by private groups and associations, and in yet others by various sorts of quasimarket organizations. If it is indeed the case that the "new competition" is going to be dominated by those manufacturers who can continuously innovate, constantly improve product quality (even at the expense of rising prices), breed new labor skills, and secure the creative collaboration of workers in production—as opposed to relentless price-cutting, deskilling, and product standardization—then the kinds of collective action described above are going to have to be taken seriously (Best 1990; Cohen and Zysman 1987). In a recent book, Florida and Kenny (1990) have gone so far as to describe the sorts of unrestricted competition associated with places like Silicon Valley as a destructive war of attrition, and they have suggested as a remedy the need for higher levels of internalization of production in larger firms. Oddly, however, they do not consider a third and possibly more effective alternative—whose lineaments are in any case already beginning to emerge in Silicon Valley as Saxenian (1990) has argued—which is to stimulate habits of cooperation by means of collective action and programs of social coordination, and thus to combine the merits of the small entrepreneurial firm with the strategic capacities of the large organization.

All of this discussion about remedial intervention in industrial agglomerations presupposes that we are dealing with places where industrialization is in some sense already under way. What of places that have not yet begun to grow and where industrial development on any significant scale remains only a prospective vision? Is it possible to deploy policies that will create new agglomerations *ex nihilo*? The kinds of institution-building described above are not likely to be of much avail in this regard. Certainly, and to repeat, where an agglomeration of a particular sort has already risen to the fore, its first-mover advantages and external economies probably make it unwise to attempt to clone similar agglomerations elsewhere. This is not to say that underdeveloped regions should simply be abandoned. Where there are local endowments of special kinds (e.g., particular sorts of craft skills, potentialities for tourism and resort development,[2] or an existing industrial structure onto which new forms of manufacturing activity can be grafted) then there are real possibilities of building a developmental process on these foundations. But where such initial advantages are lacking, only massive, concerted, and extremely expensive action by central government authorities is likely to produce results, and even then, as the experience of regional development programs in the period of fordism suggests, the net effects are apt to be ambiguous. Rather than aiming for the impossible and probably undesirable vision

2. Tourist resorts typically display all the features of flexible-production agglomerations, and probably more than any other sort of agglomeration they are dependent for their prosperity on socially agreed-upon quality-control standards.

of industrial growth for all regions, some means of spreading the benefits of locationally differential growth needs to be found—a sentiment that suggests that some sort of redistributive regional policy may well be firmly back on the agenda if current trends continue.

By way of summing up the entire discussion thus far, let us consider a practical example of local collective action and attempts at regional development, namely, emerging plans and coalitions to create and sustain an electric-car industry in Southern California. If an electric-car industry is successfully launched in the region, this could help to absorb some of the excess productive capacity and labor that has been created as the aerospace-electronics industries continue to decline. The challenge represents, in addition, a critical laboratory experiment that could provide much useful practical experience in the tasks of collective action and organizational restructuring for the purposes of local economic development.

LOCAL ECONOMIC DEVELOPMENT AND STRATEGIC CHOICE IN ACTION: A PROSPECTIVE ELECTRIC-CAR INDUSTRY FOR SOUTHERN CALIFORNIA?

Of all the world's major urban regions, Southern California is close to being the one that will benefit most in environmental terms from the development of alternative-fuel vehicles. Several different technologies are currently contending in the race to replace the gasoline-powered car, but it is the electric car that seems most likely eventually to attain commercial supremacy while meeting increasingly stringent emissions criteria. If Southern California will unquestionably benefit from the electric car in environmental terms, might it not also make some claim on the employment opportunities that will flow from this new technology?

An electric-car industry is by all accounts on the verge of making its appearance in the United States, and in its early phases of development the industry is likely primarily to serve small-scale niche markets, and to adopt highly flexible production technologies and organizational forms in order to allow it maximum latitude of maneuver (Morales et al. 1991). This means that the industry will in all probability be vertically disintegrated, and that it will be linked to a dense network of many different subcontractors and specialized service providers. As the industry grows, it may retain this disintegrated configuration, or, more probably, it may evolve into a flexible mass-production sector in the style of modern Japanese car manufacturers with well-organized just-in-time relations to a streamlined hierarchy of upstream suppliers. In either case, the industry is likely to be marked by definite locational agglomeration.

The eventual development of such an industry in the near future is scarcely in doubt at this point. Already, prototype manufacturing is under way in many different parts of the world, and a number of firms have announced plans to embark on production for final consumer markets. The major questions for present purposes are, where will the main concentration(s) of production occur, and within what sorts of collective frameworks? One obvious and plausible answer to these questions is: somewhere in Japan under the institutional umbrella already worked out by major Japanese car producers in association with various governmental agencies. Another possible response is: in the Northeast of the United States where domestic car producers are grappling with the problem of building manufacturing systems capable of meeting the Japanese competition on equal terms. General Motors has actually announced that it is planning to manufacture an electric car (the Impact) at its Reatta plant in East Lansing, Michigan. What chances, then, does Southern California have of becoming a major world center of electric-car production?

In the first place, the electric car is sufficiently different from the gasoline-powered car in terms of its internal workings, materials, and basic design that it almost certainly cannot be made in existing car-production plants without radical retooling and retraining. This suggests that there may be a small but significant window of locational opportunity for the new industry, and that it is not irredeemably anchored to existing car-producing regions. In the second place, Southern California is already one of the world's major centers of automobile design, and it has an enormous aerospace/industrial complex with many subjacent sectors that could fairly easily be converted to making products for the electric-car industry. Particularly relevant are the numerous plastics-molding firms, foundries, machine shops, tool and die manufacturers, and electronics components producers already located in Southern California. As a corollary, Southern California also has a significant pool of skilled engineering and technical workers. In the third place, there is a powerful coalition of local groups now materializing in Southern California with the objective of mobilizing the public interest in favor of supporting an electric-car industry in the region.

Much of the impetus behind the initial formation of this coalition can be traced to the long-term commitment by state and local authorities to reducing air pollution in Southern California. Part can also be traced to the realization in the region that defense spending is likely to continue to decline dramatically over the next several years with deleterious effects on employment in the local aerospace-electronics industry. The collective momentum already achieved is based on the participation of politicians at all levels of government (including the congressional delegation), powerful local agencies like the utility companies and the South Coast Air Quality Management District, lobbying groups like the Southern California Chamber of Commerce and the Aerospace Task Force (an informal association of aerospace manufacturers sponsored by the Community Development Commission of Los Angeles County), and major academic institutions like UCLA, the University of California, and the California Institute of Technology, which are all engaged in different aspects of research into the electric car. In 1989 the Los Angeles City Council adopted an initiative, through its Department of Water and Power, to sponsor the production of at least 5,000 electric passenger cars and 5,000 electric vans by 1995. Three companies were selected out of the eighteen that responded to the initiative, and one of these (a Swedish-British venture named Clean Air Transport) is now under contract to produce a hybrid gasoline-electric car, with some $7 million in financing provided by the Department of Water and Power and matching funds from private sources. Clean Air Transport is now engaged in prototype manufacturing in England, and a production facility is being planned for Southern California some time in 1992 or 1993. Amerigon is another venture that has announced intentions to manufacture electric cars in the region in the near future, and the firm is now being funded by the South Coast Air Quality Management District to produce a demonstration car using only local inputs.

Over the next few years, we are likely to see a variety of private and public efforts devoted to the development of this infant industry in Southern California. In addition to the lobbying efforts and political support reported in the previous paragraph, there may well be further evidence of a wider public commitment in the form, perhaps, of an electric-vehicle technology and manufacturing consortium (perhaps funded out of the federal Advanced Transportation Systems and Electric Vehicle Consortia Act of 1991), a publicly supported vehicle test track, local (as well as federal) legislation that will make it more expensive to operate gasoline-powered cars, and so on. There is thus a possibility that a new industrial complex may begin to take shape in Southern California over the next several years, though this possibility is unlikely to materialize without a further consolidation of the collective efforts already described. In the absence of such efforts, the industry is no more likely to grow in Southern California than in a score of other places with similar or even superior initial endowments. Even then, continued public exertions will no doubt be necessary to maintain the industry's competitive edge.

Should Southern California indeed manage to accomplish an early start in building an electric-car industry, its first-mover advantages would certainly help it ward off competitive threats from other and later entrants. By the same token, without an early start, the energies that have so far been devoted to the problem will in all probability have been stillborn. The translation of these speculative visions into a flourishing electric-car industry in the region represents a test case of and an object lesson in the theoretical ideas adumbrated above.

SOUTHERN CALIFORNIA AND THE NEW WORLD ORDER

I have contended that the long-run success of production agglomerations—like the Southern Californian technopolis—depends on their ability to build appropriate institutional frameworks to complement their central competitive tendencies. This is neither an appeal to some romantic vision of community, nor a call for central authority to keep inefficient industries running. It is a reasoned view about the underlying organizational-cum-locational tendencies of modern capitalism, and a series of deductions about how these tendencies may be harnessed to maximum advantage. There are, of course, many different ways of seeking to combine markets and institutions of collective order in particular places, and the initiation of the latent debate implied by this observation is long overdue. Inaction, by default or design, is the worst of all possible worlds, particularly as the region is now facing a critical turning point in its history, and it is entirely conceivable that a failure to act could lead to a real deterioration of Southern California's manufacturing base.

If the analysis presented here is correct, it suggests that we will in all probability witness—if not in Southern California then certainly in many other industrialized and industrializing regions in the world—a trend to concerted institution-building in the interests of enhanced competitive advantage. Indeed, the trend is already under way in most of the advanced capitalist economies and in many of the newly industrializing countries too. There will also assuredly be an escalation in the perceptible tendency for places to compete economically with one another as collectivities and not just as sets of individual and uncoordinated actors, which means that those not equipped with a suitable superstructure of institutions are running high risks of being left behind (Cox and Mair 1988; Humphrey et al. 1989; Molotch 1976). On this basis the world's industrial regions will no doubt trade more and more aggressively with one another in manufactured goods and services, while most of the left-behinds will struggle against increasing odds simply to retain their existing industrial capacity or to initiate the process of local economic development. On the other side of the coin, international systems of social regulation are coming into being at a rapid pace, and these may help to palliate some of the least-desirable aspects of the new world economic geography that is now taking shape, and provide forums for periodic adjustment of the most pernicious kinds of problems. This emerging new order of things will lead to new political tasks and alignments, new forms of regional economic activity, and eventually, no doubt, to new attempts to reformulate local economic development policies and strategies.

Appendices

Appendix A: The Calculation of Total Employment in Large Establishments

For the purposes of this analysis, a large establishment is defined as any individual manufacturing plant that employs 500 or more workers. Data on the number of establishments by establishment-size grouping and by SIC category are available on a county-by-county basis from *County Business Patterns*, published annually by the U.S. Department of Commerce. The same publication provides information on total employment by SIC category and by county. Establishment-size groupings are given by *County Business Patterns* as 1–4, 5–9, 10–19, 20–49, 50–99, 100–249, 250–499, 500–999, and 1,000+ employees.

Let us define (a) x_{ij} as the number of establishments in the ith employment-size grouping and the jth SIC category, (b) m_i as the median value of the upper and lower bounds of the ith employment-size grouping, and (c) E_j as total employment in the jth SIC category. For category j, employment in the largest (open-ended) size grouping—which is given as establishments with 1,000 and more employees—can be computed as $E_{Lj} = E_j - \sum X_{ij}m_i$ (for $i = 1, 2, \ldots, n-1$), subject to the evident condition that $E_{Lj} \geq 1000x_{Lj}$. Where the computation does not satisfy this condition (due to variations of actual establishment sizes and calculated median values) we set $E_{Lj} = 1000x_{Lj}$ and readjust all values of m_i systematically downwards to ensure consistency. To obtain aggregate employment in all establishments with 500 or more employees, we now simply add together estimated employment in plants with 1,000 or more employees and estimated employment in plants in the size-grouping 500–999 (using the median or adjusted median for this latter operation). These procedures are not entirely satisfactory, and in particular no method of identifying gross overestimates of E_{Lj} is provided, but they seem to be the best that can be accomplished given the information available.

A further problem of the estimation procedure is that it has some tendency to exaggerate growth in the large-establishment sector in times of rising employment and to exaggerate decline in times of falling employment. When employment levels rise, some establishments will be reassigned from the smaller establishment-size grouping to the larger, and when employment levels fall, some establishments will be reassigned downwards. Such reassignments will thus surreptitiously magnify cyclical trends.

Fortunately, the recommended estimation procedure does not seem to result in undue bias. This judgment is supported by the observation that the percentage of high-technology workers employed in the large-establishment sector correlates extremely significantly with (a) the number of establishments with 500 or more workers as a percentage of all establishments ($r = 0.79$), and (b) average size of establishment ($r = 0.84$). Note that the former of these two variables is also subject to exaggerated cyclical amplitude, but that the latter is not.

It must be added that *County Business Patterns* occasionally suppresses total employment data for reasons of confidentiality, and instead gives estimates in terms of minimum and maximum ranges. Where this is the case, total employment has been estimated as the median value of the given range.

Program	Type	Start	End	Agency	Prime Contractor(s) (Southern Californian contractors set bold)
A-3A/B	LV	1950	1955	Army	General Electric
Honest John	Tactical	1950	1978	Army	**Douglas Aircraft**
AIM-4(A-G) Falcon	AIM	1950	1990	AF/Navy	**Hughes**
M-9A/B Sidewinder	AIM	1951	1962	Navy	Philco (**Ford**)/Raytheon
BOMARC A	SAM	1951	1965	USAF	Boeing/Michigan Aeronautical Research Labs
Redstone	MRBM/LV	1951	1962	Army	Chrysler
Petrel	Anti-sub	1952	1958	Navy	Fairchild Aircraft
Grebe	Anti-sub	1952	1956	Navy	Goodyear Missile Div.
Regulus II	SLCM	1953	1964	Navy	Chance Vought (LTV)
Atlas (A-D)	ICBM/LV	1953	1964	AF/NASA	**Convair (GD-Pomona)**
Nike-Ajax	SAM	1953	1958	Army	**Western Electric/Douglas**
ASM-N-7 Bullpup	AGM	1954	1960	Navy/AF	Martin-Orlando Div.
Mace	ICBM	1954	1965	USAF	Martin Co.
Typhon	SAM	1954	1963	Navy	**Douglas Aircraft/Bendix**
Nike-Zeus	SAM	1954	1960	Army	**Western Electric/Douglas**
Wagtail	AGM	1954	1958	USAF	*Minneapolis-Honeywell*
Hound Dog	AGM	1955	1963	USAF	**North American-Downey**
SUBROC	Anti-sub	1955	1990	Navy	Goodyear Aerospace
Lacrosse	Tactical	1955	1962	USMC	Cornell Aero Labs/Martin

APPENDIX B (cont.)

Program	Type	Start	End	Agency	Prime Contractor(s) (Southern Californian contractors set bold)
Thor	IRBM	1955	1962	AF/NASA	**Douglas Aircraft (Santa Monica)**
Sergeant	Tactical	1955	1978	Army	**Jet Propulsion Lab/Sperry**
Utah AIM-2A Genie	AIM	1955	1962	USAF	**Douglas/McDonnell Douglas**
Juno I	LV	1956	1960	Army	Chrysler
Juno II	LV	1956	1960	Army	Chrysler
Agena (A-D)	LV	1956	1990	AF/NASA	Lockheed Missiles & Space
GAM-67 Crossbow	AGM	1956	1960	USAF	**Radioplane (Northrop)**
AIM-26A/B Falcon	AIM	1956	1979	USAF	**Hughes**
Tartar	SAM	1956	1968	Navy	**Convair (GD Pomona)**
ASROC	Anti-sub	1956	1990	Navy	Honeywell
Little John	Tactical	1956	1962	Army	Redstone Arsenal/Emerson
ASM-N-8 Corvus	AGM	1957	1960	Navy	Temco Aircraft-Dallas
Eagle	AIM	1957	1960	Navy	Bendix Systems Div.
Polaris A1	SLBM	1957	1965	Navy	Lockheed Missiles & Space
AIM-47A Falcon	AIM	1958	1986	USAF	**Hughes**
Minuteman I	ICBM	1958	1969	USAF	Boeing Aircraft Co.
Hawk	SAM	1958	1978	Army	Raytheon
Nike-Hercules	SAM	1958	1974	Army	**Western Electric/Douglas**
Jupiter	IRBM	1958	1961	Army	Army Ballistic Missile
Agency Little Joe	LV	1958	NA	NASA	Redstone Arsenal

Centaur	LV	1959	AF/NASA	General Dynamics-Convair
Saturn I	LV	1959	NASA	Chrysler/McDonnell Douglas
Delta	LV	1959	NASA	McDonnell Douglas
Atlas-Able	LV	1959	AF/NASA	Convair/Lockheed Missile and Space Division
BOMARC B	SAM	1959	USAF	Boeing
AGM-28A/B Skybolt	AGM	1959	USAF	Douglas Aircraft
Atlas-Centaur	ICBM/LV	1959	NASA	General Dynamics
MGM-51 Shillelagh	AIM	1959	Army	Aeronutronic (Ford)
Redeye	SAM	1959	Army	Convair (GD-Pomona)
AGM-12E Bullpup	AGM	1959	USAF	Martin-Orlando
AIM-54A Phoenix	AIM	1960	Navy	Hughes
Atlas E	ICBM/LV	1960	NASA	Convair (GD Pomona)
Pershing	Tactical	1960	Army	Martin-Orlando Div.
AGM-12B Bullpup A	AGM	1960	Navy/AF	Martin-Orlando/W. L. Maxson
AIM-9G Sidewinder	AIM	1961	Navy	Aeronutronic (Ford)
AIM-9D/E Sidewinder	AIM	1961	Navy	Aeronutronic (Ford)
Atlas SLV-3/3A/3C	LV	1961	NASA/AF	Convair (GD-Pomona)
AGM-45A/B Shrike	AGM	1961	Navy/AF	Texas Instruments/Sperry/Naval Weapons Center–China Lake
Centaur D-1A/D1T	LV	1961	NASA	Convair (General Dynamics)
Saturn V-5D	LV	1961	NASA	Martin Co.
AIM-9C Sidewinder	AIM	1961	Navy	Motorola
Saturn S-II	Booster	1962	NASA	Rockwell Space Division

APPENDIX B *(cont.)*

Program	Type	Start	End	Agency	Prime Contractor(s) (Southern Californian contractors set bold)
Saturn S-IC	Booster	1962	NA	NASA	Boeing
Saturn V	LV	1962	1973	NASA	**Boeing/Rockwell/McDonnell Douglas**
Titan I	ICBM	1962	1965	USAF	Martin-Denver
Lance	Anti-tank	1962	1979	Army	Vought
Polaris A2	SLBM	1962	1973	Navy	Lockheed Missiles and Space Div.
Lance	Tactical	1962	1979	Army	Vought (LTV)-Michigan
Saturn IB	LV	1962	1968	NASA	**Chrysler/McDonnell Douglas**
Saturn S-IVB	LV	1962	NA	NASA	**McDonnell Douglas**
AGM-12C Bullpup B	AGM	1962	1980	USAF	Martin-Orlando
AGM-12D Bullpup	AGM	1962	1980	USAF	Martin-Marietta
Safeguard	ABM	1963	1975	AF/Navy	**McDonnell Douglas Astronautics**
Standard MR	SAM	1963	NA	Navy	**Convair (GD Pomona)**
Standard ER	SAM	1963	NA	Navy	**Convair (GD Pomona)**
Titan II	ICBM	1963	1990	USAF	Hill AFB/Martin-Marietta
Gemini-Titan II	LV	1963	1967	NASA	Martin Co.-Baltimore
AGM-62 Walleye	AGM	1963	1990	Navy	**Martin-Marietta/Hughes**
Minuteman I	ICBM	1963	1975	USAF	**Boeing Aircraft Co.**
Hornet	Anti-tank	1963	1970	USAF	**North American Rockwell**
Sea Sparrow	SAM	1964	1978	Navy	Raytheon

Titan III	LV	1964	NA	USAF	Martin-Denver
Titan IIIC	LV	1964	NA	USAF	Martin-Marietta
Titan IIIB	LV	1964	NA	USAF	Martin-Marietta
Polaris A3	SLBM	1964	1985	Navy	Lockheed Missiles & Space Div.
AIM-7E Sparrow	AIM	1964	1976	Navy	Sperry/Douglas
Minuteman II	ICBM	1964	1977	USAF	Boeing Aircraft Co.
AGM-45 Shrike	AGM	1964	1976	Navy	Naval Weapons Center-China Lake
AGM-53A Condor	AGM	1964	1976	Navy	Rockwell North American
Titan III Transtage	Booster	1965	197?	USAF	Martin-Denver
Improved Delta	LV	1965	1990	NASA	Douglas Missile & Space
Patriot	SAM	1965	1980	Army	Martin-Orlando
FGM-77A Dragon	Anti-tank	1965	1977	Army	McDonnell Douglas/Raytheon
AIM-9H Sidewinder	AIM	1965	NA	Navy	Aeronutronic (Ford)
BGM-71A TOW	Anti-tank	1965	1990	Army	Hughes
Chaparral	SAM	1965	1990	Army	Aeronutronic (Ford)
Viper	Anti-tank	1965	1970	Army	Convair (GD-Pomona)
Mark VI	SLM/ALM	1965	1970	Navy	Aerojet-General
Standard ARM	AGM	1966	1978	Navy/AF	Convair (GD Pomona)
AGM-78 Standard ARM	AGM	1966	1990	Navy/AF	General Dynamics
Pershing 1A	Tactical	1967	1979	Army	Martin-Marietta
Long Tank Thor	LV	1967	NA	NASA/AF	Douglas Missile & Space
AIM-9H Sidewinder	AIM	1968	1990	Navy/AF	Ford Aerospace
Improved Hawk	SAM	1968	1981	Army	Raytheon

Program	Type	Start	End	Agency	Prime Contractor(s) (Southern Californian contractors set bold)
AIM-9J-N Sidewinder	AIM	1968	1990	AF/Navy	**Ford Aerospace**
AGM-65 Maverick	AGM	1968	NA	USAF	**Hughes**
AGM-83A Bulldog	AGM	1969	NA	Navy	Texas Instruments
ADATS	SAM	1969	1989	Army/MC	Martin-Marietta
AGM-84A/C Harpoon	AGM	1970	1990	Navy	**McDonnell Douglas**
Minuteman III	ICBM	1971	1980	USAF	Boeing Aircraft Co.
Poseidon C3	SLBM	1971	1979	Navy	**Rockwell**
Hellfire	Anti-tank	1971	1990	Army/MC	**McDonnell Douglas**
Harpoon	Sub	1971	1990	Navy	**Lockheed Missiles & Space Div.**
Trident I C4	SLBM	1972	1990	Navy	Boeing Co.
AGM-69A SRAM	AGM	1972	NA	USAF	**Convair/Aeronutronic**
Stinger	SAM	1972	1990	Army	**Lockheed Missiles & Space Div.**
AGM-86A/B ALCM	ALCM/AGM	1972	1990	USAF	Boeing
Sprint	ABM	1973	1975	DOD	Martin-Marietta
Spartan	ABM	1973	1975	DOD	Western Electric Co.
Sea Phoenix	SAM	1974	1978	Navy	**Hughes**
AGM-109 TALCM	ALCM	1974	1990	Navy/AF	**General Dynamics**
Tomahawk GLCM	GLCM	1974	1990	Navy/AF	**Convair (GD-Pomona)**
Tomahawk SLCM	SLCM	1974	1990	Navy/AF	**Convair (GD-Pomona)**
MIM-115 Roland	SAM	1975	1983	Army	Hughes/Boeing

Atlas F	ICBM/LV	1976	1978	NASA	Convair (GD Pomona)
AGM-88A/B HARM	AGM	1976	1990	Navy/AF	Texas Instruments
Improved Chaparral	SAM	1976	1990	Army	Aeronutronic (Ford Aerospace)
ASALM	SAM	1976	1981	USAF	Martin-Marietta
AIM-7F Sparrow	AIM	1977	1989	Navy/AF	Raytheon/GD-Pomona
AIM-54B Phoenix	AIM	1977	1982	Navy	Hughes
Titan IV	LV	1977	1990	AF/NASA	United Technologies (UTC)
BGM-71C ITOW	Anti-tank	1978	1982	Army	Hughes
AIM-120(A) AMRAAM	AIM	1978	1990	AF/Navy	Hughes/Raytheon
Inertial Upper Stage	Booster	1979	1990	AF/NASA	Boeing Aerospace
Pershing 2	Tactical	1979	1984	Army	Martin-Marietta
AIM-54C Phoenix	AIM	1982	1990	Navy	Hughes
Titan 34D	LV	1982	1990	NASA/AF	Martin-Marietta
BGM-71E TOW2	Anti-tank	1983	1990	Army	Hughes
MX Peacekeeper	ICBM	1985	1990	USAF	TRW/Martin-Marietta
AGM-130A/B	AGM	1986	1990	USAF	Rockwell
GBU-15	AGM	1987	1990	USAF	Rockwell
TOW2A	Anti-tank	1988	1990	Army	Hughes
Trident II D5	SLBM	1988	1990	Navy	Lockheed Missiles & Space Div.
Pegasus	LV	NA	1990	Commercial	Orbital Sciences

SOURCES: *Aerospace Facts & Figures* (various years); Baker (1978); Birtles and Beaver (1985); Bowman (1963); Bowman, N. (1980); Gatland et al. (1981); Gunston (1979); Ordway and Wakeford (1960); Taylor and Taylor (1972); Ulanoff (1959); Wilson (1982); Yenne (1987).

APPENDIX C: U.S. SPACE VEHICLE AND EQUIPMENT PROGRAMS, 1956–1991

Program/Vehicle	Start	End	Agency	Prime Contractor(s) (Southern Californian contractors set bold)
Pioneer	1958	1978	NASA	**TRW Systems Group**
Orbiting Solar Observ.	1960	1969	NASA	Ball Brothers Research
Ranger	1960	1965	NASA	**Jet Propulsion Laboratory**
Mariner	1961	1978	NASA	**Jet Propulsion Laboratory**
Apollo	1962	1973	NASA	**North American Space Division**
Apollo Command Module	1962	1973	NASA	**N.A. Rockwell (Space Division)**
Apollo Service Module	1962	1973	NASA	**N.A. Rockwell (Space Division)**
Apollo Lunar Module	1962	1973	NASA	Grumman Aerospace Corp.
Gemini	1962	1966	NASA	McDonnell Co.
Lunar Landing Veh.	1963	1967	NASA	**Textron Bell Aerosystems**
Skylab Observatory	1963	1974	NASA/DOD	**McDonnell Douglas**
M2F1/M2F2 Lift Body	1963	1968	NASA	**Northrop Corp.**
Surveyor	1964	1968	NASA	**Jet Propulsion Lab/Hughes**
Voyager	1965	1990	NASA	**Jet Propulsion Laboratory**
Lunar Orbiter	1965	1967	NASA	Boeing Co.
Manned Orbiting Lab.	1965	197?	DOD/USAF	**Douglas Missile & Space**
Space Shuttle	1965	1991	DOD/NASA	**Rockwell North American**
Shuttle Orbital Veh.	1965	1991	NASA	**TRW Systems Group**

Shuttle Orbiter	1965	1991	NASA	Rockwell International
Viking Probe	1968	1980	NASA	JPL/Martin-Marietta
Lunar Rover	1968	197?	NASA	Boeing Co.
Space Station	1980	1991	NASA	Rockwell International
Space Platform	1990	1991	NASA	McDonnell Douglas Astronautics

SOURCES: *Aerospace Facts & Figures* (various years); Aerospace Industries Association of America (various years); *Aviation Week* (various issues); Baker (1978); Birtles and Beaver (1985); Bowman (1963); Ezell (1989); Gatland et al. (1981); Gunston (1979); Nicks (1985); Osman (1983); Taylor and Taylor (1972); Van Nimmen (1970); Yenne (1987).

Appendix D: Specialized Tasks in Printed Circuits Production

This appendix provides brief descriptions of the eight subcontracting functions analyzed in the main body of chapter 10. The descriptions are derived largely from Clark (1985) and Kear (1987).

Copper-plating. Double-sided and multilayer printed circuit boards have circuitry on different layers of the base laminate material. Circuit connections thus have to be made between the layers, and this is achieved by copper-plating the walls of the holes drilled through the board. Copper-plating occurs in two stages. After the board is drilled and scrubbed, a thin coating of copper is chemically deposited on the hole walls. Because the deposit obtained in this way is normally very thin, the board is then placed in a copper-electroplating bath to build greater metal thickness on the walls. If copper-plating is not wanted in the tooling holes of the board, they must be masked during these operations.

Drilling. Printed circuit boards have holes drilled into them to facilitate the mounting of electronic components at the assembly stage. The number of holes drilled in any given board may range from only a few to upwards of many thousands. Narrowly defined hole location tolerances together with the need for high production rates have encouraged the development of specialized numerically controlled drilling machines for the printed circuits industry. The machines are governed by programs that identify precisely the location and size of every hole to be drilled. The capital investment per machine is high (of the order of $100,000 to $150,000), and an experienced operator is needed to run the machine.

Gold-plating. The edge-connector fingers of any printed circuit board are usually gold-plated in a two-stage electroplating operation. The connectors are first plated with nickel and then with gold. The nickel provides a wear-resistant surface, and the gold provides good conductivity and low levels of friction.

Laminating.   Laminating is a process used in the production of multilayer boards. It involves bonding layers of double- and single-sided panels into one composite board. The panels are bonded together with layers of epoxy-impregnated glass cloth, and then laminated by the application of great heat and pressure in a mechanical press. After laminating, the boards are drilled.

Plasma etch.   This process consists in the etching back of laminate resin smear that accumulates in the holes of multilayer boards during drilling. By this means the copper connections to inner-layer circuits are fully exposed, thus allowing good electrical junctions to be formed. The plasma-etch technique involves the exposure of the boards to a gaseous mixture of oxygen and carbon tetrafluoride transformed into a plasma state. As this mixture passes through the holes of each board, it removes the smear and epoxy resin from the hole walls.

Solder-leveling.   In this process, a layer of solder is deposited on the copper pads (small annular areas around circuit holes) of the circuit board, thus facilitating the mounting of components. The board is first of all cleaned and a hot-air leveling flux applied to prepare the copper pads for the solder. Molten solder is then put on the board and the copper pads appropriately coated. Hot-air leveling is required to ensure an adequate thickness of solder around the pads and to prevent the hole walls from being soldered. The requisite equipment is expensive and requires careful maintenance.

Solder-masking.   Solder-masking seals the surface of the circuit board with a solder-resistant material. This provides a permanent protective cover over the circuitry of the board, thus minimizing damage from molten solder at later stages of fabrication. Solder masks are applied as liquid film or as dry film. Liquid films are silk-screened onto the board. Dry films are laminated onto the board's surface and then photographically processed. The latter operation permits the removal of mask material where it is not wanted (i.e., over the pads). The mask is cured by heat and usually allowed to set for a day or two before further processing of the board.

Testing.   Circuit boards are frequently tested by electronic means before assembly. Testing seeks to locate defective circuits in the form of unwanted opens, shorts, and capacitative couplings. The testing machine usually prints out a listing of diagnostic results, which identify the node points of any failure along with an indication of the failure mode.

References

Acs, Z. J., and D. B. Audretsch. 1990. "Small firms in the 1990s." In Z. J. Acs and D. B. Audretsch (eds.), *The Economics of Small Firms*, 1–22. Dordrecht: Kluwer.

Aerospace Industries Association of America. Annuals. *Aerospace Facts and Figures*. Washington, D.C.: American Aviation Publications.

Ahlbrandt, R. S. 1990. "The revival of Pittsburgh—a partnership between business and government." *Long Range Planning* 23:231–40.

Aircraft Industries Association of America. 1957. *Aviation Facts and Figures*. Washington, D.C.: American Aviation Publications.

Air Force Systems Command. n.d. *Space and Missile Systems Organization: A Chronology, 1954–1979*. Los Angeles: Air Force Systems Command, Space Division, History Office.

Aglietta, M. 1979. *A Theory of Capitalist Regulation: The US Experience*. London: New Left Books.

Allen, A. P., and B. V. H. Schneider. 1956. *Industrial Relations in the California Aircraft Industry*. Berkeley: Institute of Industrial Relations, University of California.

Allen, D. N., and V. Levine. 1986. *Nurturing Advanced Technology Enterprises: Emerging Issues in State and Local Economic Development*. New York: Praeger.

Allen, G. C. 1929. *The Industrial Development of Birmingham and the Black Country, 1860–1907*. Hemel Hempstead: Allen and Unwin.

Alonso, W. 1989. "Deindustrialization and regional policy." In L. Rodwin and H. Sazanami (eds.) *Deindustrialization and Regional Economic Transformation*, 221–237. London: Unwin Hyman.

American Aviation Magazine. 1956. *Missile Progress Handbook*. Washington, D.C.: American Aviation Magazine.

American Aviation Publications. 1958. *Missile Market Guide and Directory Edition*. Washington, D.C.: American Aviation Publications.

Amin, A., and K. Robins. 1990. "The re-emergence of regional economies? The mythical geography of flexible production," *Environment and Planning D: Society and Space* 8:7–34.

Anderson, F. 1976. *Northrop: An Aeronautical History*. Los Angeles: Northrop Corporation.

Anderson, G. 1974. *Networks of Contact: The Portuguese in Toronto*. Waterloo: Wilfrid Laurier University Press.

Angel, D. P. 1989. *Production, Labor Markets and Location: A Case Study of the US Semiconductor Industry*. Ph.D. diss., Department of Geography, University of California, Los Angeles.

Angelucci, E. 1980. *The Rand McNally Encyclopedia of Military Aircraft: 1914–1980*. New York: Military Press.

Applegate, J. W. 1984. "County in forefront as an industry's pulse quickens." *Los Angeles Times*, Orange County Edition, June 13, pt 5.

Armacost, M. H. 1969. *The Politics of Weapons Innovation: The Thor-Jupiter Controversy*. New York: Columbia University Press.

Arnold, R. K., R. G. Spiegelman, N. T. Houston, O. F. Poland, and C. A. Trexel. 1960. *The California Economy, 1947–1980*. Menlo Park, CA.: Stanford Research Institute.

Arthur, W. B. 1988. "Urban systems and historical path dependence." In J. H. Ausubel and R. Herman (eds.) *Cities and Their Vital Systems*, 85–97. Washington, D.C.: National Academy Press.

———. 1990. "Silicon Valley locational clusters: when do increasing returns imply monopoly?" *Mathematical Social Sciences* 19:235–251.

Atkinson, J. 1985. *Flexibility, Uncertainty and Manpower Planning*. Brighton: University of Sussex, Institute of Manpower Studies, Report no. 89.

Austin, E. T. 1965. "Rohr's first 25 years." *Rohr Magazine* 15, no. 2:6–14.

Aviation Week. 1956. "Forecast and inventory: specifications." *Aviation Week* (12 March): 217.

Aviation Week and Space Technology. 1989. "Reduced spending on military aircraft spurs decline in aerospace employment." *Aviation Week & Space Technology* (29 May): 78–87.

Baker, D. 1978. *The Rocket: The History and Development of Rocket and Missile Technology*. New York: Crown Publishers.

Ball, J. 1962. *Edwards: Flight Test Center of the USAF*. New York: Duell, Sloan, and Pearce.

Barlett, D. L., and J. B. Steele. 1979. *Empire: The Life, Legend and Madness of Howard Hughes*. New York: Norton.

Becattini, G. 1987. "Introduzione: il distretto industriale marshalliano: cronaca di un ritrovamento." In G. Becattini (ed.) *Mercato e Forze Locali: Il Distretto Industriale*, 7–34. Bologna: Il Mulino.

Beneira, L. 1987. "Gender and the dynamics of subcontracting in Mexico City." In C. Brown and J. A. Pechman (eds.) *Gender in the Workplace*, 159–188. Washington, D.C.: The Brookings Institution.

Benko, G. 1991. *Géographie des Technopôles*. Paris: Masson.

Berger, S., and M. J. Piore. 1980. *Dualism and Discontinuity in Industrial Societies.* Cambridge: Cambridge University Press.

Best, M. H. 1989. "Sector strategies and industrial policy: the furniture industry and the Greater London Enterprise Board." In P. Hirst and J. Zeitlin (eds.) *Reversing Industrial Decline? Industrial Structure and Policy in Britain and Her Competitors,* 191–222. Oxford: Berg.

———. 1990. *The New Competition: Institutions of Industrial Restructuring.* Cambridge: Polity Press.

Bianchi, P. 1992. "Levels of policy and the nature of post-fordist competition." In M. Storper and A. J. Scott (eds.) *Pathways to Industrialization and Regional Development.* London: Routledge.

Bilstein, R. E. 1974. *The Saturn Management Concept.* Washington, D.C.: National Aeronautics and Space Administration, Report no. NASA CR–129029.

———. 1980. *Stages to Saturn: A Technological History of the Apollo/Saturn Launch Vehicles.* Washington, D.C.: National Aeronautics and Space Administration.

Birch, D. L., 1987. *Job Creation in America: How Our Smallest Companies Put the Most People to Work.* New York: The Free Press.

Birtles, P., and P. Beaver. 1985. *Missile Systems.* Shepperton, Surrey: Ian Allan.

Bland, W. M. 1964. "Project Mercury." In E. M. Emme (ed.) *The History of Rocket Technology,* 212–240. Detroit: Wayne State University Press.

Bloch, R. 1987. *Studies in the Development of the United States Aerospace Industry.* Los Angeles: Graduate School of Architecture and Urban Planning, University of California. Discussion paper no. D875.

von Böhm-Bawerk, E. 1891. *The Positive Theory of Capital.* New York: G. E. Stechert.

Bolton, R. E. 1986. *Defense Purchases and Regional Growth.* Washington, D.C.: Brookings Institution.

Bonacich, E. 1989–90. *Asian and Latino Immigrants in the Los Angeles Garment Industry: An Exploration of the Relationship between Capitalism and Racial Oppression.* Los Angeles: University of California, Institute for Social Science Research. Working paper no. 13.

Boston, T. D. 1990. "Segmented labor markets: new evidence from a study of four race-gender groups." *Industrial and Labor Relations Review* 44:99–115.

Bowman, M. W. 1980. *The Encyclopedia of U.S. Military Aircraft.* London: Bison Books.

Bowman, N. J. 1963. *The Handbook of Rockets and Guided Missiles.* Newtown Square, PA: Perastadion Press.

Boyer, R. 1986. *La Théorie de la Régulation: Une Analyse Critique.* Paris: Editions la Découverte.

Bright, C. D. 1978. *The Jet Makers: The Aerospace Industry from 1945 to 1972.* Lawrence, Kansas: The Regents' Press of Kansas.

Brusco, S. 1986. "Small firms and industrial districts: the experience of Italy." In D. Keeble and E. Wever (eds.) *New Firms and Regional Development in Europe,* 184–202. London: Croom Helm.

———. 1990. "The idea of the industrial district: its genesis." In F. Pyke, G. Becattini, and W. Sengenberger (eds.) *Industrial Districts and Inter-Firm Cooperation in Italy*, 10–19. Geneva: International Institute for Labour Studies.

M. Caidin. 1959. *Spaceport U.S.A.* New York: E.P. Dutton & Co.

California Manufacturers Association. 1955. *California Manufacturers Annual Register*. Los Angeles: Times-Mirror Press.

———. 1989. *California Manufacturers Register*. Newport Beach, CA.: Database Publishing Co.

California State Chamber of Commerce. 1952. *An Examination of California's Electronics Industry*. Sacramento: Research Department, California State Chamber of Commerce.

Camagni, R., P. C. Cheshire, J. P. de Gaudemar, and J. R. Cuadrado-Roura. 1990. *Europe's Regional Policies, Past and Present*. University of Reading, Department of Economics, Discussion Papers in Urban and Regional Economics. Series C, vol. 2, no. 48.

Carlton, D. W. 1979. "Vertical integration in competitive markets under uncertainty." *Journal of Industrial Economics* 27:189–209.

Castells, M., L. Goh, and R. Y-W. Kwok. 1991. *The Shek Kip Mei Syndrome: Economic Development and Public Housing in Hong Kong and Singapore*. London: Pion.

Chapin, S. L. 1966. "Garrett and pressurized flight: a business built on thin air." *Pacific Historical Review* 35:329–343.

Christopherson, S., and T. Noyelle. 1992. "The US path toward flexibility and productivity: the remaking of the US labor market in the 1980s." In H. Ernste and V. Meier (eds.) *Regional Development and Contemporary Industrial Response: Extending Flexible Specialisation*, 163–178. London: Belhaven.

Clapp, E. J. 1926. *Los Angeles Should Be the Home of Aircraft Industries*. Los Angeles: Chamber of Commerce.

Clark, C. 1951. "Urban population densities." *Journal of the Royal Statistical Society, A* 114:490–496.

Clark, D. L. 1981. *Los Angeles: A City Apart*. Woodland Hills, CA.: Windsor Publications.

Clark, G. 1988. "Using an outside drilling service." *Printed Circuit Fabrication* 11 (June): 48–55.

Clark, R. H. 1985. *Handbook of Printed Circuit Manufacturing*. New York: Van Nostrand and Reinhold.

Clark, W. A. V. 1982. "Recent research on migration and mobility: a review and interpretation." *Progress in Planning* 18:1–56.

Clark, W. A. V., and J. E. Burt. 1980. "The impact of workplace on residential location." *Annals of the Association of American Geographers* 70:59–67.

Clarke, M. K. 1990. "Recent state initiatives: an overview of state science and technology policies and programs." In J. Schmandt and R. Wilson (eds.) *Growth Policy in the Age of High Technology: The Role of Regions and States*, 149–170. Boston: Unwin Hyman.

Clayton, J. L. 1962. "Defense spending: key to California's growth." *Western Political Quarterly* 15:280–293.

———. 1967. "The impact of the Cold War on the economies of California and Utah, 1946–1965." *Pacific Historical Review* 36:449–473.

Coase, R. H. 1937. "The nature of the firm." *Economica* 4:386–405.

Cochran, C. 1988. "The aerospace industry in California." Sacramento, CA: California Department of Commerce, Office of Economic Research.

Cohen, S. S., and J. Zysman. 1987. *Manufacturing Matters: The Myth of the Post-Industrial Economy.* New York: Basic Books.

Collier, R. P., and L. B. Perry. 1953. "A study of the effect upon the Los Angeles area of defense expenditure reduction." *Proceedings of the Twenty-Eighth Annual Conference of the Western Economic Association,* 34–37.

Committee on Armed Services. 1959. *Military Procurement.* Hearings before a Subcommittee of the Committee on Armed Services, United States Senate, Eighty-sixth Congress, First Session, Washington, D.C.: Government Printing Office.

Commuter Transportation Services. 1990. *The State of the Commute: Research Findings from the 1989 Commuter Survey.* Los Angeles: Commuter Computer.

Cooper, A. C. 1985. *The Role of Incubator Organizations in the Founding of Growth-Oriented Firms.* West Lafayette, IN: Krannert Graduate School of Management, Purdue University.

Cornelius, W. A. 1982. "Interviewing undocumented immigrants: methodological reflections based on fieldwork in Mexico and the US." *International Migration Review* 16:378–411.

———. 1989–90. *Mexican Immigrants in California Today.* Los Angeles: University of California, Institute for Social Science Research. Working paper no. 10.

Courlet, C., and B. Pecqueur. 1992. "Les systèmes industriels localisés en France: un nouveau modèle de développement." In G. Benko and A. Lipietz (eds.), *Les Régions Qui Gagnent: Districts et Réseaux, les Nouveaux Paradigmes de la Géographie Economique,* 81–102. Paris: Presses Universitaires de France.

Covault, C. 1988. "Commercial space ventures face harsh market realities." *Aviation Week & Space Technology* (19 December): 34–43.

Cox, K. R., and A. Mair. 1988. "Locality and community in the politics of local economic development." *Annals of the Association of American Geographers* 78:307–325.

Cunningham, W. G. 1951. *The Aircraft Industry: A Study in Industrial Location.* Los Angeles: Lorrin L. Morrison.

Dangler, J. F. 1989. "Electronics subassemblers in central New York: nontraditional homeworkers in a nontraditional homework industry." In E. Boris and C. R. Daniels (eds.) *Homework: Historical and Contemporary Perspectives on Paid Labor at Home,* 147–164. Urbana and Chicago: University of Illinois Press.

David, P. 1975. *Technical Choice, Innovation and Economic Growth.* New York: Cambridge University Press.

———. 1985. "Clio and the economics of QWERTY." *The American Economic Review* 75:332–337.

Day, J. S. 1956. *Subcontracting Policy in the Airframe Industry*. Boston: Division of Research, Graduate School of Business Administration, Harvard University.

de Bernardy, M., and P. Boisgontier. 1990. "Les technopôles dans la technopôle: effets d'entente cordiale." In G. Jalabert and C. Thouzellier (eds.) *Villes et Technopoles: Nouvelle Urbanisation, Nouvelle Industrialisation*, 43–55. Toulouse: Presses Universitaires du Mirail.

DeFreitas, G. 1988. "Hispanic immigration and labor market segmentation." *Industrial Relations* 27:195–214.

Del Monte, A., and F. Martinelli. 1987. "The organizational structure of small and medium firms in the electronics industry: regional differentials in Italy." Paper presented at the conference on Innovation Diffusion in the Regional Experience of Europe and the United States, Istituto Universitario Orientale, Naples (February): 20–21.

Dertouzos, M. L., R. K. Lester, and R. M. Solow. 1989. *Made in America: Regaining the Productive Edge*. Cambridge, MA: The MIT Press.

De Vet, J. M. 1990. *Innovation and New Firm Formation in Southern California's Medical Device Industry*. Master's thesis, Department of Geography, University of California, Los Angeles.

Directory Systems. 1987. *Medical Device Register*. Greenwich, CT: DSI.

Dore, R. P. 1986. *Flexible Rigidities: Industrial Policy and Structural Adjustment in the Japanese Economy, 1970–1980*. London: Athlone.

———. 1987. *Taking Japan Seriously*. Stanford, CA: Stanford University Press.

Dosi, G. 1988. "The nature of the innovative process." In Dosi et al. (eds.) *Technical Change and Economic Theory*, 221–238. London and New York: Pinter Publishers.

Doyle, E. J., and K. Friedenreich. 1988. "Cardiovascular: Orange County's world class technology." *High-Technology*. Official Orange County Centennial Magazine.

Economic Roundtable. 1992. *Los Angeles County Economic Adjustment Strategy for Defense Reductions*. A report to the Community Development Commission of Los Angeles County, Los Angeles: Economic Roundtable.

Eisenschitz, A., and D. North. 1986. "The London industrial strategy: socialist transformation or modernising capitalism?" *International Journal of Urban and Regional Research* 10:419–440.

Employment Development Department. 1991. *Annual Planning Information*. Los Angeles: Employment Development Department of the State of California. (Individual reports by county).

Ezell, L. N. 1989. *NASA Historical Data Book, Vol. III: Programs and Projects 1969–1978*. Washington, D.C.: NASA Scientific & Technical Information Division.

Fernandez-Kelly, M. P. 1987. "Economic restructuring in the United States: the case of Hispanic women in the garment and electronics industries of Southern California." A paper presented at the thematic panel on *The*

New International Division of Labor: Implications for Working Women and Working Men. Meetings of the American Sociological Association, August.

Fernandez-Kelly, M. P., and A. M. Garcia. 1989. "Hispanic women and homework: women in the informal economy of Miami and Los Angeles." In E. Boris and C. R. Daniels (eds.) *Homework: Historical and Contemporary Perspectives on Paid Labor at Home,* 165–179. Urbana and Chicago: University of Illinois Press.

Florida, R., and M. Kenny. 1990. *The Breakthrough Illusion: Corporate America's Failure to Move from Innovation to Mass Production.* New York: Basic Books.

Francillon, R. J. 1982. *Lockheed Aircraft Since 1913.* Annapolis, MD: Naval Institute Press.

Friedman, M., and R. Friedman. 1980. *Free to Choose.* New York: Harcourt Brace Jovanovich.

Friedmann, D. B. 1988. *The Misunderstood Miracle: Industrial Development and Political Change in Japan.* Ithaca: Cornell University Press.

Gaffard, J-L. 1990. *Economie Industrielle et de l'Innovation.* Paris: Dalloz.

Gansler, J. S. 1980. *The Defense Industry.* Cambridge, MA: The MIT Press.

Gatland, K. et al. 1981. *The Illustrated Encyclopedia of Space Technology.* New York: Crown Publishers.

Gibson, L. J. 1970. "An analysis of the location of instrument manufacturers in the United States." *Annals of the Association of American Geographers* 60:352–367.

Gibson, T. A., and C. M. Merz. 1971. *Impact of the Space Shuttle Program on the Economy of Southern California.* Downey, CA: North American Rockwell Space Division.

Goodman, R. 1979. *The Last Entrepreneurs: America's Regional Wars for Jobs and Dollars.* New York: Simon and Schuster.

Gordon, D. M., R. Edwards, and M. Reich. 1982. *Segmented Work, Divided Workers: The Historical Transformation of Labor in the United States.* Cambridge: Cambridge University Press.

Gordon, R. 1991. "Innovation, industrial networks and high technology regions." In R. Camagni (ed.) *Innovation Networks: Spatial Perspectives,* 174–195. London: Belhaven.

Gordon, R., A. Dilts, and L. M. Kimball. 1990. "High-technology innovation and the global milieu: small and medium-sized enterprises in Silicon Valley." In J. C. Perrin and D. Maillat (eds.) *Milieux Innovateurs et Processus d'Innovation dans les Entreprises* (forthcoming).

Granovetter, M. S. 1974. *Getting a Job: A Study of Contacts amd Careers.* Cambridge, MA: Harvard University Press.

Grant, M. 1988. "The genesis of Orange County's biomed industry." *Technology Business* (First Quarter): 25–26.

Green, S. S. 1983. "Silicon Valley's women workers: a theoretical analysis of sex segregation in the electronics industry labor market." In J. Nash and M. P. Fernandez-Kelly (eds.) *Women, Men and the International Division of Labor,* 273–331. Albany, NY: State University of New York Press.

Gunston, B. 1979. *The Illustrated Encyclopedia of the World's Rockets and Missiles.* London: Salamander Books.

Hagen, J. P. 1964. "The Viking and the Vanguard." In E. M. Emme (ed.) *The History of Rocket Technology,* 122–141. Detroit: Wayne State University Press.

Hall, P. 1962. *The Industries of London since 1861.* London: Hutchinson.

———. 1988. "The creation of the American aerospace complex, 1955–65." In M. J. Breheny (ed.) *Defence Expenditure and Regional Development,* 102–121. London: Mansell.

Hall, P., and P. Preston. 1988. *The Carrier Wave: New Information Technology and the Geography of Innovation, 1846–2003.* London: Unwin Hyman.

Hamilton, A. 1962. "Shangri-La for deep thinkers." *Westways* 54 (February): 4–6.

Hammond, E. H. 1941. "The localization of the aircraft industry in the United States." *Yearbook of the Association of the Pacific Coast Geographers,* 33–40.

Hanson, S., and G. Pratt. 1988. "Reconceptualizing the links between home and work in urban geography." *Economic Geography* 64:299–321.

———. 1990. "Geographic perspectives on the occupational segregation of women." *National Geographic Research* 6:376–399.

———. 1991. "Job search and the occupational segregation of women." *Annals of the Association of American Geographers* 81:229–253.

Harlan, N. E. 1956. *Management Control in Airframe Subcontracting.* Boston: Harvard University, Division of Research, Graduate School of Business Administration.

Harr, M., and R. Kohli. 1990. *The Commercial Utilization of Space: International Comparison of Framework Conditions.* Columbus: Battelle Press.

Harvey, D. 1989. "From managerialism to entrepreneurialism: the transformation in urban governance in late capitalism." *Geografiska Annaler* 71B:3–17.

Hatfield, D. D. 1973. *Los Angeles Aeronautics, 1920–1929.* Inglewood, CA: Northrop University Press.

Hatfield Collection. 1943. *List of Planes: Consolidated Aircraft Corporation.* Pamphlet PAM 2004. D. D. Hatfield Collection, Northrop University Alumni Library, Los Angeles.

Hekman, J. S. 1980. "Can New England hold onto its high-technology industry?" *New England Economic Review* (March/April): 35–44.

Hirschman, A. 1958. *The Strategy of Economic Development.* New Haven: Yale University Press.

Holmes, J. 1986. "The organization and locational structure of subcontracting." In A. J. Scott and M. Storper (eds.) *Production, Work, Territory: The Geographical Anatomy of Industrial Capitalism,* 80–106. Boston: Allen and Unwin.

Hoyt, E. P. 1971. *The Space Dealers.* New York: John Day Company.

Hughes Aircraft Company. 1986. *The History, Culture, and Organization of the Hughes Aircraft Company*. Los Angeles: Hughes Aircraft Company, Corporate Human Resources, Research and Development.

Humphrey, C. R., R. A. Erickson, and E. J. Ottensmeyer. 1989. "Industrial development organizations and the local dependence hypothesis." *Policy Studies Journal* 17:624–642.

Hund, J. M. 1959. "Electronics." In M. Hall (ed.) *Made in New York: Case Studies in Metropolitan Manufacturing*, 241–326. Cambridge, MA: Harvard University Press.

Hyman, R. 1991. "Plus ça change? The theory of production and the production of theory." In A. Pollert (ed.) *Farewell to Flexibility?* 259–283. Oxford: Blackwell.

Ikle, D. 1960. *Southern California's Economy in the Sixties*. Report no. P–2077. Santa Monica, CA: RAND Corporation.

Ingells, D. J. 1979. *The McDonnell Douglas Story*. Fallbrook, CA: Aero Publishers.

Isard, W., and J. Ganschow. 1963. *Awards of Prime Military Contracts by State, County, and Metropolitan Areas of the United States, Fiscal 1960*. Philadelphia: Regional Science Research Institute.

Izzard, A. E. 1961. *The Factors Influencing the Agglomeration of the Electronics Industry in the San Fernando Valley*. Master's thesis, Department of Geography, University of California, Los Angeles.

Jayet, H. 1983. "Chômer plus souvent en région urbaine, plus longtemps en région rurale." *Economie et Statistique* 153:47–57.

Jones, L. S. 1968. *U.S. Bombers: B1–B70*. Los Angeles: Aero Publishers.

———. 1975. *U.S. Fighters: 1925 to 1980s*. Fallbrook, CA: Aero Publishers.

Kaldor, N. 1970. "The case for regional policies." *Scottish Journal of Political Economy* 17:337–348.

Karaska, G. J. 1967. "The spatial impacts of defense-space procurement: an analysis of subcontracting patterns in the United States. *Papers of the Peace Research Society (International)* 8:109–122.

Kear, F. W. 1987. *Printed Circuit Assembly Manufacturing*. New York: Marcel Dekker.

Keller, J. F. 1983. "The division of labor in electronics." In J. Nash and M. P. Fernandez-Kelly (eds.) *Women, Men and the International Division of Labor*, 346–373. Albany, NY: State University of New York Press.

Kidner, F. L., and P. Neff. 1945a. *An Economic Survey of the Los Angeles Area*. Los Angeles: The Haynes Foundation.

———. 1945b. *Statistical Appendix to an Economic Survey of the Los Angeles Area*. Los Angeles: The Haynes Foundation.

———. 1946. *Los Angeles: The Economic Outlook*. Los Angeles: The Haynes Foundation.

Kucera, R. P. 1974. *The Aerospace Industry and the Military: Structural and Political Relationships*. Beverly Hills, CA: Sage Administrative and Policy Studies Series 2.

Lamden, C. W., and L. A. Pemberton. 1962. *A Study of the Problems of Small Electronics Manufacturing Companies in Southern California*. San Diego: Bureau of Business and Economic Research, San Diego State College.

Lilley, T., P. Hunt, J. K. Butters, F. G. Gilmore, and P. F. Lawler. 1946. *Problems of Accelerating Aircraft Production During World War II*. Boston, MA: Division of Research, Graduate School of Business Administration, Harvard University.

Los Angeles Chamber of Commerce. 1950. *Directory of Manufacturing, Los Angeles County*. Los Angeles: Industrial Departmaent, Los Angeles Chamber of Commerce.

Los Angeles Chamber of Commerce. 1955. *Report on the Electronics Industry, Los Angeles Metropolitan Area*. Los Angeles: Electronics Committee, Industrial Department, Los Angeles Chamber of Commerce.

Lipietz, A. 1986. "New tendencies in the international division of labor: regimes of accumulation and modes of social regulation." In A. J. Scott and M. Storper (eds.) *Production, Work Territory: The Geographical Anatomy of Industrial Capitalism*, 16–40. Winchester, MA: Allen and Unwin.

Lotchin, R. W. 1992. *Fortress California, 1910–1961*. New York: Oxford University Press.

Loveman, G. W., and W. Sengenberger. 1990. "Introduction: economic and social reorganisation in the small and medium-sized enterprise sector." In W. Sengenberger, G. W. Loveman, and M. J. Piore (eds) *The Re-Emergence of Small Enterprises: Industrial Restructuring in Industrial Countries*, 1–61. Geneva: International Institute for Labour Studies.

Lund, W. S. 1959. *Orange County: Its Economic Growth, 1940–1980*. South Pasadena, CA: Southern California Laboratories of Stanford Research Institute.

Malecki, E. J. 1985. "Industrial location and corporate organization in high technology industries." *Economic Geography* 61:345–369.

Malina, F. J. 1964. "Origins and first decade of the Jet Propulsion Laboratory." In E. M. Emme (ed.) *The History of Rocket Technology*, 46–66. Detroit: Wayne State University Press.

Marchand, B., and A. J. Scott. 1991. "Los Angeles en 1990: une nouvelle capitale mondiale." *Annales de Géographie* 560:406–426.

Markusen, A. R., and R. Bloch. 1985. "Defensive cities: military spending, high technology, and human settlements." In M. Castells (ed.) *High Technology, Space, and Society*, 106–120. Beverly Hills: Sage.

Markusen, A. R., P. Hall, and A. Glasmeier. 1986. *High Tech America: The What, How, Where and Why of the Sunrise Industries*. Boston: Allen and Unwin.

Markusen, A. R., P. Hall, S. Campbell, and S. Deitrick. 1991. *The Rise of the Gunbelt: The Military Remapping of Industrial America*. New York: Oxford University Press.

Markusen, A. R., and J. Yudken. 1992. *Dismantling the Cold War Economy*. New York: Basic Books.

Marshall, A. 1919. *Industry and Trade*. London: Macmillan.

Martin, R. 1989. "The new economics and politics of regional restructuring: the British experience." In L. Albrechts, F. Moulaert, P. Roberts, and E. Swyngedouw (eds.) *Regional Policy at the Crossroads: European Perspectives*, 27–51. London: Jessica Kingsley.

Martinelli, F. 1989. "Business services, innovation and regional policy: consideration of the case of Southern Italy." In L. Albrechts, F. Moulaert, P. Roberts, and E. Swyngedouw (eds.) *Regional Policy at the Crossroads: European Perspectives*, 10–26. London: Jessica Kingsley.

Masser, I. 1990. "Technology and regional development policy: a review of Japan's Technopolis program." *Regional Studies* 24:41–53.

Mattingly, D. 1991. *Local Labor Market Dynamics of Production Workers in a Southern California Aircraft Plant.* Masters thesis, Department of Geography, University of California, Los Angeles.

Maynard, C. 1962. *Flight Plan for Tomorrow: The Douglas Story.* Santa Monica, CA: Douglas Aircraft Company Inc.

Mettler, R. F. 1982. *The Little Brown Hen That Could: The Growth Story of TRW Inc.* New York: The Newcomen Society in North America.

Miller, R. E., and M. Cote. 1987. *Building the Next Silicon Valley: A Guide for Successful Regional Planning.* Lexington, MA: Lexington Books.

Miller, R., and D. Sawers. 1968. *The Technical Development of Modern Aviation.* New York: Praeger.

Molotch, H. 1976. "The city as a growth machine: toward a political economy of place." *American Journal of Sociology* 82:309–332.

Morales, R., M. Storper, M. Cisternas, C. Quandt, A. J. Scott, J. Slifko, W. Thomas, M. Wachs, and S. Zakhor. 1991. *Prospects for Alternative Vehicle Use and Production in Southern California: Environmental Quality and Economic Development.* University of California, Los Angeles, Lewis Center for Regional Policy Studies. Working paper no. 2.

Morrison, P. S. 1990. "Segmentation theory applied to local, regional and spatial labour markets." *Progress in Human Geography* 14:488–528.

Munson, K. 1972. *Airliners since 1946.* New York: Macmillan.

Myers, S., and D. G. Marquis. 1969. *Successful Industrial Innovation.* Washington, D.C.: National Science Foundation.

Myrdal, G. 1957. *Economic Theory and Underdeveloped Regions.* London: Duckworth.

NASA. 1989. *NASA Subcontracts Awarded by NASA Major Prime Contractors and Their First-Tier Subcontractors.* Washington, D.C.: National Aeronautics and Space Administration, Office of Procurement.

———. 1990. *NASA Pocket Statistics: January 1990.* Washington, D.C.: National Aeronautics and Space Administration, Office of Headquarters Operations.

Neufeld, J. 1990. *Ballistic Missiles in the United States Air Force, 1945–1960.* Washington, D.C.: Office of Air Force History, USAF.

Nicks, O. W. 1985. *Far Travelers: The Exploring Machine.* Washington, D.C.: National Aeronautics and Space Administration, (NASA SP–480).

Oakey, R. 1983. "High-technology industry, industrial location and regional development: the British case." In F. E. I. Hamilton and G. J. R. Linge (eds.), *Spatial Analysis, Industry and the Industrial Environment*, 179–296. Vol. 3. Chichester: John Wiley.

———. 1984. *High Technology Small Firms.* New York: St. Martin's Press.

Oakey, R., R. Rothwell, and S. Cooper. 1988. *The Management of Innovation in High-Technology Small Firms.* New York: Quorum Books.

OECD. 1985. *The Space Industry: Trade Related Issues.* Paris: Organisation for Economic Cooperation and Development.

———. 1985. *La Politique d'Innovation en France.* Paris: Economica.

Office of Technology Assessment. 1984. *Federal Policies and the Medical Devices Industry.* New York: Pergamon Press.

O'Green, F. W. 1988. *Putting Technology to Work: The Story of Litton Industries.* New York: The Newcomen Society in North America.

Ong, P. 1989. *The Widening Divide: Income Inequality and Poverty in Los Angeles.* Research Group on the Los Angeles Economy. Graduate School of Architecture and Urban Planning, University of California, Los Angeles.

Ong, P. M., and R. Morales. 1988. "Mexican labor in Los Angeles." In J. H. Johnson and M. L. Oliver (eds.) *Conference on Comparative Ethnicity: Ethnic Dilemmas in Comparative Perspective*, 109–121. Institute for Social Science Research, University of California, Los Angeles.

Osborne, D. 1988. *Laboratories of Democracy.* Boston: Harvard Business School Press.

OTA. 1984. *Technology, Innovation, and Regional Economic Development.* Washington, D.C.: Office of Technology Assessment.

Morrison, P. S. 1990. "Segmentation theory applied to local, regional and spatial labour markets." *Progress in Geography* 14:488–528.

Ordway, F. I., and R. C. Wakeford. 1960. *International Missile and Spacecraft Guide.* New York: McGraw-Hill.

Osman, T. 1983. *Space History.* New York: St. Martin's Press.

Parson, N. A. 1962. *Missiles and the Revolution in Warfare.* Cambridge, MA: Harvard University Press.

Peck, M. J., and F. M. Scherer. 1962. *The Weapons Acquisition Process: An Economic Analysis.* Boston: Harvard University, Division of Research, Graduate School of Business Administration.

Pegrum, D. F. 1963. *Urban Transport and the Location of Industry in Metropolitan Los Angeles.* Bureau of Business and Economic Research, University of California, Los Angeles.

Peltz, M., and M. A. Weiss. 1984. "State and local government roles in industrial innovation." *Journal of the American Planning Association* 50:270–279.

Phillips, A. 1971. *Technology and Market Structure.* Lexington, MA: D. C. Heath.

Piore, M. J., and C. F. Sabel. 1984. *The Second Industrial Divide: Possibilities for Prosperity.* New York: Basic Books.

Pollert, A. 1991. "The orthodoxy of flexibility." In A. Pollert (ed.) *Farewell to Flexibility?* 3–31. Oxford: Blackwell.

Porter, M. 1990. *The Competitive Advantage of Nations.* New York: The Free Press.

Prais, S. J. 1976. *The Evolution of Giant Firms in Britain: A Study of the Growth of Concentration in Manufacturing Industry in Britain, 1909–70.* Cambridge: Cambridge University Press.

Premus, R. 1982. *Location of High Technology Firms and Regional Economic Development.* Washington, D.C.: Report prepared for the Subcommittee on Monetary and Fiscal Policy of the Joint Economic Committee.

Quigley, J. M., and D. H. Weinberg. 1977. "Intra-urban residential mobility: a review and synthesis," *International Regional Science Review* 2:41–66.

Rae, J. B. 1968. *Climb to Greatness: The American Aircraft Industry, 1920–1960.* Cambridge, MA: MIT Press.

Ramo, S. 1988. *The Business of Science.* New York: Hill and Wang.

RAND Corporation. 1963. *The First Fifteen Years.* Santa Monica, CA: The RAND Corporation.

Rees, J., and T. Lewington. 1990. "An assessment of state technology development programs." In J. Schmandt and R. Wilson (eds.) *Growth Policy in the Age of High Technology: The Role of Regions and States,* 195–210. Boston: Unwin Hyman.

Renard, J. 1989. "La crise dans les industries chôletaises." *La Lettre d'Odile* 0:3.

Ride, S. 1987. *Leadership and America's Future in Space: A Report to the Administrator.* Washington, D.C.: NASA.

Roberts, E. B. 1988. "Technological innovation and medical devices." In K. B. Ekelman (ed.), *New Medical Devices: Invention, Development and Use,* 35–50. Washington, D.C.: National Academy Press.

Roberts, E. B., and O. Hauptman. 1986. "The process of technology transfer to the new biomedical and pharmaceutical firm." *Research Policy* 15:107–119.

Robischon, T. 1988. "Orange County, CA: A hotbed of medical-technology entrepreneurship." *MD & DI* (January): 36–39.

Romeo, A. A. 1988. "Private investment in medical device innovation." In K. B. Ekelman (ed.), *New Medical Devices: Invention Development, and Use,* 62–72. Washington, D.C.: National Academy Press.

Rothwell, R., and W. Zegveld. 1981. *Industrial Innovation and Public Policy.* Westport, CT: Greenwood Press.

Russo, M. 1985. "Technical change and the industrial district: the role of interfirm relations in the growth and transformation of ceramic tile production in Italy." *Research Policy* 14:329–343.

Sabel, C. F. 1989. "Flexible specialization and the re-emergence of regional economies." In P. Hirst and J. Zeitlin (eds.) *Reversing Industrial Decline? Industrial Structure and Policy in Britain and Her Competitors,* 17–70. Oxford: Berg.

———. 1990. "Studied trust: building new forms of cooperation in a volatile economy." Department of Political Science, Massachusetts Institute of Technology, Boston, MA. Typescript.

Sabel, C. F., G. Herrigel, R. Kazis, and R. Deeg. 1987. "How to keep mature industries innovative." *Technology Review* (April): 27–35.

Saxenian, A. 1990. "Regional networks and the resurgence of Silicon Valley." *California Management Review* 33:89–112.

Sassen-Koob, S. 1982. "New York City's informal economy." In A. Portes, M. Castells, and L. A. Benton (eds.) *The Informal Economy: Studies in*

Advanced and Less Developed Countries, 60–77. Baltimore: The Johns Hopkins University Press.

Sayer, A. 1990. "Postfordism in question." *International Journal of Urban and Regional Research* 13:666–695.

Schiesl, M. J. 1984. "Airplanes to aerospace: defense spending and economic growth in the Los Angeles region, 1945–1960." In R. W. Lotchin (ed.) *The Martial Metropolis: U.S. Cities in War and Peace*, 135–149. New York: Praeger.

Schmandt, J., and R. Wilson. 1987. *Promoting High Technology Industry: Initiatives and Policies for State Governments*. Boulder and London: Westview.

Schoneberger, W. A. 1984. *California Wings*. Woodland Hills, CA.: Windsor Publications.

Schoneberger, W. A., and R. R. H. Scholl. 1985. *Out of Thin Air: Garrett's First 50 Years*. Los Angeles: The Garrett Corporation.

Schreuder, Y. 1989. "Labor segmentation, ethnic division of labor, and residential segregation in American cities in the early twentieth century." *Professional Geographer* 41:131–143.

———. 1990. "The impact of labor segmentation on the ethnic division of labor and the immigrant residential community: Polish leather workers in Wilmington, Delaware, in the early twentieth century." *Journal of Historical Geography* 16:402–424.

Schumpeter, J. A. 1934. *The Theory of Economic Development*. Cambridge, MA: Harvard University Press.

Scott, A. J. 1983. "Industrial organization and the logic of intra-metropolitan location II: a case study of the printed circuits industry in the Greater Los Angeles region." *Economic Geography* 60:3–27.

———. 1988a. *Metropolis: From the Division of Labor to Urban Form*. Berkeley and Los Angeles: University of California Press.

———. 1988b. *New Industrial Spaces: Flexible Production Organization and Regional Development in North America and Western Europe*. London: Pion.

———. 1991. "Electronics assembly subcontracting in Southern California: production processes, employment, and location." *Growth and Change* 22:22–35.

Scott, A. J., and D. Angel. 1987. "The US semiconductor industry: a locational analysis." *Environment and Planning A* 19:875–912.

Scott, A. J., and A. S. Paul. 1990. "Industrial development in Southern California, 1970–1987." In J. F. Hart (ed.) *Our Changing Cities*, 189–217. Baltimore: The Johns Hopkins University Press.

Scott, A. J., and M. Storper. 1992. "Regional development reconsidered." In H. Ernst and V. Meier (eds.) *Regional Development and Contemporary Industrial Response: Extending Flexible Specialisation*, 3–24. London: Belhaven.

Security First National Bank. 1960. *The Growth and Economic Stature of the San Fernando Valley*. Los Angeles: Research Department of the Security First National Bank.

Seitz, F., and L. W. Steele. 1985. *The Competitive Status of the US Civil Aviation Manufacturing Industry: A Study of the Influences of Technology in Determining International Industrial Competitive Advantage*. Washington, D.C.: National Academy Press.

Select Committee on Small Business. 1956. *The Aircraft Industry*. Hearings Before Subcommittee No. 4 of the Select Committee on Small Business, House of Representatives, 84th. Cong., 2d. sess. Washington, D.C.: Government Printing Office.

Sheard, P. 1983. "Auto production systems in Japan: Organizational and locational features." *Australian Geographical Studies* 21:49–68.

Simonson, G. R. 1964. "Missiles and creative destruction in the American aircraft industry, 1956–1961." *Business History Review* 38:302–314.

Simpson, W. 1987. "Workplace location, residential location, and urban commuting." *Urban Studies* 24:119–128.

Snow, R. T. 1983. "The new international division of labor and the US workforce: the case of the electronics industry." In J. Nash and M. P. Fernandez-Kelly (eds.) *Women, Men and the International Division of Labor*, 39–69. Albany, NY: State University of New York Press.

Soja, E. W. 1989. *Postmodern Geographies: The Reassertion of Space in Critical Social Theory*. London: Verso.

Southern California Association of Governments. 1989. *City of Los Angeles Jobs with Peace Initiative: Defense Spending Cutbacks and the Los Angeles Economy*. Los Angeles, CA: Economic Analysis and Development Program, SCAG.

Starr, K. 1990. *Material Dreams: Southern California through the 1920s*. New York: Oxford University Press.

State of California. 1981. *The Aerospace Industry in California*. Office of Economic Policy, Planning, and Research, Department of Economic and Business Development.

State of California Commission on State Finance. 1990. *Defense Spending in the 1990s: Impact on California*. Sacramento: Commission on State Finance.

Steiner, G. A. 1961. *National Defense and Southern California, 1961–1970*. Los Angeles: Southern California Association of the Committee for Economic Development.

Stekler, H. O. 1965. *The Structure and Performance of the Aerospace Industry*. Berkeley and Los Angeles: University of California Press.

Sternberg, R. 1989. "Innovation centres and their importance for the growth of new technology-based firms: experience gained from the Federal Republic of Germany." *Technovation* 9:681–694.

———. 1990. "Innovation centres in West Germany: transferring technology from universities to enterprises." *Industry and Higher Education* 4:23–29.

Stevenson, R. W. 1990. "Foreign role rises in military goods." *New York Times* (23 October): 1.

Storper, M., and S. Christopherson. 1987. "Flexible specialization and regional industrial agglomerations: the case of the US motion picture industry." *Annals of the Association of American Geographers* 77:104–117.

Storper, M., and B. Harrison. 1991. "Flexibility, hierarchy and regional development: the changing structure of industrial production systems and their forms of governance in the 1990s." *Research Policy*, vol. 20.

Storper, M., and A. J. Scott. 1990. "Work organisation and local labour markets in an era of flexible production." *International Labour Review* 129:573–591.

Storper, M., and R. Walker. 1989. *The Capitalist Imperative: Territory, Technology and Industrial Growth*. Oxford: Blackwell.

Subcommittee on Economic Stabilization. 1989. *Internationalization of the Aerospace Industry: Hearing before the Subcommittee on Economic Stabilization, Committee on Banking, Finance and Urban Affairs, U.S. House of Representatives*. Serial 101–23. Washington, D.C.: U.S. Government Printing Office.

Swanborough, G. 1973. *North American: An Aircraft Album*. New York: Aero Publishing.

Tatsuno, S. 1986. *The Technopolis Strategy: Japan, High Technology and the Control of the Twenty-First Century*. New York: Prentice-Hall.

Taylor, M. J. H. 1980. *Jane's Encyclopedia of Aviation*. London: Jane's Publishing Co.

Taylor, M. J. H., and J. W. R. Taylor. 1972. *Missiles of the World*. New York: Charles Scribner's Sons.

Tiebout, C. M. 1966. "The regional impact of defense expenditures: its measurement and problems of adjustment." In R. E. Bolton (ed.) *Defense and Disarmament: The Economics of Transition*, 125–139. Englewood Cliffs, NJ: Prentice-Hall.

Tienda, M., and P. Guhleman. 1985. "The occupational position of employed Hispanic women." In G. J. Borjas and M. Tienda (eds.) *Hispanics in the US Economy*, 243–273. Orlando, FL: Academic Press.

Tirole, J. 1988. *The Theory of Industrial Organization*. Cambridge, MA: MIT Press.

Topel, R. H. 1986. "Local labor markets." *Journal of Political Economy* 94:S111–S143.

Trigilia, C. 1990. "Work and politics in the Third Italy's industrial districts." In F. Pyke, G. Becattini, and W. Sengenberger (eds.) *Industrial Districts and Inter-Firm Cooperation in Italy*, 160–184. Geneva: International Institute for Labour Studies.

Ulanoff, S. 1959. *Illustrated Guide to U.S. Missiles and Rockets*. Garden City, NY: Doubleday.

Urbanomics Research Associates. 1969. *Southern California Economic Trends, 1940–1970*. Claremont, CA: Urbanomics Associates.

U.S. Department of Commerce. 1989. *U.S. Industrial Outlook*. Washington, D.C.: Government Printing Office.

U.S. Department of Labor, Bureau of Labor Statistics. 1986. *Technology and Its Impact on Labor in Four Industries*. Washington, D.C.: U.S. Government Printing Office.

Uto, R. 1990. *Immigrants in a High Technology Industrial Complex: A Case Study of Vietnamese and Mexican Workers*. Master's thesis, Department of Geography, University of California, Los Angeles.

Van Nimmen, J. 1970. *NASA Historical Data Book, 1958–1968*. Washington, D.C.: Science and Technical Information Office, NASA SP–4012.

Vartabedian, R. 1990. "Aerospace industry trend: flight from the Southland." *Los Angeles Times* (10 May): 1, 41.

Venture Economics. 1985 and 1989. *Venture Capital Yearbook*. Wellesley, MA: Venture Economics.

Von Hippel, E. 1976. "The dominant role of users in the scientific instrument innovation process." *Research Policy* 5:212–239.

Von Hippel, E., and S. N. Finkelstein. 1979. "Analysis of innovation in automated clinical chemistry analysers." *Science and Public Policy* (February): 24–37.

Warner, S. B. 1989. "The evolution of high technology in the Boston region 1920–1980." In A. E. Andersson, D. F. Batten, and C. Karlsson (eds.) *Knowledge and Industrial Organization*, 133–141. Berlin: Springer-Verlag.

Wiewel, W., J. S. deBettencourt, and R. Mier. 1984. "Planners, technology, and economic growth." *Journal of the American Planning Association* 50:290–296.

Wilburn, J. R. 1971. *The Social and Economic Aspects of the Aircraft Industry in Metropolitan Los Angeles During World War II*. Ph.D. diss., Department of History, University of California, Los Angeles.

Wilkinson, F. (ed.). 1981. *The Dynamics of Labor Market Segmentation*. London: Academic Press.

Williamson, O. E. 1975. *Markets and Hierarchies: Analysis and Antitrust Implications*. New York: The Free Press.

———. 1985. *The Economic Institutions of Capitalism*. New York: The Free Press.

Wilson, A. 1982. *The Eagle Has Wings: The Story of American Space Exploration*. London: Unwin.

Witze, C. 1965. "The USAF missile program: a management milestone." In E. G. Schwiebert (ed.) *A History of the U.S. Air Force Ballistic Missiles*, 165–183. New York: Praeger.

Wren, C. 1990. "Regional policy in the 1980s." *National Westminster Bank Quarterly Review* (November): 52–64.

Yenne, B. 1987. *Lockheed*. Greenwich, CT: Crescent Books.

Index

Designer: U.C. Press Staff
Compositor: Asco Trade Typesetting Ltd.
Text: 10/13 Sabon
Display: Sabon
Printer: Edwards Brothers, Inc.
Binder: Edwards Brothers, Inc.